"With eloquence and ecumenical hospitality—
Edith Humphrey has given us a much-needed b
for entering into the worship of the Triune God. Anyone who participates in
worship and especially anyone who leads in worship, whether traditional or
contemporary, liturgical or free, should read this timely book *now*."

—Michael J. Gorman, dean, The Ecumenical Institute of Theology,
St. Mary's Seminary & University

"In a study that is at once biblical, theological, historical, and practical, Humphrey explores the essence of true Christian worship: awed entrance, body
and soul, into the presence of the Triune God. Although Humphrey speaks
with the accent of the Eastern Church, her insights illumine a wide range
of traditional and contemporary practices, and she poses probing questions
that often challenge popular wisdom about liturgy. This is a book not only
for worship leaders but also for the whole congregation to study together."

—Ellen F. Davis, Amos Ragan Kearns Professor of Bible and
Practical Theology, Duke Divinity School

"Worship, like Bible reading, is not about finding something new but about
entering into the Old Story—something so old it overwhelms what is new,
something so old it expands our future, and something so old it reframes who
we are so that we become who we are meant to be. Don't expect Edith Humphrey's book to settle the worship wars. Expect it to go behind the wars into the
great tradition where worship was about entrance into the presence of God."

—Scot McKnight, Karl A. Olsson Professor in Religious Studies,
North Park University

"*Grand Entrance* is a monograph, a memoir, and much more. Through Scripture, the early church fathers, and the author's own personal experience,
it examines the centrality of liturgy in biblical religion and the Christian
tradition, bearing witness to the rites of East and West in the process. We
are caught up in the author's life story, too, as she traces her movement from
an evangelical background very much opposed to ritual worship toward the
biblically saturated liturgical tradition of the ancient church. A lively book
and a journal of shared discovery."

—Scott Hahn, Pope Benedict XVI Chair of Biblical Theology and Liturgical
Proclamation, St. Vincent Seminary; professor of scripture and theology,
Franciscan University of Steubenville

"Instructed by the great biblical categories of redemption, covenant, worship,
and assembly, Edith Humphrey has written a book rich in theology, contemplative wisdom, and practical insight. When I recall the ignorance, insensitivity,

and intellectual morass attendant on so much of modern 'liturgical renewal' during almost my whole lifetime, I wish Humphrey were old enough to have written this excellent work a half century earlier."

—Patrick Henry Reardon, author, Chronicles of History and Worship;
pastor, All Saints Orthodox Church, Chicago

"This is a great book—a must-read for anyone interested in a scholarly yet accessible treatment of Christian worship. Edith M. Humphrey frames her discussion of liturgy as 'grand entrance' and in so doing focuses on a fundamental motive for gathering for public prayer. In ways reminiscent of ancient Egeria, Humphrey describes a variety of Christian churches from the East and the West, noting both strengths and weaknesses in a clear and engaging narrative. Her meticulous scholarship, accessible writing, insightful questions, and balanced critique highlight the radical nature of what it means to enter—together—into God's presence for worship."

—Judith M. Kubicki, associate professor of theology, Fordham University

"This book offers a compelling account of the way that God's Spirit works through public worship to lead us from the claustrophobia of our own narcissism into the spacious, luminous reality of the Triune God—a place so expansive that we find ourselves in communion with God's people across centuries and continents and in transformative encounter with the Holy Trinity. This breadth of vision is evoked through discussions of a wide range of biblical and historical scholarship as well as Humphrey's experiences in Salvation Army, Anglican, Presbyterian, Catholic, and Orthodox communities. The book is an especially welcome tonic for all of us exhausted by the quest for endless innovation in church life—a quest that often reinforces rather than challenges the small, isolated spiritual world we occupy. Fittingly, this is not a feel-good book; rather, it is a book of prophetic insight that you will wrestle with, talk back to, argue against, and sing along with."

—John D. Witvliet, Calvin Institute of Christian Worship,
Calvin College and Calvin Theological Seminary

Grand
ENTRANCE

WORSHIP ON EARTH AS IN HEAVEN

Edith M. Humphrey

BrazosPress
a division of Baker Publishing Group
Grand Rapids, Michigan

© 2011 by Edith M. Humphrey

Published by Brazos Press
a division of Baker Publishing Group
P.O. Box 6287, Grand Rapids, MI 49516-6287
www.brazospress.com

Printed in the United States of America

Library of Congress Cataloging-in-Publication Data
Humphrey, Edith McEwan.
    Grand entrance : worship on earth as in heaven / Edith M. Humphrey.
        p.   cm.
    Includes bibliographical references (p.   ) and index.
    ISBN 978-1-58743-252-1 (pbk.)
    1. Public worship. I. Title.
BV15.H86 2010
264—dc22   2010044978

11   12   13   14   15   16   17   7   6   5   4   3   2   1

For my husband, Chris, who played Peter to my cautious John (John 20:4–6) and remains my constant and dearest companion.

Contents

Preface

I once heard a choir leader comment that there are not many true contraltos, but there are a lot of lazy sopranos. I suspect that this comment applies to me: I sing alto or middle whenever possible but am prepared to stretch to the soprano section should the need arise. The problem is, if I don't concentrate, I find myself forgetting to follow the correct line in the music; there is a confusion of identity! A similar ambivalence in voice is likely to be discerned by the perceptive reader of this book, as it was written during a period of transition in my life.

More than other pieces over which I have labored, *Grand Entrance* reflects my inquiry into the nature of the Church. It has been my companion during the last stages of a pilgrimage that began over thirteen years ago and that was fulfilled in a concrete (though not final) manner when I was received into the Orthodox Church by *"chrismation" (anointing with oil) on Pentecost, 2009. Because of this, it has been difficult for me to retain a consistent voice in the writing, and readers will note that I adopt a "we" stance with regard to several traditions. This is not an affectation or an imaginative empathy: though I am an Orthodox Christian, I feel a deep kinship especially with my Anglican and Salvation Army friends, and a sense of community, too, with other groups with whom I spend time in worship. While I was deeply engaged in the renewal and realignment of the Anglican *Communion, I began the research and writing of this volume; I completed it as an Orthodox Christian. During all this time, I have continued to have fellowship with Roman Catholics, Presbyterians, and others, at Pittsburgh Theological Seminary and elsewhere. I thought it best to leave the book as it has emerged, the strange fruit of this ecclesial and spiritual quest, rather than to start afresh from the more decided perspective that I now hold. (Though, with most Orthodox, I worship in the Eastern tradition, I remember that the Western rite is by no means to be considered a lesser form: the *"Western rite Vicariate" through which some Orthodox

Christians inhabit Western liturgy is not a concession, but a free recognition of other authentic traditions in the Church. I myself retain a special love for the hymnody of the West, an appreciation that is not out of place among the Orthodox.) If there are ambiguities and tensions that emerge because of my decision not to obscure traces of change in my own mind, perhaps this is not entirely a loss. Many Christians today are in a similar state of discovering the mystery of the Church and wondering how Christians should worship when they assemble, and so I hope that such readers will understand the different positions that I occupy in this book.

Further, I find myself in the strange position of having been not only both an informal and professional leader of church worship but also a frequent visitor in other church settings, as well as a newcomer to my Orthodox context, where I sing but do not lead. As a result, though I am not a liturgical specialist, I speak both as a leader with some experience and as an utter novice in some matters. At times, then, the "we" of the worship leader emerges, while at other times the "we" of the humble sheep comes to the fore. (This is appropriate, of course: even in the Scriptures, for example in Ephesians, it is not always clear whether St. Paul's "we" is apostolic or whether it includes the entire congregation. Sheep and rams are all lambs to God; all God's people are liturgists.) I have struggled with the difficulty of balancing worship amidst the contemporary demands for both change and continuity. Sometimes the current drive for novelty in worship has led me to empathize with C. S. Lewis, who naughtily remarked: "The charge to Peter was 'Feed my sheep,' not . . . Teach my performing dogs new tricks!"[1] The move between leader and congregant, then, is yet another point at which my "voice" changes register throughout this book.

Though I have tried to provide a fairly thorough examination of the biblical texts and have gone into some detail while tracing the history of the classical liturgies, I cannot pretend to have attempted a full account of these things. Those in the Catholic and Orthodox communities will miss a discussion of architecture, *icons, and relics, and may be surprised that I do not engage in a more robust defense of sacramentalism (though, I hope, my delight in the mysteries is clear). Orthodox brothers and sisters may wonder why I have chosen the title *Grand* (rather than "Great") *Entrance*. I hasten to assure them that I am not proposing a novel term for that solemn procession that signals the beginning of the Eucharist; rather, I am indicating the immense scope of worship—the grandeur of it all!—as we approach the Holy One, surrounded by an innumerable cloud of witnesses. My purpose in the book, to recover the theme of entrance into worship, is quite particular, and I hope that it will be of benefit to Christians in other traditions who are not looking for a discussion of these other important matters. Those in the Reformed and other Protestant traditions perhaps will be disappointed that I do not delve into the period of the Reformation, and so omit an account of the distinct roots of various Protestant forms of worship; fortunately, there are many excellent histories of worship that do this very thing. At any rate, the deeper foundations of Protestant worship predate the Reformation, since the Reformers looked to the biblical period and sometimes to the undivided Church as the basis for the different forms that they developed. Moreover, since the efforts of the liturgical renewal movement in the mainline churches and the influence of Robert Webber in the evangelical churches, many Protestant churches have recovered elements from the classic liturgies of the East and West. My hope is that though Protestant readers will not find a thorough account of the development of their varied worship services, they will find this analysis of worship in the Bible and the early Church helpful, and will benefit from the sympathetic (though searching) descriptions of various worship scenarios that I undertake in chapter 6.

Because of the varied terms that I use in this broad discussion of worship, I have not only offered brief definitions in the text and notes but have also included a glossary at the end of the book. Items found in the glossary are marked with an asterisk the first time they appear in each chapter.

Perhaps a few other words of explanation will be helpful. I have adopted, as a main point of reference, the RSV translation of the English Bible, both because I find its tone suitable to worship and because I consider it to be a version that shows more concern for the Tradition of the Church than the now more popular NRSV. Where I depart from the RSV and cite other versions, this is indicated (NRSV, KJV, etc.), and where I offer my own translation, it is marked accordingly (EH). The use of italics for emphasis in Bible references and other quotations is also my addition. I have also adopted the practice of the English Bible in which the holy name of God is indicated through the use of LORD spelled out in small capital letters. (A more thorough account of this tradition is found in the glossary under the heading YHWH.) Though readers might expect this in connection with the Old Testament, they may be startled to see that I also use it frequently to refer to the one God of the New Testament, where the divinity of Jesus as LORD also is in view. It is helpful to remember that no ancient Greek versions distinguished between small and capital letters and that to do so is an editorial decision that matches the conventions of our day. Though translators of English Bibles have not used the majuscule LORD in the New Testament, it frequently seems justified, especially in the light of St. Paul's reformulation of the Hebrew monotheistic declaration in 1 Corinthians 8:6.

Some readers may also be surprised that I have not refrained from the use of masculine language for God and Christ. My decision to retain the Church's way of speaking about God is not intended as a slight to women, nor is it sheer entrenchment in what some may consider quaint archaism. Rather, I am deferring to Jesus, who has delighted to reveal the Father to God's people (John 1:18; Matt. 12:25–27; Luke 10:22), and giving honor as well to the Son, to whom the Church is "betrothed." The question of metaphor, revelation, and the holy name of God is not as simple as some revisionists have assumed, and the alteration of these names may well be leading to an alteration of the faith that we have received.

I owe a special debt to all those who have helped me along the way and to a host of others who have made this study a good deal more clear than it would have been without their efforts. Thanks are due especially to Kathy Anderson, Lisa Sayre, Megan MacDonald, and Brian Hutchinson, who read all or most of this manuscript and made invaluable comments, and to my daughter Meredith Burnett, who always asks searching questions! I also express my gratitude to Pastor Robert Austell, Fr. Steve James, and Major David Ivany for their generous gift of time and discussion with me, as well as to the Rev. Dr. John McGuckin, the Rev. Dr. John Behr, Fr. Nicholas Alford, Fr. Alistair Stewart-Sykes, the Rev. Dr. Bogdan Bucur, Professor Paul Meyendorff, and Fr. Gregory Long, who offered invaluable advice and saved me from mistakes in areas that are still very new to me. Besides these, I could name a host of other colleagues, including those who invited me to conferences on worship at Calvin College and Trinity School for Ministry (Ambridge), where I joined in bracing conversation and careful thinking about many matters. Finally, I am extremely grateful to the Board of Directors of Pittsburgh Theological Seminary, who granted me a sabbatical during the 2008–9 academic year, and for my colleagues, who covered for my absence and have encouraged me in more ways than I can recount!

It is apt that I draw to the end of writing this book on the feast-day of God's eloquent servant who has so shaped worship, especially in the East, but also in the West (including the Anglican Communion with whom I sojourned for twenty-five years). It is my prayer, and, I am certain, the prayer of those who have gathered with me in twos and threes while working on this project, that this book should be an aid in understanding what it means to enter into worship. In the words of the "golden-mouthed," I pray: "Fulfill now, O Lord, the desires and petitions of thy servants . . . granting us in this world knowledge of thy truth, and in the world to come life everlasting."

The Feast of *St. John Chrysostom, November 13, 2009

Introduction

The Crisis of Corporate Worship and the Life of the Church

"So how was your service today?"

It is an innocent question, asked for the sake of companionable conversation around a Sunday dinner table—sadly, not everyone in our family is part of the same congregation. But my husband looks slightly pained. "It was the *Liturgy*," he responds, smiling, and I am forcibly reminded that Eastern Orthodox are not predisposed to evaluate how things "went." Worship is offered to God, in a well-known pattern, without a searching eye to creativity or novel expression, or to the effect upon the individual worshiper. (Their attitude goes back at least to the sixth century, when Leontius of Byzantium criticized Theodore of Mopsuestia for composing his own liturgy, and in this way showing his lack of reverence for "the apostles' way of worship," passed down by St. Basil and others.)[1] I *have* heard Orthodox marvel about the beauty of their liturgy and remark upon the wisdom and luminosity of the preacher's words. When they do so, however, one gets the sense of a serendipitous surprise and not an assessment of whether the prayers did what they were supposed to do. "I didn't get anything out of this morning's meeting . . . that song . . . her sermon" is not a refrain that I have heard often in the Orthodox context.

There is, of course, a just retort to such complaints: "The question is—what did *you* put into it?" The corrective is all very well and good. After all, one of the definitions of *liturgy* is that it refers to people's (*laos*) work (*ergon*)—*laos-urgy*. However, this counterresponse ("What did *you* put into the worship?"), though a helpful corrective, leaves us trapped in the same world of thought: worship, we assume, is something that people *perform*, and so it asks to be evaluated. We are to judge its success, according to aesthetics, or theology, or relevance, or utility, or earnestness, or effort. But there is something in our

1

heart that yearns for more than this evaluative approach to worship. Prompted by God's own Spirit, we long to be taken out of ourselves, even out of our role as judge. We long to inhabit worship instead of treating it as an object. We long to meet with the One who is the lover of each one of us and of the whole Church, his bride. We look to *rejoice* as God's glory fills the temple. Such a meeting surely takes place only at God's initiative, and not because of our creative, emotive, or practical interventions.

Yet everywhere one looks today, worship is spoken of in terms of creativity—novel moves for the sake of relevance or well-crafted moves for the sake of aesthetics. The "worship wars" of North America seem stalled, at an impasse, as Christians debate the relative merits of seeker-friendliness or good taste. This issue came into focus for me when I moved from Canada to the United States, from teaching at the university and college to engaging in theological formation at a seminary. As a preliminary to my first opportunity to speak at chapel, I was given a sheet of guidelines, with almost the first line of instruction reminding me, "This is your opportunity to be creative!" I understood why the words were there—after all, this seminary was a diverse place, and seminary students were learning how to lead in worship, coming from and going to different traditions. Leading in chapel provides an opportunity for candidates to share the riches of their own backgrounds and to learn from others. Yet the baldness of the statement ("This is your opportunity to be creative") struck me both as a burden and as a complication. Immediately I was tempted to question whether my prepared service would please: would it be "creative" enough? Then I wondered, what happens to the worship of God's people when it is controlled, like the publishing world, by the drive for something unique?

Are you puzzled and worried, as I have been, about what we should do concerning these ongoing and divisive debates in the contemporary church? In the American church, the debate is not simply aesthetic and cultural (concerns that are not in themselves slight), but wide-ranging and substantive. Christians debate the style of music and lyrics; the value of established liturgy over against "seeker-friendly" services; the authenticity of spontaneous versus traditional prayers; the rightful place or danger of visuals, movement, and dance; permission for "prophetic words," glossolalia (speaking in tongues), or meditative silence; the weighted importance of Word, witness, and Sacrament; and the roles of laity and professional clergy. Cutting through these particular questions, and guiding the answers to them, are conflicting expectations concerning reverence, fervency, therapeutic healing, and teaching in worship. Do we expect the service to be a time of quiet, an oasis in our purpose-driven lives? Or do we cleave to the "purpose-driven" church, expecting the Sunday gathering to be a time when more passion is inculcated so that we can be effective witnesses during the week? Do we have a model of the church as a meeting of Christians for the purpose of healing and picture the church as a hospital for those who attend? Or do we view ourselves as though we are in a classroom, gathering to better understand the Christian way?

When God's people are in widespread, deep disagreement and crisis, then we need to go back to basics. In this case, the basics include thinking about what the Church is, what worship is, and what or *who* worship *is for*. This little book is not an introduction to ecclesiology, the study of the Church, but a special study of worship, an action integrally connected with what the Church is. I will not argue but merely state, as a foundation, my presupposition that worship is *the* major purpose and action of the Church, for (in the apt words of the *Westminster Catechism) we are meant "to glorify God and enjoy him forever." To adapt that famous passage from St. Paul's chapter on love: as for evangelism, it will come to an end (for the Word himself will be known in the new Jerusalem) and as for social action, it will cease (for on that day, we shall all be healed and filled), but worship never fails! Evangelism and mission are, of course, significant to our identity as Christians, for our God is a "missional God."[2] We have been embraced by the "two hands of the Father" (as St. Irenaeus[3] says)—the Son and the Holy Spirit—who gathers up humankind to himself. In turn, Jesus has sent us, filled with the Spirit, as the Father sent him into the world.

However, evangelism and mission have their beginning and end in our adoration of the One who was, and is, and is to come. The little adage, "the church is the only institution that exists for the benefit of its nonmembers" (i.e., nonbelievers and the needy) is therefore only partly true. For we exist first of all before the face of God, because of his holy love. There are still some Christians who need to be convinced of the priority of worship, but that would be a different study. Yet the focus of this book, authentic Christian worship, may also help to clarify the nature of the Church by showing that when we gather together to worship, we are indeed becoming what we are called to be. As C. S. Lewis remarked, "Here, as in worship, in love, in moral action, and in knowing, I transcend myself; and am never more myself than when I do."[4]

The purpose of this book is not to talk about worship in all of its aspects. Instead, I want to recover a single idea, an understanding of worship that is being increasingly neglected in our day. Our corporate forgetfulness of this foundation has, I believe, given rise to a myopia that makes us see the worship wars as concerned only with surface issues like personal preference and differences in taste. Here is my hunch: the rancor and fighting found among North American Christians when they discuss worship needs to be placed in the context of a bigger idea. Worship should not be considered only in terms of relevance for today, or in terms of beautiful music and good aesthetics; rather, worship is *entry*. It is entry into something that is not primarily of our own making. Worship is entry into an action, into a company, into a reality that is ongoing and bigger than we are. When we worship, we are joining, or are joined to, something cosmic (even supercosmic!) and something trans-historical. This "something" into which we enter is not ours in the first place, but belongs to God, who issues his invitation to us. The worship into which we have been invited, the company into which we have been welcomed, and the holy place that has been opened to us are indeed grand—things beyond our unaided sight, hearing, or imagining, that "God has prepared for those who love him" (1 Cor. 2:9).

For some Christians, this is not news. Indeed, the idea of worship as *entrance* is an ancient and persistent theme, found in the Scriptures and continued throughout the worship of the whole Church, East and West. Yet among many of us who have become enamored with new approaches, "fresh" expressions, and diversity, that perspective has been all but lost. As children of the past five centuries, most of us are programmed to value what we call "original" and to apply the scientific model of discovery to everything. The academic world values research that is "groundbreaking" and looks for it in the arts as well as the sciences. Popular books are marketed based on their promise of a new solution to an old problem or a brand new way of looking at life. Art is valuable if it is avant-garde. Novelty has become a nearly unquestioned value of our age.

Beyond this drive for all that is new, we must reckon with the fact that, in our global context, the past few generations have now been trained to honor a multiplicity of approaches and stories. The modern drive to progress and the postmodern desire to be inclusive both have their strengths. Yet a mindless trajectory toward what we envision as the future, or an indiscriminate openness to every voice that clamors, makes it difficult for us to see the value of continuity and unity, characteristics essential to the Church and taken for granted by many of our forebears. We so fear the stagnation of the past that the term *conservative* has become a synonym for *fundamentalist*; we so fear the oppression of conformity that even our newest biblical translations fudge the call to uniform confession of faith when it is enjoined by St. Paul.[5]

In the following pages, with the help of our faithful siblings of the ancient and not-so-distant past, and in conversation with believers across the continents, I hope to rub some of the modernist grime off our windows and to adjust the antenna so that the postmodern static is stilled. The *catholic lenses of the Church through the ages and across the globe are helpful as correctives for today's misperceptions; the voices of God's people sing in harmony at the wonder of entering into the holy Presence, because the Lord has prepared this way, removing the veil that separates, and teaching us how to proceed.

We will begin by considering the centrality of corporate worship in the life of God's people, which calls into question the very notion of private devotions. Next, in two chapters, we will study the Scriptures (especially Psalms, Isaiah, Acts, Hebrews, and Revelation), discovering the many places where worship is pictured as a grand entrance made possible by the Lord, and where we are invited (indeed, urged!) to make this entrance. Then we will look at key places in the traditional liturgies of the Church, both East and West, where this perspective of entrance is both assumed and expressed. Next we will move on to visit some representative Christian communities of worship, asking our brothers and sisters in various places whether an understanding of worship as entrance is alive in their gatherings and what difference it makes (or *would* make). Finally, we will turn to the question of *now what?* This troubleshooting chapter will tackle some common impediments in our services that stand in the way of entrance into worship and offer tools for discernment by Christian pastors and lay leaders, particularly those who compose or lead worship. By way of conclusion, we will listen to the angels sing and consider the true origin of these songs of praise, which we are called to join. But let us begin by hearing the invitation of the psalmist:

> Make a joyful noise to the LORD, all the earth!
> Worship the LORD with gladness!
> Come into his presence with singing!
>
> Know that the LORD, he is God!
> It is he who made us, and not we ourselves;
> we are his people, and the sheep of his pasture.
>
> Enter his gates with thanksgiving,
> and his courts with praise!
> Give thanks to him, bless his name!
>
> For the LORD is good;
> his steadfast love endures forever,
> and his faithfulness to all generations. (Ps. 100)[6]

1

"Teach Us to Pray"

What Is Worship, and Where Does Corporate Worship Fit?

It is hard for us to realize how deeply we have been infected by the bug of individualism. Most naturally, "I" understand my identity in terms of who I am *over against* others and as a self-contained unit. So it is that women today cry out to be identified *not* in terms of their relationships, and men *not* in terms of their occupations. There is, we assume, a core to each one of us that is independent of every other being and action, unique to itself. As with many compelling ideas, this is a half-truth, for our uniqueness is expressed and indeed nurtured by means of our relations with others and through the roles that we take on or that come to us.

For Christians, this mystery of our uniqueness-in-community should not come as a complete surprise. At the very beginning of the Scriptures, it is revealed that we are made after the image of that God whom we later learn is one alone and yet also three. Only God is utterly "autocephalous" ("his own head") and only God is Trinity. Though God is sufficient in himself, he is the Creator of a multitude of others. In pale reflection of that mystery, each one of us human beings is of intrinsic value to God, while we are who we are through communion with God and with others. Perhaps the way we imagine ourselves, as fundamentally independent individuals, is due to our neglect of this mystery, that there is only One who is Holy (distinct) and that this God is Three-in-One. Perhaps, along with others, we tend to confuse the creature with the Creator. Whatever the causes, even we Christians easily slip into thinking about a human being as someone whose identity is best seen in isolation. Ancients, formed by polytheism, tended to think mostly in terms of the group; our culture, watering down Christianity to a practical deism-with-doubts, now fixates upon the individual.

Whose Business Is My Soul?

Even our understanding of worship has been affected by this focus on self: we consider our prayers, in their most authentic form, to be private. Protestants not only reject confession in the presence of a priest, but often also ignore the biblical injunction to "confess your sins to each other and so be healed": why confess to each other when we can speak *privately* with the Lord? And whose business is it, anyway? (The privilege of absolute privacy is a malady that may also be spreading in Catholic and Orthodox settings in North America as well, even though these communions have a time-honored tradition of the rite of reconciliation or confession.) We have manipulated David's impassioned recognition of God's primacy—"against thee, thee only, have I sinned!" (Ps. 51:4)—so as to soften our sense of responsibility. And so we forget that most of what we think, do, and say makes an impact on our brothers and sisters. A spiritual exercise that I found enormously challenging was that of asking every person present at Forgiveness *Vespers (at the beginning of Eastern Orthodox *Lent) for their forgiveness. As a guest it seemed an odd thing to do with those whom I scarcely knew or had never even met before; it was even more embarrassing to do this with members of my family, who knew me well. On reflection, it seems to me now that the corporate and personal actions involved in Forgiveness Vespers are exactly right: we can never know how what we have done (perhaps what we think in private, or in secret) has affected the whole body of Christ!

Beyond the question of confession of sin, there is our approach to worship in general. Many of us suppose that when we "go to church," what is most important even there is our solitary devotion, though we are in a corporate setting. What really matters in the service is that *I* have a vivid experience of God's presence. The practice of closing one's eyes when praying, so helpful in shutting out distraction, unfortunately also trains our gaze *within*. Most of the popular hymns or contemporary songs emphasize the first person singular. Many Christians approach the Lord's Supper, or Eucharist, assuming that it is largely a poignant or serious moment between them and the Lord. The success of the service is measured by how it has helped or challenged *me*.

"We" in the Old Testament

It was not always this way. Throughout the Old Testament, it is clear that the assembly, rather than each individual, was the basic orientation, the mode in which the Hebrews and Israelites worshiped. Though Abram is called out from his household, he is made by God into "a great nation" that itself is blessed, so that all the families of the earth may be blessed (Gen. 12:1–3). Jacob, though he has a privileged, singular vision while asleep (Gen. 28:12–17), sees in his vision a myriad of angels at the "gate of heaven," and hears the voice of the Lord speaking in terms of his ancestors and his many offspring. Even while "alone" with the Lord, he is not left alone, for his dreams place him in the midst of others and bring others to him. For Joseph, happiness and the fulfillment of his dreams are found in reconciliation with his brothers and father, so that God makes them, as he promised to Jacob, "a great nation" (Gen. 45–46). All these patriarchs, though they personally saw mysteries and heard from God prior to the emergence of Israel, looked forward to the promise of God—the forging of a holy people.

This collective identity of Israel comes about, of course, under Moses. Though alone in the desert, and indeed an outcast from Egypt, he sees the vision of the burning bush and hears the divine voice who reveals "the God of your father, the God of Abraham, the God of Isaac, and the God of Jacob" (Exod. 3:6). Heeding the cry of his own, this God purposes to bring his people out of Egypt so that they may worship him (Exod. 3:12).

God's own identity, then, is couched in terms of Moses' ancestors, and he aims to rescue all the Hebrew tribes and bring them together as a nation to worship him as the LORD. When the LORD sends Moses to Pharaoh, his instructions are not simply to demand "Let my people go!" but also to give the reason, "that they might worship me." This is not divine subterfuge. The purpose of the exodus is indeed liberation. But it is liberation so that this priestly people might freely serve God together, might worship without snares or obstacles. Worship, then, is intimately linked with freedom.

With Moses, the people later are given instructions to keep Sabbath and to construct the tabernacle. They are taught to worship under the ministry of the priest Aaron, whose very vestments symbolize the tribes, and to keep the commandments of the two tablets, worshiping God together and expressing their love for each other. "Before the eyes of all the house of Israel at each stage of their journey" (Exod. 40:38 NRSV) is the presence of the LORD, filling the tabernacle and hovering over it as they travel. (Later that same glory will fill the magnificent temple of Solomon.) God's glory is in them, before them, and behind them, the center of their community, their vanguard through the desert, and their shield of protection. They are in the presence of the Holy One during these formative forty years, as he forges the unruly tribes into a single people.

The corpus of psalms that were collected as the Hebrew people worshiped together is replete with references to adoration in the context of the whole community. Even when the "I" is used in the Psalms, it is not individualistic, though it is deeply personal. That is, the "I" does not indicate a subjective lyrical poem intended to focus only upon one person's feelings or experiences. Neither

David nor Asaph is the Hebrew equivalent of the Latin lyricist Catullus or the romantic English poet Coleridge. Instead, even the "I" psalms place their feelings, experiences, and prayers within the company of the faithful and before the face of God. Because of this, the most personal psalm is not idiosyncratic, but able to be "tried on" by each of God's people, for the sake of all. This dynamic is seen in the constant rhythm from the personal to the corporate—"*I* was glad when they said to me, Let *us* go to the house of the Lord" (Ps. 122:1); "Create in *me* a clean heart. . . . Then I will teach *transgressors* thy ways" (Ps. 51:10, 13).

Some, however, might say, what about the teaching of Jeremiah and Ezekiel? Isn't the whole point of the "new covenant" that God promises to speak internally, to the heart of each person? Isn't corporate worship an Old Testament thing ("the fathers have eaten sour grapes," Jer. 31:29), while the New Testament is profoundly interested in the individual? This contrast is a caricature that goes along with the common misconception that the Old Testament God is a God of wrath and the New Testament God is a God of love. We must actually look at those places where the prophets promise this new covenant of the heart to see what they also envision concerning persons in community.

In Jeremiah 31, the prophet does not, in fact, agree with the people that God has dealt with them according to the principle that the "fathers have eaten sour grapes, and the children's teeth are set on edge." Instead, Jeremiah quotes the people's bitter refrain (which they are probably using as a defense: "we didn't do anything to deserve this punishment—it was our fathers!"). Then he gives them hope in their darkness, witnessing to a new covenant that God will make "with the house of Israel" (v. 31), a covenant that will make God's will a vibrant reality among all of Israel, from the least to the greatest (v. 34). Here is an emphasis on each person, but also upon "them," that is, the whole "house."

Similarly, Ezekiel, the prophet of the softened heart, speaks about the resurrection of the people of God (chap. 37) and about the gathering of all the sheep under a future "shepherd, my servant David" (34:23). If Ezekiel's prophecy were really about individualistic relations with God, it could hardly have come to a consistent climax with the staggering vision that he gives of a renewed temple at the end of his book. It is from this temple that Ezekiel envisions that God will send his cleansing and healing flowing out freely to Israel and to any who sojourn with God's people (47:23). Ezekiel's final picture, the hope of Israel and the world, is the new Jerusalem, called "The Lord is there." This city encompasses all the tribes and has twelve protective gates (named for each tribe) that also open out into the world (48:21–35).

"We" in the New Testament

When we move into the pages of the New Testament, we hear holy Mary exult in God "helping Israel" according to the promises made to her fathers (Luke

1:54–55). Jesus speaks to the woman at the well concerning the "worshipers" (plural!) whom God seeks (John 4:23), and prays his high priestly prayer on behalf of the disciples and those who will believe because of them (John 17:23). In Acts, the worshipers of the Lord gather together and even pray prayers in unison (cf. Acts 4:24–30). St. Paul speaks about the entire community as the "temple" of Christ (1 Cor. 3:16–17)—though many have individualized his words, not noticing that the "you" is *plural* rather than singular in the Greek phrase "you are God's temple."

A similar unwitting editing job is often done on Jesus' words to those around him: "the kingdom of God is in the midst of you" (Luke 17:21). This proclamation, intending to alert the people of his generation to the fact that God was doing a new thing in their midst, is frequently internalized and individualized to read "within you." As a child I remember singing in our junior choir an *anthem that has, it seems, slipped into oblivion:

> Where is the Kingdom of our God? Is it beyond the sky?
> Far from the ways our feet have trod, Far from our searching eye?
> "No," says the Master, "seek not there,"—What joy His word imparts!
> "The heavenly kingdom is so near, It lies within your hearts!"[1]

The song, set to the martial music reminiscent of Elgar's "Land of Hope and Glory," may be lost, but the sentiment is often considered the most Christian of ideas. The kingdom in the heart is believed by many to be what distinguishes the Christian hope from the mistaken idea of first century Jewish people, who envisaged the kingdom of God as a concrete, social reality. After all, Jesus said, "my kingship is not of this world" (John 18:36).

Indeed, Jesus' home was with the Father, and the power of his rule did not come from the principalities of this present age. The Lord may "set up his throne" in each of our lives, and a good deal of deep spiritual advice has been given about the "spiritual kingdom"[2] within. But Jesus does not draw a sharp distinction between the physical and the spiritual, between the created visible and invisible spheres, between heaven and earth. Nor was Jesus talking to the Pharisees about the possibility of an internal place for God when he spoke to them about the present rule of God. He was, rather, challenging them to see what (or *who*) was right there among them, as plain as the noses on their faces: God was incarnate in Jesus, offering his love, and he was going unrecognized. He was here, longing like a hen to gather the chicks, his people, under his wings—and they resisted. His challenge here to the Pharisees reminds us of the lament of the Fourth Gospel: he came to his own, and his own did not receive him. God does not simply care for the human *soul*. He seeks for his people to worship in Spirit and in truth: "The Father seeks such as these to worship him" (John 4:23 NRSV). Truly, Jesus' rule is not *of* this world, for his authority does not originate in this age or realm, nor does the Son himself come from our world in the first place. But the rule of Jesus comes from God *into* this world to transform it—all of it, all of us, are meant to be healed. In this hope we pray "thy kingdom come on earth as in heaven."

The rule of Jesus is neither solely spiritual nor concerned with the individual alone. So it is that Jesus weeps over Jerusalem. So it is that he appeals, from the cross, "Father, forgive *them*" (Luke 23:34). And so it is that the disciples together come to the Lord, and ask him, "Teach *us* to pray" (Luke 11:1). When Jesus responds to them, he does not correct the *us*, but continues to model for them a collective prayer "*Our* Father . . . give *us* this day . . . forgive *us* our sins . . ." (Luke 11:2–4 KJV). It is interesting that the pronoun used to address the Lord is the second-person singular ("*thy* kingdom, *thy* will" in the Old English), even while the voice of the prayers is in the first person plural (us, we). God proves himself personal even when (could it be *especially* when?) his people pray together.

But surely, some will argue, Jesus himself gave strong warrant for private prayer in his words concerning "the closet": "But when you [singular] pray, go into your inner room and shut the door and pray to your Father who is in the hidden place; and your Father who sees in the hidden place will reward you" (Matt. 6:6 EH). But remember the context of this passage! It is not an aphorism or rule that is meant to disqualify our prayer together. Rather, Jesus is here attacking the cheap political or social use of prayer, in order to win friends and influence people, to flaunt status or giftedness, or to gossip about our neighbor. The words about the closet, or inner chamber, are the positive instructions meant to replace the course of prayer that Jesus rejects: "When you pray, you must not be like the hypocrites; for they love to stand and pray in the synagogues and at the street corners, that they may be seen by [people]. Truly, I say to you, they have received their reward" (Matt. 6:5). Jesus is not playing off private and corporate prayer, or he would not have attended synagogue himself, "as his custom was" (Mark 10:1) nor taught his disciples to pray "*Our* Father." The problem with the public prayer that he is tackling is that of motivation—"that they may be seen by [people]."

But what about Jesus' own prayer in secret, his habit of going off into the wilds or up on a mountain to pray at key moments in his ministry? We see a solitary Jesus praying before the calling of his disciples (Luke 6:12), with only three others at the Transfiguration (Luke 9:28), and in the garden (Matt. 26:36–37). Certainly there are times in our lives when we need to address God and listen to what God says to us, undistracted by the overt influences of others. Even these times are not hermetically sealed from others, however. If we have the heart of God, our times of great need will be bound up with the needs of others. So we see that the "private" prayer-moments of Jesus, even in times of extreme crisis, concerned others and were linked inextricably with them. Jesus' prayer alone in the wilderness led to the calling of the twelve. The decision was something only God—Father, Son, and Holy Spirit—could make! But God's call involved the whole of his people, for "he gave some to be apostles" (Eph. 4:11 EH). As for his prayer on the Mount of Transfiguration, this surely gave Jesus strength for the ordeal to come—strength that came from the old covenant representatives of Moses and Elijah, and strength that enveloped the three inner apostles Peter, James, and John as they entered into the cloud of his glory (Luke 9:28–36). What they saw—the glory of the Messiah-who-was-to-die-in-glory—Jesus told them to keep secret, *for the time being* (Matt. 17:9). Yet the time came when the entire event of the Transfiguration was openly proclaimed in three Gospels, for the sake of everyone! And his crisis in the garden, where Jesus was in agony known only to himself, is enveloped by Jesus' instructions to his disciples that they, too, should pray to be kept from temptation (Luke 22:40, 46). At all these times, his prayer was for them, and he invited his people to participate in his communion with the Father. His prayer in John 17:23 clinches the matter: "I in them and thou in me, that they may become perfectly one."

In the same way, those of us who are in Christ carry around with us who we are, and to whom we belong, as we pray. But perhaps putting it this way makes it sound like our relationship with others is simply a mind-trick, something that we pretend by means of our memory or our will. No, when we pray, we really *are* surrounded, and we really *are* praying in the midst of God's people. As the liturgist Robert Taft puts it, it is "not psychological recall"[3] but a spiritual reality. Jesus' very personal prayer on the Mount of Transfiguration should inform our imagination in this regard: all the covenant people of the old and new covenants are gathered, by means of Moses, Elijah, and the three, around the Lord as he prays. There are those who are truly with us, even when we might seem, physically (or emotionally), to be alone with the LORD. This is something that may seem strange to some Christians, but it is a corollary of the mysterious teaching concerning the *"communion of saints," a teaching affirmed by many Christians weekly in the creed: We believe "in the Holy Spirit, the holy catholic Church, the communion of saints, the forgiveness of sins, the resurrection of the body and the life everlasting." As the writer to the Hebrews puts it, "we are surrounded by so great a cloud of witnesses!" (Heb. 12:1).

This means that whenever we pray, in whatever circumstance, our hearts should remember the truth expressed in this morning prayer for families: "Remember, O Lord, according to the multitude of thy mercies, thy whole Church, all who join with us in prayer, and all of our brethren, wherever they may be."[4] Those whom the LORD remembers are incorporated into one body. This collection into one body is what has happened in Jesus, through his life, death, resurrection, and ascension. By the power of the Holy Spirit, we have been joined together and are being gathered into one body that prays together—even when we seem to be apart. And so, St. Paul (or perhaps his disciple) can put it this way:

For this reason I bow my knees before the Father, from whom every family in heaven and on earth is named, that according to the riches of his glory he may grant you [plural!] to be strengthened with might through his Spirit in the inner [human being], and that Christ may dwell in your hearts through faith; that you [plural!], being rooted and grounded in love, may have power to comprehend *with all the saints* what is the breadth and length and height and depth, and to know the love of Christ which surpasses knowledge, that you may be filled with all the fullness of God. Now to him who by the power at work within us is able to do far more abundantly than all that we ask or think, to him be glory *in the church* and in Christ Jesus to all generations, for ever and ever. Amen. (Eph. 3:14–21)

This luminous prayer joins together the most personal of things, "the inner *anthrōpos*," or internal human being (where God works to make each of us what we truly are), with the entire community of the redeemed, each and all of whom are being filled with the fullness of God. This comes about by prayer, through the work of God, so that in Christ Jesus God may be truly glorified, or worshiped, among all future generations. The personal and the corporate, the past, present, and future, all come together in a staggering mystery.

And the truth is even richer and more astonishing still! Christian prayer does not simply involve human beings, the sons of Adam and the daughters of Eve—for the angels, too, are glorifying God in adoration, even as they *learn* from our human drama of salvation. In Christ we have had revealed to us mysterious "things into which angels long to look" (1 Pet. 1:12). A mutual exchange goes on between the human and angelic realms!

We are not surprised that angels come to our aid, in response to our prayer, for that is everywhere imprinted upon the stories and teachings of Scripture: angels are "ministering spirits" (Heb. 1:14). Jesus, in the garden, is strengthened by an angel from God, according to some manuscripts (Luke 22:43). In Matthew 26:53, Jesus speaks about the reserve contingency of angelic legions that might save him from violent hands, though he forgoes this possible escape. (Remember how the rebel angel Satan had tempted him at the onset of his ministry, by God's promise to the faithful that they should be "borne up" by angels from danger?) In Revelation 4 and 5, the angels lead and punctuate the heavenly worship in which human beings also participate. Whenever I read such chapters, I hum the verse: "Angels help us to adore him; ye behold him face-to-face!"[5]

But there is still more. Revelation 5:8 speaks about the human elders who hold bowls brimming with the prayers of the saints, and all of Revelation 5 centers around *the* Human Being, Jesus, who took on flesh and even died to "ransom" saints "for God" from every tribe and people (5:9). This human being is of greater honor than the angels, and those who are ransomed by the incarnate One know something of the love of God that angels have not experienced, for God did not become an angel. First Corinthians 11:1–16, a very complex passage that we will consider later, assumes that what we do in worship affects the angels (v. 10) as well. Remarkably, human worship somehow needs to take into consideration the presence of these usually unseen beings. Even more pointedly, Ephesians 3:10 says that part of the role of the Church is to make known the riches of God's gifts and blessings even to the unseen hosts!

All of God's servants, then, are bound up together in prayer and worship, so that God's glory may be seen more and more. This miracle occurs as all of us pray and as each of us prays, joined with the other, because "in [Jesus] the whole structure is joined together and grows into a holy temple in the Lord . . . built into it for a dwelling place of God in the Spirit" (Eph. 2:21–22). What I think I do in secret affects the whole cosmos if I am joined to Christ! Indeed, as redeemed humans, we are bound up not only with the angels but also with those created beings that we think of as "below" humanity. Paul envisages us, by the Holy Spirit, giving voice to the inarticulate and inanimate creation that "groans" under the bonds of the Fall and stands "on tiptoe"[6] to see our complete redemption. Our redemption is, indeed, the harbinger of an entire new creation, a newly redeemed world (Rom. 8:18–27).

Finding Our Faces

The danger of thinking of prayer as mostly a private matter can be seen when we look at places in the Bible where worship goes very wrong. In the Bible, false worship is practically synonymous with self-absorption, self-worship. This is true from the very beginning of human history through to the visions of the end. Indeed, in Western theology, sin has been often described as coming about because God's creature becomes *curvatus in se*—turned in on himself or herself. This human condition is pictured in various places throughout the Scriptures. The mysterious Lamech, in Genesis 4:23, sings a boastful song of triumph about the murder(s?) that he has committed and assumes that the Lord is listening and will avenge anyone who tries to bring him to justice. His "sword-song" is hardly a prayer, yet clearly he believes that he can conscript the Almighty by it. Just as God warned that anyone harming Cain would be avenged by God, so Lamech assumes that God will protect him.

> Adah and Zillah, hear my voice; you wives of Lamech, hearken to what I say:
> I have slain a man for wounding me, a young man for striking me. If Cain is
> avenged sevenfold, truly Lamech seventy-sevenfold. (Gen. 4:23–24)

In Ezekiel, the prince of Tyre is likened by God himself to a guardian cherub who becomes infatuated with his own beauty and wisdom. What should be a hymn morphs into self-celebration, as the fallen angel sings "I am a god, I sit in the seat of the gods, in the heart of the seas" (28:2). Jesus tells the story of the proud Pharisee who "thanked God" for his "righteousness" using these ironic terms: he "prayed thus *with himself*" (Luke 18:11). Paul tells the Roman Christians that the first misstep among humans was that they refused "to give thanks" but rather "gave glory" to images "resembling a corruptible human being" (Rom. 1:21–22 EH). Finally, in the last book of the Bible, we see a visionary epitome of human pride in the figure of the unclean woman-city Babylon, who delights in her own glory: "A queen I sit . . . mourning I will never see" (Rev. 18:7). Inward-turning "prayer" is easily turned into idolatry of self and separates us not only from God but from others. It makes for disintegration, not for the building up of who we are in Christ. Turned in on myself, I will implode.

We might be reminded of the self-absorbed complaint of C. S. Lewis's complex main character, Orual, in the novel *Till We Have Faces*.[7] Orual becomes wholly consumed by a possessive type of love through which she objectifies and misuses those close to her, assuming that they are her very own possessions rather than gifts for her to receive with gratitude. Disappointed by life, jealous of the gifts of others, and jaded by experience, she addresses to the God of the Mountain what she intends to be a strong, brutally honest, courageous prayer of resistance. The more Orual indulges her pride, defiantly nursing her wounds, the more she becomes a swirling mass of whining, self-seeking rhetoric. The deity allows her this verbal and passionate fury, until, with words flowing over and over, the river is exhausted, and she dwindles into silence. What could have been the death of her spirit, the swallowing of her whole self down the drain of self-indulgence, does not occur. For she is lifted out of her self to see things, and to see others, as they really are. It is not all about her, though she has had much to bear. Her life is intertwined, in this great mystery, with the lives of those whom she loves. Somehow, truth breaks into her cycle of inward-seeking death, and Orual, like Job (when he encounters the Almighty directly), comes to herself and so is reconciled with those dearest to her. Finally, she becomes truly human. She has a face, and faces are made to face others!

My plea in this chapter is for us to put away the idea that the most authentic type of prayer is what we would call "private," an exchange simply between Jesus and myself. (Indeed, the common contemporary habit of adding the word "just" to petitions suggests this attitude: "Lord, I don't want to bother you; I *just* ask this and that. . . .") Of course, God does not deal with us only as part of a group. Clearly, he calls to each of us, deep unto deep, as he called Mary's name in the garden on that first Easter morning (John 20:16). But this personal call is in harmony with his love for us all as the body of Christ, this holy temple that he is making, which becomes more glorious the more it looks to the glorious One. St. Mary Magdalene, when Jesus calls her, is given the commission to "go to my brethren and say to them" that their Lord, and hers, has arisen (John 20:17). She willingly embraces this task, playing her part in

God's great undoing of the curse of alienation that was enacted in that first garden. By her service to the apostles, she participates in the undoing of that primal separation between God and us, between male and female, between people and nature. Mary realizes that her teacher is also "our Lord" and that God is doing a new thing.

Only the Holy Spirit can help us to get the "we" back into our prayers and our worship. I suspect that, as *we* pray with each other, realizing that we are never alone in our prayers, each of us will also receive a face that is more distinct, the special personal identity that each of us has in Christ Jesus.

> Where the Spirit of the Lord is, there is freedom. And we all, with unveiled face, beholding (and reflecting) the glory of the Lord as in a mirror, are being transformed into the same image from one degree of glory to another: for this comes from the Lord, the Spirit. (2 Cor. 3:17–18 EH)

So What Is Worship?

If even prayer "in the closet" is not a solo thing, then, what *is* worship? Worship is responding to God's own invitation, that we should see more and more clearly who God is, hear more and more clearly what he is saying, be more and more thankful about his mighty actions, and *enter* more deeply into his communion with us and his care for the world. It is to be thrilled at the wonder of it all, to be astonished and silenced by the weighty glory of God-among-us, and to want it never to end. It is, in the words of Reepicheep, that unlikely *psychopomp mouse from *The Chronicles of Narnia, to come "further up and further in" and to know that this life is never-ending and always deepening for those who are joined to Christ Jesus.

Worship is to celebrate reality as it truly is, placing at the center, or rather acknowledging at the center, the only real One from whom all good things come. It is to respond completely and in truthfulness to the One who is All-in-all and Truth itself. One Greek word for worship (*proskyneō*) describes it as "coming forward to kiss" the One who is all-lovely. Another word in the New Testament (*latreia*) suggests that worship is our "service" offered to God, as Samuel and the high priests served the Lord in the awe of the temple. (So mighty was God's presence that, according to Jewish tradition, the high priest was told to wear a string around his ankle, in case he should fall prostrate before that wonder and have to be pulled back out to the people for whom he was interceding!) The Old English word *worðscip* pictures it as ascribing "worth" or "worthiness" to the worthy One. The French verb *adorer* (Latin, *adorare*) suggests an engaged beseeching, an intimate and abject appeal for help and for love. We adore God as we would turn our unveiled faces toward our Lover. All these words are helpful, for they point to different aspects of worship to which our minds, hearts, and bodies are called.

Worship, responding to the Lord as he speaks to us and as he shows himself to us, affects all of us and each of us. Because Jesus is the One who has gone before us, we are called to enter—personally and as a company—into the beauty of God's presence. Such a summons is no light matter. John was in the Spirit on the Lord's Day and found himself on his face before the shining Glory who was pacing among the churches, each pictured as candlesticks. The Lord's voice, speaking to John, summoned the seven churches, the whole Church, with all its foibles, treachery, and weakness, to worship and to glory. So, as we worship together, you and I will discover that Jesus' goodness as well as his love and sustenance are matched to each one of us. We are in this together, and yet for each one of us, there is with the Lord a particular intimacy that "no one knows except [the one] who receives it" (Rev. 2:17). So, let us move on to see what the Bible says about that great entrance into worship!

Questions for Discussion

1. If God frees the Israelite people from the Egyptians so that they might worship him, what conclusions can we draw about the connection between freedom and worship? Is it possible that people are most free while in worship? What of the person who insists upon the freedom to refrain from worship? Might the capacity to worship be a measure of our true freedom?

2. What can be said about human identity in the light of Paul's prayer in Ephesians 3:14–21? What is the relationship between the "inner human being" and the people of God in the context of worship?

3. How are prayer and worship related? Are all forms of true prayer worship? Or is worship a distinct category of prayer?

4. When it comes to worship, what is the role of the imagination, the mind, and the emotions? How are they properly related to realities that we enter when we pray and worship?

2

"Praise God in His Sanctuary"

Worship as Entrance in the Old Testament

Entry Shock

> In the year that King Uzziah died I saw the Lord sitting upon a throne, high and lifted up; and his train filled the temple. Above him stood the seraphim; each had six wings: with two he covered his face, and with two he covered his feet, and with two he flew. And one called to another and said: "Holy, holy, holy is the LORD of hosts; the whole earth is full of his glory." And the foundations of the thresholds shook at the voice of him who called, and the house was filled with smoke. And I said: "Woe is me! For I am lost; for I am a man of unclean lips, and I dwell in the midst of a people of unclean lips; for my eyes have seen the King, the LORD of hosts!" (Isa. 6:1–5)

Isaiah's mysterious vision has fired the imaginations and nourished the worship of God's people throughout the ages. It reveals that the boundary between heaven and earth is startlingly permeable when God wants it to be so. The prophet, an unclean man living in the midst of an unclean people, is somehow ushered into a place where he sees the glory of the King, the LORD of hosts. Entry is foundational to Isaiah 6.

Part of this chapter has appeared in more "scholarly dress" in Edith M. Humphrey, "Grand Entrance: Entrance into Worship as Rhetorical Invitation and Liturgical Precedent in the Older Testament," in Vahan Hovhanessian, ed., *The Old Testament as Authoritative Scripture in the Early Churches of the East* (New York: Peter Lang, 2010), 79–89.

The prophet is whisked into the divine presence, a crisis so startling[1] that he marks it in time—the year when King Uzziah died. Does his vision occur in the earthly temple of Jerusalem or is it concerned with the heavenly sanctuary? This scholarly debate is moot. As Fr. Christopher Seitz declares, the vision "takes place within the temple itself, even as it explodes the limitations of that sacred space."[2] Both the Hebrew and Greek nouns[3] for the place where the prophet finds himself have ordinary workaday meanings—heykal (Heb.) is used for "palace" and oikos (Gk.) for "house." Here, though we are certainly in God's palace, or house, a temple also is in view: elements of the vision, or Isaiah's earthly context, include smoke (of incense and offering), doorposts, prayers, worship, and an altar. Isaiah sees into the heaven of heavens, where the Lord is on high—and yet, his glory fills the earthly temple, irradiating the house where his people worship. Transcendence and *immanence join together in the Lord's presence. This is confirmed by the seraphim, who speak with one breath of the "holy" (separate) God, whose glory fills *the earth*. Fr. Alexander Schmemann reminds us, "Standing in the temple we stand in heaven."[4]

In this vision, there is a shocking juxtaposition of the eternal, immense God with time and space—a specific time in Judean history, and a specific place at the Jerusalem altar. It seems that the sight of the great Glory is more than the prophet can bear, and so he diverts his gaze to the seraphim. The seraphim are like and unlike us, with faces and feet like humankind, but with wings by which they both fly and exhibit modesty (over against characteristic human shamelessness). In their actions of seeing, covering, and moving, they are living symbols of awe, humility, and action. By God's grace they see the living God—and so they cover in reverence. Because of their creatureliness, they are aware of their distance from God—and so they humbly cover their most intimate and personal parts.[5] And yet they are meant to fly and to cry out—and so they do God's will while they praise him. Their very song speaks of the Lord who is wholly other and yet also with his creation. Perhaps we are meant to imagine the one seraph exclaiming, "Holy, holy, holy is the LORD" while the other responds, "The whole earth is full of his glory!" Their demeanor and action proclaim the nature of the One for whom they sing.

By means of this song, Isaiah—and we readers too!—are not left entirely on our own to discern the substance of the vision. Embedded within the detailed description of the seraphim, in the midst of what Isaiah sees and hears, are theological truths, or propositional statements about the mysterious One on the throne. The prophet has diverted his eyes to watch the seraphim, yet to look on them is to be drawn back to worship the Source of their light and life. The staggering vision is interpreted by their antiphonal hymn, "Holy, holy, holy." Isaiah beholds utter Holiness, the One who is Creator and who is different from every other being. Still, this Holy One draws near, or catches us up into his presence: "The whole earth is full of his glory!" The vision and the song reinforce God's holy otherness and God's generous immanence. God is one.

Yet we understand him with "double vision" and in stereo. The psalmist, too, understands this dynamic when he cries out, "One thing God has spoken; two things have I heard: that you, O God, are strong, and that you, O Lord, are loving!" (Ps. 62:11–12 NIV; cf. Tanakh JPS).

Even the form of the heavenly song underscores this mystery. Strangely, though two seraphim[6] have been singing, the prophet speaks in the singular of the "one whose voice calls." At *that* voice, there is both a shaking and a smoke. The impact of the Almighty is felt and seen, but in such a way that feeling and seeing are disturbed. To perceive that One is to know that perception is inadequate, and so the revelation is both positive and negative, a matter of disoriented sensibilities and sight. We come into a larger place, and it is not comfortable. In this shaking and smoking, the major actor is the "Voice of the one who calls," the initiator of all. To follow the pyrotechnics back to their origin is to adore the hidden One on the throne.

The prophet embodies the only appropriate human reaction: he is undone. And so Isaiah acknowledges his personal sinfulness, the sinfulness of his community, and the disjunction between himself and the One whom he has glimpsed. Each and all are seen in relief against the heavenly Glory. What a shame that some readers of this passage have fixated only upon the prophet's experience or humankind's ability to sense the mysterious. Though there is material here for the historian or the anthropologist, the Church has read otherwise. Every part of the vision, including Isaiah's reaction, becomes a catalyst for worship, directing us back to the thrice-holy One. Indeed, *St. John Chrysostom remarks that the details in the vision concerning the seraphim and the other angels are offered by the prophet only so that we might recognize God's enormity:

> Tell me this. Why do the seraphim stretch forth their wings? There is no other reason than the statement made by the apostle: "Who dwells in unapproachable light." And these heavenly virtues, who are showing this by their very actions, are not the only ones. . . . What, then, do you think? Do you think that the angels in heaven talk over and ask each other questions about the divine essence? By no means! What are the angels doing? They give glory to God, they adore him.[7]

> Do you desire to learn how the powers above pronounce that name; with what awe, with what terror, with what wonder? . . . But you, in your prayers and supplications, call upon him with much listlessness; when it would become you to be full of awe and to be watchful and sober.[8]

Just as the golden-mouthed preacher called his people not to be distracted by speculation, but to adore the Lord, Brevard Childs chides our age, so turned in on itself: "To focus on [ecstatic] . . . individual, personal evaluations completely misses the point of the narrative. Isaiah . . . is not concerned with reimagining God!"[9] No, Isaiah's reaction is reported to us for one reason alone: that we might, with him, glorify the One who is seen so far as human eyes are able to bear it.

The great Glory responds to human need:

> Then flew one of the seraphim to me, having in his hand a burning coal which he had taken with tongs from the altar. And he touched my mouth, and said: "Behold, this has touched your lips; your guilt is taken away, and your sin forgiven." And I heard the voice of the Lord saying, "Whom shall I send, and who will go for us?" Then I said, "Here am I! Send me." (Isa. 6:6–8)

From the altar is brought a living coal that is both touched and not touched. It is both in the hand of the angel and placed upon lips, yet is removed, indirectly, by tongs from the altar. Again, the imagery is both negative and positive: live but burning, mediated and immediate, touched and yet not to be touched.[10] In the application to his lips, Isaiah's personal sin is purged, so that the prophet may respond to the Voice who is about to speak. The voice of the Lord, speaking initially in first-person singular and then in the plural, sets up our expectations: the question "Whom shall *I* send and who will go for *us*?" ideally would be answered by "Here am *I*; Send *us*." But Isaiah can't answer for the community. He only, in all honesty and humility, can reply, "Send *me*."

Blind, deaf, and heartless, Isaiah's people will not raise their voice for God. This leads to the dark mystery of God's commission—Isaiah, the prophetic mouthpiece of the Lord, will speak, but the effect will be to harden. God's people will not hear, see, or be moved. . . . Or will they?

> And he said, "Go, and say to this people: 'Hear and hear, but do not understand; see and see, but do not perceive.' Make the heart of this people fat, and their ears heavy, and shut their eyes; lest they see with their eyes, and hear with their ears, and understand with their hearts, and turn and be healed" [LXX: "and be turned, and I shall heal them"]. Then I said, "How long, O Lord?" And he said: "Until cities lie waste without inhabitant, and houses without men, and the land is utterly desolate, and the LORD removes men far away, and the forsaken places are many in the midst of the land. And though a tenth remain in it, it will be burned again, like a terebinth or an oak, whose stump remains standing when it is felled." The holy seed is its stump [or, LXX: "and as an acorn when it falls out of its husk"]. (Isa. 6:9–13)

The absolute indictment, "hear, but do not understand," must be matched to other Scriptures, where God is known to overcome human hardness, even to change his *own* mind. Think of the apparently unconditional judgment uttered by the prophet Jonah, which comes to a happy ending for Ninevah, if not for the prophet. Through his prophets, the Lord sometimes pronounces unchangeable certainties, but often such absolute-sounding declarations function as warnings of judgment or even offers of blessing. To be sure, utter desolation is in full view in Isaiah's oracle. The land will be burnt, hacked down to a stump. Yet there is at the end a sign of hope—a bare acorn ready to sprout, a holy seed. Lurking behind the judgment is the astonishing hope of resurrection. Again we see God with "double vision"—he is just; he is merciful.

The old Greek version, the *Septuagint (LXX), of Isaiah 6:10 offers a surprise. As Christians we often read Isaiah 6 through the lenses of Matthew, Luke, and John (Matt. 13:14–15; Acts 28:26–27; John 12:40). And in verse 10, all three Gospels follow the astonishing Greek version. The prophetic word has hampered the people's eyes, ears, and/or heart, "lest they should repent, or be turned—*and I shall heal them.*" (I here offer my own translation, since most versions obscure the oddness of the future tense.) The Hebrew text offers less of a sense of hope than the Greek, but it is by way of this strange Greek version, with its future tense, that Isaiah 6 has come into our New Testament. The strange sentence envisions, hope against hope, the future action of God, against all grammatical rules and against all probabilities. Proper grammatical structure would of course be "lest they should repent, for in that case I *would* heal them." Yet the Greek Old Testament and the evangelists hear God say, *I shall heal them.* (If you can't find this in your English Bible, it is simply because the translators don't think that the future tense makes sense, and so they mistranslate it as "and I would heal them.")

Herein lies the wonder of Isaiah 6: we enter God's presence. The Almighty is seen yet does not finally destroy, the coal burns yet does not in the end consume, the word makes deaf yet still speaks, people are sinners and unlikely to turn; they will die and yet God will heal them.

Because of the numerous times Isaiah 6:10 is quoted in the New Testament, we may discern that it was a key verse in the apostolic preaching. It is a luminous passage, illustrating the mystery of evil, the contrast of dark humanity with the glory of the LORD, and God's astonishing embrace and healing of those who seem not to want him. Isaiah 6 fed the early Christian imagination with deep truths about the LORD who had shown himself in the Son: he is a God of holiness and plenitude, transcendence and immanence, justice and mercy. He invites us to enter his presence, so that we may learn to repent, so that he might do something about our unworthiness. Therefore we ought not to be surprised that it finds an honored place in many worship services. "Holy, holy, holy," the song of the angels, has been echoed in liturgies of the East and West, in the traditional English hymn ("Holy, holy, holy . . . early in the morning our song shall rise to thee") and in African spirituals ("We-e-e-e-e see the Lord. . . . The angels cry 'holy,' the angels cry 'holy,' the angels cry 'holy is the Lord!'"). This is a vision not limited to Isaiah, but a revelation that has embraced the whole of the Church. For God's glory fills the whole earth.

If such a hope lies beyond the death of God's people, then why is the prophet given such a dire word? Is God playing with us? Is the threat of destruction purely heuristic, a stick to drive Israelite spirits, or our spirits, to obedience?

No, it corresponds to reality. It is *through* death that we may be brought to enter life, and death is no light thing. We must not be like lazy schoolchildren who look at the back of the math text and copy the answer—without really working through the sum. We are not to be like my youngest daughter, who at age four heard about a friend's grief because her pet had died and asked in bewilderment: "Why is she crying? Doesn't she know that Fluffy will 'arise on the third day'?" My little prodigy had embraced Easter morning with her imagination—but it wasn't truly Easter, because she had not come to terms with death or Good Friday. Isaiah 6 is strong medicine for those of us who think that entry into the presence of God is natural, our right, and an easy thing. There is an entry shock that we must undergo. The LORD is holy. The weight of his glory bears down upon us. There is a burning coal. Disappointment and death lie before us. And yet, the Lord says, "I shall heal them."

Roads Not Taken

This commixture of realism and mystery makes Isaiah's vision an ideal starting point. There are several other places in the Scriptures where we could have begun. Why not alight upon an explicit passage about worship in the New Testament, such as 1 Corinthians 14:26–32, and use it as a template or pattern for worship? In doing this, some readers might think, we would return to the pristine time of the apostles, before worship was developed into something complicated, and when every Christian was free to offer his or her gifts, unencumbered by institutional regulation.[11] Or, why not begin with such New Testament descriptions and then add to them a clearly defined biblical theology, one that centers around Christ, or the Holy Trinity, or the mission of the Church in the world, so that worship can be related to this center? Or, why not read both Testaments, working out a consistent pattern for worship that is seen in the Old Testament, but suitable also for Christians who see Jesus as the *telos*—both the fulfillment and the conclusion—of Hebrew and Israelite practices?[12]

All of these methods have their merits, and we can learn from them. But we are talking about a mystery—that human beings might actually *enter* into worship, invited by God. For the purposes of our study, Isaiah's vision beckons. It does not shy away from the grandeur and strangeness of God, nor the lack of human preparation, nor even the rebellion of the human heart and of human society. Yet the human heart can be healed, and it is not for this fallen society that we are made, but for something bigger! Isaiah traces the wonder of this entrance into worship, and through his eyes we glimpse a larger space, action, and company of worshipers—a larger theater of God's glory.

By beginning with Isaiah 6 we give due emphasis to both the old and new covenants, to the preaching of the early Church, and to the worship of Christians of various traditions, who have entered into both the awe of Isaiah and the joy of the seraphim. In starting here, we push back against the assumption that the bare-naked New Testament provides self-sufficient teaching about worship. For "no New Testament book was written to be a complete manual of liturgics."[13] Beginning with a vision that has been fully knitted into the imagination of the Church lifts from us the burden of constructing an entire biblical theology of worship from scratch. We do not have to weigh Old Testament passages against New by our own ingenuity and come up with something novel. Instead, we base our study of worship upon a passage that for two millennia has found its place in hymnody and prayer, in the proclamation of the Word and in the Eucharist. Here in Isaiah 6, amidst the Thrice-Holy Song of the angels and the strong word of the LORD, we find that which quickens our minds, hearts, and imaginations, as it has our brothers' and sisters' throughout the ages. God draws near to draw us into his presence—by his initiative, we find an entrance.

Entrance into Worship, Old Testament Style

Isaiah was not alone in understanding worship as a response to God's unexpected invitation. We may find this emphasis in other Old Testament texts, where entrance emerges as a visual symbol, as a rhetorical invitation aimed to move us to action, and as a theological insight, or as a combination of these. Indeed, the idea is deeply embedded in tabernacle and temple worship. In particular, we will see that Psalms, Chronicles, and Isaiah picture the boundary between heaven and earth as potentially open in the act of adoration, so that these two realms are joined together by the will of God. God's ancient people are taught to understand themselves as gathering together in a grand action of worship that is not confined even to the human domain.

We begin with the beginning. In the garden of Eden, prior to the Fall of humanity, God was said to "walk" with the first human couple, in the cool of the evening (Gen. 3:8). Here was the LORD entering their human realm, a world that he had made and that he understood. They had regular and expected intimacy with God—presumably an intimacy that was to grow as the couple matured and as they entered more fully into their role as vice-regents in God's world. Some Christian thinkers have wondered whether the time would have come when, once human beings had "passed the test," God would indeed open to them the Tree of the Knowledge of Good and Evil, alongside the Tree of Life. (For an absorbing story that depicts such a fulfillment of human potential, see C. S. Lewis's second novel of the "space-trilogy," called alternately *Perelandra* or *Voyage to Venus*.)

Whether or not entrance into God's will, purpose, and life included the goal of such a lofty initiation, the original intimacy between humankind and our loving Creator was spoiled by human refusal to give thanks (Rom. 1:21). At the instigation of the tempter, humans questioned the goodness of God and desired for other or more than what God was giving to them in their daily round of life. Worship was spoiled because they brought the enemy into their council. So what was meant to be a place of entrance, an ideal gate-world into the Lord's presence (the garden with its Tree of Life and easy concourse with the LORD), was closed to them. Beyond the gates, they were exiled from this idyllic place where God walked, in order to restrain the inevitable effects of their now corruptible and corrupting condition, and in order to stem their presumption.

The gate was closed. The angels were stationed to guard it with swords. This may seem punitive, but it is "a severe mercy."[14] In our current condition, the weight of God's presence would easily consume us. God has regard for our weakened condition, a mercy that we can see in his immediate action to clothe the newly vulnerable human couple, at the cost of animal life. Nor does he take away from them all the signs of their connection with the LORD; still they can pray, still they can work with the land and the animals, still they can bear children. Yet, a restriction now is in place: we do not always see God's hand in our lives, nor do we bask in his ineffable glory. To those of us who would complain that this seems unfair and who clamor for unhampered access—"Send me a vision!" "Where is the sign?"—one wise pastoral voice warns:

> A meeting face to face with God is always a moment of judgment for us. We cannot meet God in prayer or in meditation or in contemplation and not be either saved or condemned. . . . To meet God face to face . . . is a critical moment in our lives, and thanks be to Him that He does not always present Himself to us when we wish to meet Him, because we might not be able to endure such a meeting. Remember the many passages in Scripture in which we are told how bad it is to find oneself face to face with God, because God is power, God is truth, God is purity. Therefore, the first thought we ought to have when we do not tangibly perceive the divine presence, is a thought of gratitude. God is merciful; He does not come in an untimely way.[15]

No, God knows what he is doing. The closed gate, along with death and vulnerability, remind us of our need to cry, "Lord, have mercy!" All humanity since the expulsion from Eden does not walk naturally with God. We need to knock so that the gate may open. We need mercy; we need help; we need instruction concerning true worship of the Holy One.

Christians might be tempted to retort, *but the gate now is open!* That was the old covenant! Certainly, the advent of Jesus has torn the restrictive curtain in the temple and opened the door. Indeed, he *is* that door, and we will come to this wonder in the next chapter of this study. Even so, the Old Testament remains part of our Scriptures. Let us hear these words, directed to Christians just like us, who presumed upon God's mercy:

I want you to know, brothers [and sisters!], that our fathers were all under the cloud, and all passed through the sea, and all were baptized into Moses in the cloud and in the sea, and all ate the same spiritual food and all drank the same spiritual drink. For they drank from the spiritual Rock which followed them, and the Rock was Christ. Nevertheless with most of them God was not pleased; for they were overthrown in the wilderness. Now these things are *examples* for us, not to desire evil as they did. . . . Now these things happened to them as an example, but they were written down for our instruction, upon whom the end of the ages has come. Therefore let any one who thinks that he stands take heed lest he fall. (1 Cor. 10:1–6, 11–12 RSV, with a few alterations)

Paul here directs the Corinthians, and so those of us who read his letters in the Church today, to look to the Old Testament. In the Old Testament are both positive and negative patterns (*typoi*, "examples"). Though they did not know Christ by name, the Hebrews entered God's presence, ate and drank of Christ, and yet rebelled. Paul considered their state as an apt cautionary tale for Corinthian Christians who were tempted to be eclectic, to mix the worship of the LORD with rites and acts alien to God's people (1 Cor. 10:21–22). These patterns stand in the Old Testament for us, too, helping us to understand more about the holiness of God, more about the awe meant to accompany worship, and more about the danger of being in God's presence unprepared. The beginning of worship is the fear of the LORD.

Meeting at the Footstool of the LORD

How, then, did the holy God call his covenant people to enter into his gates? Throughout the Old Testament, worship is located at places of access, chosen by the LORD. God appears to the patriarchs by means of revelatory dreams on "holy ground," where they build an altar or make a sacrifice. He appears to Moses on his holy mountain, at the tabernacle for which he gives detailed construction plans. Later, the LORD shows himself at the threshold of the gates of the Holy City and the great gate into the temple courts. The inner part of the temple, built in concentric circles, was especially understood to be a place of access. Throughout his covenant history with the people, the LORD did not normally appear to them directly but instead raised up leaders to serve as mediators and anointed ones to represent himself to them. After a period of some development, the holy offices of prophet, priest, and king are carefully separated, again to restrain human pride, and to remind the people of their dependence upon a holy God, whom they do not know face-to-face, but by witness and by covenant membership.

God's people are not to worship as they see fit. Rather, they are to worship "at the place which the LORD your God will choose" (Deut. 16:6), that is, where God can be said to "rest his feet." The worship is to be conducted within the human realm at the place where God in his goodness reveals himself: God's people must worship at God's footstool. Of course, the entire world belongs to God in the Old Testament, but there is a measured way in which God shows himself to the Hebrew, or Israelite, people. His instructions remind them that worship is not something to be created by their own imaginations, instituted at some sacred grove or other where pagan gods have been said to visit. God's divine reserve speaks of the *wonder* that human beings—and fallen humans at that!—are called to have communion with their Creator.

The holiness of God is further underscored by two ways of speaking about "God's footstool" in the Old Testament. The first is positive: Jerusalem, or especially the temple, is *the* footstool of God, the place where human beings may meet with the King of kings. The second is negative: *not even* the temple can provide this place of rest, because God cannot be contained. Rather, the entire earth is God's own footstool, even if not all races of humanity acknowledge God's reign yet.

We see the first idea, *the temple as God's footstool*, both in the stories of King David, and in the Psalms. Psalm 99:5 exhorts the people, "Extol the LORD our God; worship at his footstool! Holy is he!" Psalm 132, one of the "Songs of Ascent" sung by pilgrims going to the Holy City, cries out with enthusiasm in verse seven, "*Let us go* to his dwelling place; let us worship at his footstool." These psalms assume a knowledge that the phrase "God's footstool" refers to the temple in Jerusalem. Both the stories in 2 Samuel 7 and 1 Chronicles 17 relate that King David had always hoped to enshrine the ark of the covenant within a special temple for the Lord.

The ark of the covenant was that sacred object that doubled as a throne for the unseen God and a treasure chest for the holy objects of the past. Toward the end of his life, King David, now a mature man, lives in a palace, and the Hebrew people have been established as a nation, no longer a nomadic group of motley tribes. The ark that accompanied them on battles and expeditions has been brought home to David's own city, and the king desires for it to be placed in a special house for the Lord. God has finally settled them as a blossoming nation in the land of promise, and so David wants to put the ark at rest too in its own temple or sacred place. This is a fulfillment of Abraham's call, a direction recovered under Moses and now coming to fuller expression under David. But, in 1 Chronicles, we are told that this task is a solemn responsibility, something that David cannot fulfill because he has "shed blood" as a warrior (1 Chron. 28:3). It is a "great work," because the edifice is not "for humans but for the LORD God" (1 Chron. 29:1 EH). Listen to David's heart-cry, his words as he passes the responsibility over to his son, the young Solomon. Here we discover the meaning of the temple—not a house to confine God, but his footstool, the place where he will condescend to be at home to guide the people.

Then King David rose to his feet and said: "Hear me, my brethren and my people. I had it in my heart to build a house of rest for the ark of the covenant of the LORD, and for the footstool of our God; and I made preparations for building. . . . And you, Solomon my son, know the God of your father, and serve him with a whole heart and with a willing mind; for the LORD searches all hearts, and understands every plan and thought. If you seek him, he will be found by you; but if you forsake him, he will cast you off for ever. Take heed now, for the LORD has chosen you to build a house for the sanctuary; be strong, and do it." (1 Chron. 28:2, 9–10)

David's instructions closely link the belief that God will rest his feet with the chosen people with the conviction that God is not limited but searches his people's heart and their motivations. Significantly, the Israelites, unlike the nations around them, never put an idol in the tabernacle or the temple as a representation of the LORD. Later, in the time of David's grandson Rehoboam, when the rebellious northern tribes follow this procedure under their leader Jeroboam by putting golden calves at Dan and Bethel, God classifies their action with other abominations (2 Kings 23:13–15). God had honored Jerusalem as the place where David's son would build the temple, but the very covenant, the stone tablets within the ark, warned that there should never be a visual representation of God. The ark served to signal God's ineffable presence, which usually remained unseen.

Several centuries later, when the Babylonian invaders sacked the temple, they would be surprised to find no idol in that impressive fortress but only an empty throne—the ark that held the covenant. This golden throne was similar to the places where *their* earthly ruler sat, and had holy cherubim holding it up on either side, with their faces covered by tapering wings, cast also in gold. And there is one more detail: though at rest in the temple for generations, the ark still sat fitted with poles, those very poles by which it was carried through the wilderness and with the Hebrews as they wandered. This empty throne, fitted for movement, constantly spoke to the Israelites of their dependence upon God for the promised land, and of the truth that their God was radically free. He had visited them, and settled with them, by his own good pleasure: he was not a pet god but the Ruler of heaven and earth, who had chosen them. Their blessings, and their entry into his presence, were at his request and invitation, and not by right. God is not a mascot. We do not own God—*he* blesses and welcomes us.

The Hebrews, later named the Israelites, worshiped in a countercultural way. They had a temple without a central statue and with a divine throne prepared for travel. It is important to remember that the Israelites did not eschew idols because they thought that the peoples around them actually worshiped the stone or the wooden images. (The latter half of the book of Isaiah describes idolatry in this way, but the words here are ironic.) Clearly, even pagan idols are meant as representatives of a deity, as a focal point for a worshiping people to concentrate upon when they invoke their god. So Jeroboam set up the golden calves in Bethel and in Dan, saying "Behold your gods, O Israel, who brought you up out of the land of Egypt" (1 Kings 12:28). Clearly, Jeroboam did not mean that those bronze images had themselves brought the Hebrews out of Egypt: the calves were meant to represent the Deity who had. But even to represent the Holy One is presumptuous, because it is to try to contain him, to use him, or to force him to be present where the image is placed. And it may well lead to polytheistic idolatry: "Your God" becomes "your gods," both here and in Exodus 32:4, where the people are only honoring a single calf.

In contrast, the Israelites were called to worship so as to remember the might and otherness of the God who had given them leave to approach him. They worshiped this way because God alone is God, because he is worthy, and because he had done great things for them. God's "is-ness" (he alone is the "self-existing one") means that he alone is God. This is, indeed, the main thing that is communicated by God's very name, for which the temple was built. ("A house for [or to] my *name*," God calls the proposed temple, 2 Sam. 7:13; 1 Chron. 22:8.) The sacred name *YHWH was not even pronounced when the Hebrew Bible was read aloud. Instead, the reader substituted the Hebrew word for Lord (*Adonai), but the congregation knew that this was spoken in place of the mysterious YHWH, which means "I am who I am," "I will be who I will be," or even "I cause to be what I cause to be." (In English Bibles, we have normally preserved the tradition by capitalizing the word LORD wherever it stands in the place of the divine name YHWH.) The holy name speaks of sheer reality, and so it also speaks about the narrative that God has given, in which we find ourselves named, and by which we understand our relation to God, to others, and to the world. The strange character of the temple also enshrined what God is like—a great and merciful God calling the people to worship, but with great awe. Even its architecture conveyed to the people, by means of its nesting courts (courts within courts, growing more and more holy), that there is always a way further in toward God's holy presence. To grasp what God is like—holy and merciful—is to worship him.

Finally, there is within the temple, within the very ark, a tangible reminder of what God has done. Within the ark had been placed Aaron's miraculous rod that budded, the two tablets of the commandments, and some manna left from God's provision for them in the wilderness (Exod. 16:33; 25:16; Num. 17). These accoutrements of the temple, kept like relics within the ark, moved the people to thanksgiving. To remember that God is God is to look reality squarely in the face. To consider God's qualities is to be moved to worship. To remember what God has done is to be filled with thanksgiving. The temple, as the footstool of God, was Israel's way of understanding that great truth embedded by C. S. Lewis within his children's novels—like Aslan, the LORD is not safe or tame; but he *is* good.[16]

So then, the temple was never seen as actually containing God. Rather, it was a place where God consented to rest with his people. This was an unusual witness among other nations, which thought that they could represent their gods visually and use them as mascots to rally the troops or as insurance to guarantee safety and prosperity. Instead, the God of the Hebrews, YHWH, was radically free, and it was he who had Israel to himself. So the psalmist exclaims: "Extol the LORD our God; worship at his footstool! Holy is he!" (Ps. 99:5). And the Psalter also gives the invitation: "Let us go to his dwelling place; let us worship at his footstool" (Ps. 132:7).

Along with this positive evaluation of the temple as God's footstool, there is a competing tradition, a minority and cautionary view. This is found in the second half of Isaiah, where, amidst much rhetoric, again and again the Israelites are forcibly reminded that *no* temple, not even the one in Jerusalem, could enclose or tame this God of glory. Truthfully, no one place can be God's footstool: "Thus says the LORD: 'Heaven is my throne and the earth is my footstool; what is the house which you would build for me, and what is the place of my rest?'" (Isa. 66:1). This prophetic word hints at the theme found earlier in the great vision of chapter 6: worship is entry into a bigger space! This is the same passage that St. Stephen quotes just prior to his martyrdom (Acts 7:49), when he is warning those who have not recognized God's holy presence in Jesus of Nazareth. (But we are running ahead of ourselves—let's stay with the Old Testament for now.)

Here is the point: because of the subtle nature of sin and our human tendency not to worship God as he is, the people were given careful instructions with regard to worship. And even those instructions were not to take the place of God's very own rule and will and presence: the ark, the tabernacle, and the temple were signs of God's goodness, and not themselves to be adored. They pointed to God, they provided for God's people a place of access, by which worship could be entered into, because it was God's will to meet with his people. The Scriptures make this clear both in the way that the temple is given a positive role and in the prophetic words that qualify this modest role. God rested with his people, whom he had called. God is holy. Yet he is the LORD of the whole cosmos. It is because of God's nature and actions that entrance into worship becomes a possibility.

Luminous Old Testament Moments of Access

We have seen, then, that the purpose of the temple in Old Testament times was not to domesticate God, nor to suggest that God had concourse with his people only in circumscribed ways. The holiness of the ark, the tabernacle, and the temple were, so to speak, at the service of the holy LORD, who remained free in visiting humanity, and in calling people into his presence. God's meeting of his people in the temple was, so to speak, provisional. It held forth the promise of a greater summons: Israel was given "as a blessing" to the nations, and their God was never to be conceived as a tribal deity.

Because of this, there are poignant passages in the Old Testament that picture not only the representatives of Israel, not only the whole of God's people, but indeed the entire earth at the verge of the presence of God. Among these are the following: the forging of the covenant at Sinai (Exod. 24), the homecoming song when God's ark was brought into the city of David (2 Sam. 6; 1 Chron. 15–16, which is interconnected with Ps. 96), various accounts of God's glory filling the tabernacle and the temple of Solomon (e.g., 2 Chron. 7), and Ezekiel's vision of the Lord in which a recommitted people are led back from exile to the place of worship (Ezek. 37). Each of these passages, though different in detail and emphasis, concerns entry into the presence of God during the context of worship. Let's consider them in more detail.

Exodus 24: A Mystical Narrative of Assent and Ascent

In this chapter where the LORD forges his covenant with the house of Israel, some contemporary liturgists have seen a template, complete with constituent parts, for our worship today.[17] Some have thought that this places too great a burden upon covenant as *the* foundation for Christian worship. However, at the very least, Exodus 24 provides an intriguing picture of the graduated ascent of God's people as they enter his presence. The mysterious passage begins with God's invitation:

> And he said to Moses, "*Come up* to the LORD, you and Aaron, Nadab, and Abihu, and seventy of the elders of Israel, *and worship afar off.* Moses alone shall come near to the LORD; but the others shall not come near, and the people shall not come up with him." (Exod. 24:1–2)

The contemporary reader might, at first blush, find herself irritated by the privilege afforded the seventy, the three, and Moses. The people are not to come near, says the LORD. As Christians we might be appalled at this and overlook the passage for any other value that it might offer, except as a foil or contrast to the new covenant. The veil is lifted now, so why should we pay attention to the standoffishness of an Old Testament deity? This response, though natural, borders on what we might call Marcionism. Marcion was a second-century theologian who, in order to preserve what he believed was a pure version of the gospel, excised the entire Old Testament and honored only those new covenant writings that had little connection with Judaism. (For example, the birth narratives of Jesus, featuring Anna and Simeon, were removed.)

A closer reading of Exodus 24, however, may lead us beyond mere irritation, especially when we see that the people give their assent. In the first verse, there is a strange juxtaposition: "Come up to the LORD; worship afar." This dual command is given to the entire people, including Moses. There is something about the LORD that requires our response to his summons; yet he is holy, and so "distance" is part of that worship. In terms of the entire flow of the chapter, it is also important to remember that Moses, the elders, and the people are one. It is true that Moses alone climbs to the pinnacle and that the people do not breach the boundary at the bottom of the holy mountain. Yet they are in no way offended! Indeed, several chapters earlier (20:19) the people have begged Moses to be the intercessor, because of God's great majesty. Instead, they respond to God's invitation to Moses and their other representatives with enthusiasm: "All the words which the LORD has spoken we will do" (Exod. 24:3).

Following their assent, Moses builds an altar at the foot of the mountain and twelve pillars to represent the tribes, at which Moses and all the people hear the words of God and enter into a covenant marked with blood. Following the ceremony, Moses, the three, and the seventy ascend and enter into an ineffable vision. The vision incorporates a shared meal with God, who is here named "the God of Israel." (This is a verbal indication that those who see the vision are indeed representing the whole people and that the meal benefits all, not just the seventy.) Finally, Moses ascends (accompanied, it seems, by Joshua) and enters the cloud at the height of the mountain. For seven days he waits, until the "appearance of the glory of the LORD" (Exod. 24:17) shines so brightly that even the people at the base of the mountain know God is there. After the theophany on the seventh day, Moses sojourns there for forty days and nights, where he receives instructions about the building of the tabernacle and about worship in general (Exod. 25–31) as well as the two tablets.

We discern this pattern: the people hear God's words, revering and worshiping the LORD from afar; the elders come closer to eat and drink with the God of Israel (yet there is still awe and distance); Moses enters into a mysterious intimacy with the LORD, accompanied by verifying signs in the sight of the people. With Moses, though the presence of God is weighty and intense, there remains a distance: he beholds "the appearance of the glory of the LORD," cautiously expressed in terms of reserve. Together, the people illumine the mystery of God's concourse with humanity, including the apt response of awe, the staggering promise of a shared life with God, and the nearly unimaginable prospect of intimacy with a God who nevertheless remains (to use a theological phrase) *totaliter aliter* (wholly different and other than us). In worshiping this God, as he has invited them, the people join with a larger company that is gathered together and focused upon the same Lord; their worship also touches upon a bigger space, glimpsed by the elders, but entered into by Moses (at least in part) as he goes into the cloud of glory.

Triumphal Homecoming and Divine Invitation

Both the rhetorical injunction, "come up; worship afar," solemnly spoken by the divine voice, and the complex narrative of Exodus 24 give us some insight into entrance as fundamental to Hebrew worship. As we move further along in the story of the development of Israel, we take note of the dramatic incident in which David danced before the ark as it was brought into his own city and of the exuberant psalm associated with this homecoming. The story is told both in 2 Samuel 6:15–23 and 1 Chronicles 15:1–16:36. We know the story best from the first account, because it is briefer and because it is remarkable for highlighting the sacredness of the ark along with the drama of Michal's scorn for her exuberant husband. Even in 2 Samuel, however, the principal actor is not David. Rather, his dancing is accompanied by "all the house of Israel . . . making merry," and the homecoming of the ark ends with the people being blessed "in the name of the LORD of hosts" (2 Sam. 6:18) and given gifts of meat, bread, and fruit cake. All the people are incorporated into the fellowship of the Lord: his ark enters, and so they enter his presence, a joy punctuated by a psalm of invitation to worship.

The Chronicler's account deepens these latent themes of incorporation. David assembles all of Israel to "bring up the ark" (1 Chron. 15:3), though it is of course the Levites, painstakingly numbered, who are to actually carry the sacred object, while their kindred are to sing and play. As with the account in Samuel, we are told of David's sheer joy (but only briefly of Michal's scorn) and of how David blesses the people "in the name of the Lord," distributing to everyone, whether man or woman, celebratory food. The installation of the ark is prefaced by music and concluded by music, with portions of three interspliced psalms (cf. Pss. 96, 105, and 106) recited with rejoicing. David's own joy has played the spiritual Pied Piper, as the people join in the train. (In our Christian imagination, we may flash forward to that great victory celebration of Jesus, who by his death, resurrection, and ascension, "led captivity captive, and gave gifts to his people" [Eph. 4:8 EH].) The people, all of them, enter into worship as the ark enters their midst, and the psalm of joy invites this entry:

> O give thanks to the LORD, call upon his name, make known his deeds among the peoples! . . . Honor and majesty are before him; strength and joy are *in his place*. Ascribe to the LORD, O families of the peoples, ascribe to the LORD glory and strength! [*Come before him! Worship the LORD in the beauty of holiness* (LXX *in his holy court*); tremble in his presence, all the earth.] (1 Chron. 16:8, 27–28, 29b–30a, bracketed portion is my translation)

By their song, Asaph and his kindred not only give voice to all the people of Israel, but they embrace the peoples, or nations, whom they desire should know the LORD as well. The Chronicler has adapted three psalms to suit the story that he is narrating: reference to the "sanctuary" or "temple" of the Lord has been generalized, for example, to speak about God who is "in his place." One might have expected, then, that the book would concentrate wholly upon the joy of the Israelite people and their honor of housing the ark of the LORD in the city of David. It would be natural in such a story to omit reference to the other nations, for surely the homecoming of the ark was an in-house event.

But nothing could be further from the case. Though God's people are especially privileged to house the ark of the LORD's presence, this joyful occasion is not only for their benefit but for the illumination of the whole earth. The Lord is not their possession; his worship is not their exclusive "right." Instead, God's strength and joy are "in *his* place" for *all* to see. And so all the "families of the peoples" (16:28) are invited to come before the LORD with offerings to "worship the Lord in the beauty of holiness" (16:29 KJV). (Other translations render this "in holy array" [RSV] or "in holy splendor" [NRSV].) Does this phrase "beauty of holiness" refer to the LORD? Yes, but the invitation, "Worship the Lord in the beauty of holiness" is worded so as to also suggest that humankind enters the radiance, and the beauty, as we worship. As we "come before him" we are "in his place," "in the beauty of holiness." Interestingly, the Greek translation of this passage ascribes the holiness directly to the "temple courts," which are holy places of beauty. God's people, as they move further into the presence, or the courts of the LORD, are transformed. C. S. Lewis remarks upon the biblical hope of actual entry into beauty, expressing our human yearning:

> We do not merely want to *see* beauty, though, God knows, even that is bounty enough. We want something else which can hardly be put into words—to be united with the beauty we see, to pass into it, to receive it into ourselves, to bathe in it, to become part of it.[18]

So then, in this story of the early monarchy, the song that "David first appointed" (1 Chron. 16:7) to be sung has been shaped by the understanding of the *later* Israelite people who knew both the temple and the need of the nations for God's truth. When we turn from the psalm as it is embedded in the Chronicler's narrative to its honored place in the Psalter, there are slight variations so that general themes of the holy place and other people become crystal clear. Consider the telling differences between Psalm 96 (LXX 95) and 1 Chronicles 16:23–33. First, there is the editorial heading to the Greek version of Psalm 95 (Hebrew 96), which titles the psalm "A Psalm of David, *when the house had been rebuilt after captivity.*" Here are some selections showing in boldface type its differences with its Chronicles counterpart:

> O sing unto the LORD a new song. . . . Honour and majesty are before him: strength and beauty are **in his sanctuary.** . . . O worship the LORD in the beauty of holiness [LXX "in his holy court"]; let the whole earth stand in awe of him. . . .

For he cometh . . . with righteousness to judge the world, and the peoples with his truth. (Ps. 96:1, 6, 9, 13)[19]

In the Psalter's version, references to the holy dwelling of the Lord and entry into it abound, especially in the Greek translation. The Psalter also speaks even more clearly of the truth of God operating on behalf of all people: "he shall judge the peoples [nations] righteously" (v. 10b). The phrase, "he cometh . . . with righteousness to judge the world, and the peoples with his truth" (v. 13) includes a cosmic dimension to the psalm that is not so patent in the Chronicles story, though it is retained there to some extent.

The return of the ark to the midst of the people of Israel, then, is adorned by psalms (in particular, Psalm 96) that consider worship as entry into a larger space and company. The Chronicler suggests that the use of these three psalms before the ark became a tradition, something understood as handed down by David himself: "on that day David first appointed that thanksgiving be sung to the Lord" (1 Chron. 16:7). This was a duty committed to the singing Levites, but done on behalf of all the people, who say their "Amen!" and praise the Lord (1 Chron. 16:36b). Before leaving this scene of solemn corporate joy, we should pause also to remark upon the obvious: David pictures for us an *action* that is bigger than ourselves as well. David's ecstasy before the ark is, in Jewish and Christian tradition, a forceful reminder of a dimension without which worship would be false—worship takes us *out of ourselves*. (The very word "ecstasy" means to stand or go outside of myself, as though drawn out by compulsion.)[20] All of the house of Israel joins in this dancing and rejoicing, with the exception of David's wife Michal, who does not join the party but stands aloof from the ceremony, observing it from her window. The worship appointed for the Lord involves entrance into a large company, space, and action; to objectify and critique worship, as Michal does, precludes any such entrance. Worship, in the style of David's psalm, is exhibited in lavish praise, utter humility, and trust in the goodness of the Lord, who has made his name known. From the Christian perspective, these things are captured in the well-known English hymn by John S. B. Monsell, first written in 1863 and revised by Monsell himself in his Parish Hymnal of 1873:

> Worship the Lord in the beauty of holiness,
> Bow down before Him, His glory proclaim;
> Gold of obedience and incense of lowliness,
> Bring and adore Him—the Lord is His Name.
> Low at His feet lay Thy burden of carefulness,
> High on His heart He will bear it for thee;
> Comfort thy sorrows and answer thy prayerfulness,
> Guiding thy steps as may best for thee be.
> Fear not to enter His courts in the slenderness
> Of the poor wealth thou wouldst reckon as thine;

Truth in its beauty, and love in its tenderness,
These are the offerings to lay on His shrine.
These though we bring them in trembling and fearfulness,
He will accept for the Name that is dear,
Mornings of joy give for evenings of tearfulness,
Trust for our trembling, and hope for our fear.

The Glory of the LORD: God Makes His Presence Clear

What is this magnetism, this drawing force that induces such a lavish show of affection and praise? It is, of course, the LORD's weighty dignity, his potent presence among us. The display of his beauty, the indication of his mercy, the illumination of his truth calls for a response. We are so used to the subtle ways in which God intimates his presence that we are startled when his coming is accompanied by dramatic signs more suited to his grandeur. But our family history registers a few points at which the utter glory of the LORD shines through at the places where God's people are worshiping. C. S. Lewis has spoken about such revelations in terms of "the weight of glory"[21]—the solidness, the utter realness of God seen at such moments, at such "entry points" into God's presence.

In Deuteronomy, the ancient Moses reflects upon this glory when he reminds those who will go into the promised land about the experience that the Hebrew people had while sojourning in the desert: "The LORD came from Sinai, and dawned from Seir upon us; he shone forth from Mount Paran, he came from the ten thousands of holy ones, with flaming fire at his right hand" (Deut. 33:2). The glory of Sinai was not confined to that place but came also to adorn the "tent" or "tabernacle of meeting," as it was so aptly called. When that portable shrine was dedicated, "the glory of the LORD filled the tabernacle." Indeed, "Moses *was not able to enter* the tent of meeting, because . . . the glory of the LORD filled the tabernacle" (Exod. 40:34–35). This same energy of God was seen when Moses passed the baton to Joshua, for "the LORD appeared in the tent in a pillar of cloud; and the pillar of cloud stood *by the door of the tent*" as Joshua was commissioned (Deut. 31:15). Or fast-forward in Israel's history to Solomon's dedication of the temple, the permanent sanctuary that David had wanted to build: "When Solomon had ended his prayer . . . the glory of the LORD filled the temple. And the priests *could not enter* the house of the LORD, because the glory of the LORD filled the LORD's house" (2 Chron. 7:1–2).

This palpable radiance of the Lord, we shall see in the following chapter, is not simply an Old Testament concept. The theme is there when the three disciples see the LORD Jesus for who he really is on the Mount of Transfiguration. They are so affected by the divine glory that they are drawn into it: "As he was praying, the appearance of his countenance was altered, and his raiment became dazzling white. . . . A cloud came and overshadowed them; and they were afraid *as they entered* the cloud" (Luke 9:29, 34). Indeed, this

magnetic and weighty radiance that impedes human sense is attached not
only to earthly sanctuaries but also to the heavenly archetype, in the heaven
of heavens: "The temple of the tent of witness in heaven *was opened*, . . . and
the temple was filled with smoke from the glory of God and from his power,
and *no one could enter the temple*" (Rev. 15:5, 8). Passages like this take us
back to the words of *Metropolitan Anthony Bloom, who cautions us against
a casual longing to enter God's presence, to see the LORD in an "immediate"
way. Even the children's carol reminds us that we need preparation:

> Be near me, Lord Jesus, I ask thee to stay
> Close by me forever, and love me, I pray;
> Bless all the dear children in thy tender care,
> *And fit us for heaven to live with thee there.*

Worship as Our Prepared Response: Prophetic Warning in Ezekiel

The natural result of God's self-revelation of glory is, of course, worship.
When Solomon finishes his prayer of dedication, punctuated by the descent
of God's glory, worship inevitably follows:

> When Solomon had ended his prayer, fire came down from heaven and consumed
> the burnt offering and the sacrifices, and the glory of the LORD filled the temple.
> And the priests could not enter the house of the LORD, because the glory of the
> LORD filled the LORD's house. When all the children of Israel saw the fire come
> down and the glory of the LORD upon the temple, they bowed down with their
> faces to the earth on the pavement and worshiped and gave thanks to the LORD,
> saying, "For he is good, for his steadfast love endures forever." Then the king
> and all the people offered sacrifice before the LORD. (2 Chron. 7:1–4)

Nothing could seem more natural. The people respond to the Lord's majestic
presence, both praising him and acknowledging their sinfulness by means of
sacrifice.

But this natural response is not so very natural for sinful people. We have
constricted and numbed hearts that have forgotten our first love, wayward
wills that are out of line with our truest desires and deepest knowledge. How,
then, can we truly enter into worship? Psalm 95, which has served as a psalm
of entrance for both the Jewish and the Christian communities for centuries,
acknowledges the impediments that we face, even when we have been invited
by God himself to worship:

> O come, let us sing to the LORD; let us make a joyful noise to the rock of our
> salvation! Let us come into his presence with thanksgiving; let us make a joyful
> noise to him with songs of praise! For the LORD is a great God, and a great King
> above all gods. . . . Harden not your hearts, as at Meribah [in the provocation],
> as on the day at Masseh [in the day of temptation] in the wilderness, when your

fathers tested me, and put me to the proof, though they had seen my work. For forty years I loathed that generation and said, "They are a people who err in heart, and they do not regard my ways." Therefore I swore in my anger that they should not enter my rest. (Ps. 95:1–3, 8–11)

The psalm breathes a note of caution: "harden not your hearts, . . . they do not regard my ways." The anger of the LORD against Israel's stubbornness provides those who read the Scriptures with a cautionary tale—unless we turn, we may not enter God's rest. Even the worship book of God's people, the Psalter, contains a realism about our potential to miss out on God's good gift. And so, the early history of Israel, with its first generation that did not enter into the promised land, stands as a warning to all worshipers (to Israel and to us) that it is possible to be barred from God's ultimate Sabbath—the Sabbath of restful worship.

The prophets in general, and especially Jeremiah and Ezekiel, tackled the problem of hardened hearts. Their books are replete with words of judgment and warning. Yet they also register that the LORD does not simply mark sin but does something about it. And so, to the people suffering in exile, hoping to return and to reenter the holy land after punishment, they relayed God's promise that he would heal the heart and enlarge the capacity of his people to truly worship. Ezekiel's vivid language makes this promise especially memorable. In chapters 20 and 36, Ezekiel speaks of the presence of God with the exiled people, how he has in mind to bring them back to the holy mountain, back into the land, to dwell among them and to lodge his Spirit deeply within his people:

For on my holy mountain, the mountain height of Israel . . . there all the house of Israel, all of them, shall serve me in the land. . . . As a pleasing odor I will accept you . . . and gather you . . . and I will manifest my holiness among you . . . when I bring you into the land of Israel. (Ezek. 20:40–42)

A new heart I will give you, and a new spirit I will put within you; and I will take out of your flesh the heart of stone and give you a heart of flesh. And I will put my Spirit within you. (Ezek. 36:26–27)

In these passages, worship is allowed to take place as God is revealed to the people. Ezekiel reminds the exiles that this revelation does not occur randomly, but after a time of preparation: God will remove their heart of stone, so that with a new heart, and by the Holy Spirit, they will be able to worship. English speaking readers today may muse over the single "heart" promised by God, yet the Hebrew here is instructive. In the phrase "give you a heart of flesh," the "you" is plural while the "heart" is singular. We can translate this both in terms of the Spirit being placed "within" each heart and "among" the Israelites, within their corporate heart. The personal and corporate come together.

Moreover, Ezekiel patterns this return from exile to God's mount after the earlier story of the exodus. Remember the length of time that the Hebrews trekked the wilderness, waiting forty years until those who had not trusted God had passed on. Only then were they brought to the land, gathered by God to worship. There is an emphasis on God drawing near to them—"I will put my Spirit within/among you"—as well as an emphasis on the people's return and on entry into God's presence—"On my holy mountain . . . in the land . . . into the land." This is God's work, God's own initiative, which they are asked to accept. Yet they are not simply passive recipients: they move into God's presence, and so they also act.

Some of the exiles from Jerusalem no doubt received Ezekiel's promise in their own day, happy to know that God had not abandoned them but held forward a future for the people of Israel. They could hardly have known that Ezekiel's words, with the words of the prophet Jeremiah, would be understood in a fuller light after the Messiah came. St. Paul, reflecting upon the promise of a new heart, but in deeper knowledge of God, through Christ and by the power of the Holy Spirit, saw that the ancient promises of God had a profound fulfillment in the Church (2 Cor. 2–3). God is the great initiator, coming into our midst. Liberated by God, we make our exodus and enter into worship. Enabled by God, we return, and we enter into worship, into the very presence of God.

Gathering the Strands

Our quick journey from Genesis through to the later prophets of the exile has yielded several recurring themes or principles, some of them surprising:

- Worship is in a large company, yet involves each of us personally.
- God takes up residence in physical things and in history, yet is not contained.
- God takes the initiative even in our worship.
- God adapts to meet our weaknesses.
- God doesn't leave us where we are.
- God promises to change us from *within*—within the heart, within the worshiping community.
- God uses the present to point to the full future.

These themes and principles are shown in great variety throughout the Scriptures, in exuberant psalm and song, in invitation and promise, in mystical narrative, in prophetic vision and warning. *In all this, we have seen that God is our gracious host and invites us to worship.* Part of the answer to hard hearts is to turn to God and actually enter into worship—for it is in the entrance to worship itself, as we have learned from our Hebrew brothers and sisters of the past, that we are transformed.

> I am coming to gather all nations and tongues; and they shall come and shall see my glory. . . . For as the new heavens and the new earth which I will make shall remain before me, says the LORD . . . all flesh shall come to worship before me. (Isa. 66:18, 22–23)

Questions for Discussion

1. Is entrance into God's presence through worship only necessary because of the Fall, because we have *departed* from his presence in the first place? Or is entrance a necessary part of worship for the created order *because* it is created, and not divine in its nature?
2. Why might visual representations of God lead to polytheistic idolatry for the Israelite people? In what ways is this a live danger today?
3. What is it that we find challenging today when we read of Moses' special privilege in encountering God in Exodus 24? Do we have a sense of entitlement with respect to the divine that is particular to our time, while the Hebrews begged Moses to intercede for them? Is this sense that we ought to encounter God "face to face" ourselves justifiable?
4. If God cannot be *contained* in particular physical things and localized places, then why do you think that the LORD makes himself accessible to us through them?
5. Should we think of worship more as rest (entering God's "Sabbath") or as work (as entering into the "liturgy," literally, the work of the people)?

3

"In Spirit and in Truth"

Entrance in the New Testament

From Older Testament to New

In the previous chapter we observed that many passages of the Old Testament approach worship in terms of entrance. God through his prophets directed the Israelite people to seek him at his footstool, and in the heyday of the monarchy they entered by the gates of the holy city and the temple into the courts of the LORD. Whether personal devotion or a collective festival was in view, Israelite worship was performed with an eye to the whole company of God's people. Moreover, those visionaries who were granted special insight into the holy majesty of *YHWH, such as the prophet Isaiah, understood that entry into worship went even beyond a human action in the temple precincts. Rather, they viewed worship as *entrance into a company, space, and action bigger than human imagination*. The worship of God's people went beyond the confines of Judea or Israel because it was celebrated in a space larger even than that of the promised land: the actions of those who worship the LORD are envisaged as joined with the ministrations of the heavenly angels and with the general (but not always articulate) joy of the rest of creation.

The Old Testament prophets understood participation in a realm, company, and action proximate to the holy God as leading to transformation: repentance, cleansing, healing, and purpose, all given by the LORD. Moreover, God shows his mysterious presence to the people at those rare but poignant moments of worship where they see his ineffable glory—at the top of the holy mountain, adorning the tabernacle, and filling the entire temple.

However, the vision of God's glory, entrance into worship, and transformation do not occur automatically because of those two enemies of humanity: sin and death. Human beings share the problem of squeezed, constricted hearts. Yet the Old Testament intimates that God intends to do something about humanity's inability truly to enter into worship and so to be transformed. Jeremiah and Ezekiel look forward to God's Spirit, by whom God's people may be turned, and who will change the heart, the inner core. That work takes place in the LORD who is the Son, whose glory the prophets glimpsed from afar and whose cleansing fire (say later theologians and liturgists) touched Isaiah's lips even prior to the Incarnation.

It is a frequent temptation to compare negatively Old Testament worship with worship in the new covenant by strongly contrasting the physical with the spiritual. For example, some assume that in the Old Testament God's people concentrated upon the *physical* tabernacle and temple, but that since Jesus enacted the new covenant, worship is now something wholly spiritual. And by "spiritual" they mean nonmaterial, that which is wholly internal or cerebral. In this vein, Christian critics of the Old Testament read Jesus' words to the Samaritan woman (John 4) and interpret worship "in Spirit and in truth" to mean that true worship requires or concerns nothing physical.

This would be a mistake. Just as the spiritually enlivened coal actually touched Isaiah's lips, so today God's Spirit truly touches his people, changing them wholly, in body as well as in mind and spirit. The New Testament *temple* is just as physical as that of the Old Testament—not a building, surely, but the body of our Lord Jesus Christ himself, and (by extension) the body made up of those who are joined together in Christ. There is a physical aspect to our worship because it includes embodied Christians gathered together, joined to the Christ who took on a real human body, in which he lived and died on the wood of a cross, which was transformed into a risen body, and in which he ascended, carrying humanity with him into the glorious presence of the Father. The continued practices of baptism and *Communion in nearly every Christian community signify that our worship goes beyond the material world *without* abandoning that world; rather, we gather up the physical with the spiritual when we worship in Spirit and in truth.

Entering with Our Bodies: The Transfiguration

The transformation of the physical world appears most clearly in the luminous narrative concerning Jesus' own Transfiguration, found in Matthew, Mark, and Luke, and shining its glory (though not recounted as a narrative) through every page of the Gospel of John. In this remarkable account, we encounter many of the features already noted in the Old Testament passages where worship is portrayed as entrance. Let us focus especially on Luke's version:

> Now about eight days after these sayings he took with him Peter and John and James, and went up on the mountain to pray. And as he was praying, the appearance of his countenance was altered, and his raiment became dazzling white. And behold, two men talked with him, Moses and Elijah, who appeared in glory and spoke of his departure [literally, *exodus*], which he was to accomplish at Jerusalem. Now Peter and those who were with him were heavy with sleep, and when they wakened they saw his glory and the two men who stood with him. And as the men were parting from him, Peter said to Jesus, "Master, it is well that we are here; let us make three booths, one for you and one for Moses and one for Elijah"—not knowing what he said. As he said this, a cloud came and overshadowed them; and they were afraid as they entered the cloud. And a voice came out of the cloud, saying, "This is my Son, my Chosen; listen to him!" And when the voice had spoken, Jesus was found alone. And they kept silence and told no one in those days anything of what they had seen. (Luke 9:28–36)

Jesus has ascended to a remote mountain to pray, alone with Peter, James, and John. Despite this theme of solitude, the people of God are gathered around Jesus: old covenant believers are represented by Moses and Elijah, and the new covenant Church by the three apostles. Their actions speak of communion together with the Lord. They meet for prayer (Luke 9:28); they engage in encouraging conversation (9:31); they receive God's instruction (9:35). The narrative follows the pattern of separation, vision, audition, awe, response, enlightenment, participation, and command. All these same elements appear in the ascent of Moses to receive the commandments (Exod. 24) and in the temple-vision of Isaiah (Isa. 6). Luke, however, highlights some differences between the two covenants in an astonishing way. Not only are the disciples given a vision that shows their lives to be interconnected through Jesus with Moses and Elijah, but they also bodily *enter* the glory of the One who *alone* they must heed. Indeed, their entrance into the divine glory will be matched by God's incursion into the depth of their being. St. Paul describes this transformation, linking it with Jesus' transformation, when he declares "God . . . has shone in our hearts to give the light of the knowledge of the glory of God in the face of Christ" (2 Cor. 4:6). Here, at the Mount of Transfiguration, the disciples (and we with them) learn that God's people need not build shrines to hold God's presence because they themselves will become portable tabernacles of the glory.

Whereas the LORD spoke with truth to Moses and Isaiah in the time of the Old Testament, in the Transfiguration Jesus' disciples learn (together with their Old Testament counterparts) something more: truth is a Person, truth is the Holy One, Jesus. Jesus not only brings light, but *is* the Light; Jesus not only speaks words, but *is* the Word; Jesus not only shines with glory but also transforms everything and everyone around him, bathing all with glory. We might comment that Moses' encounter with the LORD also culminated in his "catching" God's glory. However, that glory was caught up with the oral/ written Torah, was impermanent, and was borne only by Moses himself, who was the custodian of the Law. Not every Hebrew face shone. Paul deals with these differences between the covenants, describing Moses and the Israelite people over against those who are in Christ:

> Since we have such a hope, we are very bold, not like Moses, who would put a veil over his face so that the Israelites might not gaze at the outcome of what was being brought to an end. But their minds were hardened. For to this day, when they read the old covenant, that same veil remains unlifted, because only through Christ is it taken away. (2 Cor. 3:12–14 EH)

> And we all, with unveiled face, beholding the glory of the LORD, are being transformed into the same image from one degree of glory to another. For this comes from the LORD who is the Spirit. (2 Cor. 3:18 EH)

> For God, who said, "Let light shine out of darkness," has shone in our hearts to give the light of the knowledge of the glory of God in the face of Jesus Christ. (2 Cor. 4:6 EH)

The Transfiguration account indicates that entering into worship has a greater effect than even the reception of cleansing and spiritual help. Jesus' own face and clothing shine as he prays. The disciples' attention upon the One whom they truly see for the first time, and whom they are directed to hear in a new way, issues in their total response—the only response possible in the light of his majesty. Their human intent to "build" becomes superfluous. To see the glory and to hear God's voice is to enter into rest, and so to look even more deeply to the One who gives all understanding and life. "Only one thing is needful," Jesus said at another occasion. The Transfiguration thus offers a New Testament deepening of Isaiah's great temple vision. It adds an invigorating dimension to Isaiah's wonder concerning purged lips and the remote possibility of repentance: not only are God's people called into God's council but they are also called into God's glory, because of Jesus, who is God's glory. Isaiah's lips were purged; those in the company of Jesus are given real faces, fitting them to enter the mysterious divine glory. "And we all . . . are being transformed . . . from one degree of glory to another" (2 Cor. 3:18 EH).

Entering into Communion with the Body of Christ

Because of Jesus, then, the new covenant people of God may enter more profoundly into worship, into communion with God, and so more truly into communion with each other. Acts 2 is helpful in explaining how God has provided this intensification, moving us from the Old Testament into the New.

In this chapter of Acts, we read the story of the giving of the Holy Spirit, Peter's proclamation of the gospel, the appearance of the first Christian community, and the wondrous signs performed by its members. Indeed, we track the change that God has brought about in the world through Jesus. As we read the chapter, we may listen in on Peter's preaching, which explains how this change has occurred (2:14–36), consider the interaction between Peter and the pilgrims gathered in Jerusalem (2:37–41), and pause over Luke's thumbnail sketch of the fledgling Christian community (2:42–47).

Peter's sermon (2:14–36) takes the form of a long narrative-with-appeal that addresses the pilgrims to Jerusalem (and Luke's readers), bringing them up-to-date concerning God's mighty deeds:

Men of Judea and all who dwell in Jerusalem, let this be known to you, and give ear to my words. For these men are not drunk, as you suppose, since it is only the third hour of the day. But this is what was uttered through the prophet Joel: "And in the last days it shall be, God declares, that I will pour out my Spirit on all flesh, and your sons and your daughters shall prophesy, and your young men shall see visions, and your old men shall dream dreams; even on my male servants and female servants in those days I will pour out my Spirit, and they shall prophesy. And I will show wonders in the heavens above and signs on the earth below, blood, and fire, and vapor of smoke; the sun shall be turned to darkness and the moon to blood, before the day of the Lord comes, the great and magnificent day. And it shall come to pass that everyone who calls upon the name of the Lord shall be saved."

Men of Israel, hear these words: Jesus of Nazareth, a man attested to you by God with mighty works and wonders and signs that God did through him in your midst, as you yourselves know—this Jesus, delivered up according to the definite plan and foreknowledge of God, you crucified and killed by the hands of lawless men. God raised him up, loosing the pangs of death, because it was not possible for him to be held by it. For David says concerning him, "I saw the Lord always before me, for he is at my right hand that I may not be shaken; therefore my heart was glad, and my tongue rejoiced; my flesh also will dwell in hope. For you will not abandon my soul to Hades, or let your Holy One see corruption. You have made known to me the paths of life; you will make me full of gladness with your presence."

Brothers, I may say to you with confidence about the patriarch David that he both died and was buried, and his tomb is with us to this day. Being therefore a prophet, and knowing that God had sworn with an oath to him that he would set one of his descendants on his throne, he foresaw and spoke about the resurrection of the Christ, that he was not abandoned to Hades, nor did his flesh see corruption. This Jesus God raised up, and of that we all are witnesses. Being therefore exalted at the right hand of God, and having received from the Father the promise of the Holy Spirit, he has poured out this that you yourselves are seeing and hearing. For David did not ascend into the heavens, but he himself says, "The Lord said to my Lord, Sit at my right hand, until I make your enemies your footstool." Let all the house of Israel therefore know for certain that God has made him both Lord and Christ, this Jesus whom you crucified. (Acts 2:14–36 ESV)

It is helpful to retain Peter's discourse in the back of our mind as we go on to consider the character and commitment of the fledgling Church reflected in this chapter. Peter's sermon places the description of the Church, with its signs and wonders, within the context of the victory of Jesus, the Holy One, by whose exaltation the Holy Spirit had been poured out. The Spirit of the Lord was upon them, so that the communion that they had with God and with each other was different from anything humanity (including Israel) had ever experienced. We are told, in Acts 2:42: "And they devoted themselves to the apostles' teaching and fellowship, to the breaking of the bread and the prayers" (EH). The community, living together, is devoted to

- The Teaching of the Apostles
- The *koinonia (communion) of the Apostles
- Thanksgiving (or blessing)[1] and Participation ("breaking *the* bread")
- The Prayers

Let's pause over this brief description because there is much to digest here.

The Greek text of Acts paints for us a word picture, literally placing the word *apostles* in the middle of the words for *teaching* (*didachē*) and *communion* (*koinōnia*). The early Christians were to learn about Jesus by the teaching that the apostles had received and were passing on; they also entered into their identity, their life with Jesus, by means of the communion of the apostles.

They dedicated themselves

to the *didachē*   **of the apostles**   and to the *koinōnia.*

To be apostolic meant to listen to the apostles' words and to cling to their community, to be one family with them. This first description is supplemented and paralleled by a second feature of the new community, portrayed in identical word order and syntax.

They dedicated themselves

to the breaking   **of the bread**   and to the prayers.

Notice that little article "the" before the word *bread*, and before the word *prayers*. Among New Testament scholars, there is some controversy about

Luke's meaning, but I would argue that the definite article "the" tips us off: it is not just *any* eating, not just *any* prayers, not just the generic version of these things to which this group gave themselves. After all, that would hardly be anything new—many religious groups ate together and prayed together. Members of Jewish households and of the synagogues did this all the time. No, it was the breaking of *the* bread that was so important to them, and it was *the* prayers.

Scholars continue to debate the development of the Lord's Supper in the first century of the Church's existence. Many still consider plausible the suggestion of Joachim Jeremias that by the time Acts was written, the rite of the breaking of the bread had been separated from the Christians' communal meal.[2] Some feel that this conclusion goes beyond what we can know with confidence. This much seems clear: by the time that Luke wrote Acts, many Christians participated in a special meal, an "agape," or "love-feast" that expressed God's love for his people and their love for him and for each other. The act of breaking *this* bread must have involved a thanksgiving, a blessing, or both, as the generosity of the Lord was acknowledged. In my view (though others question this), it seems unlikely that this thanksgiving would only have centered around the love of the community members for each other, without reference to God's greatest act of clemency, that is, Christ Jesus' death and resurrection. Entrance into worship in the early Church could hardly have included thankfulness for God's love in general without also a focus upon the cross, by which access to the Father was dramatically and thoroughly restored.

Moreover, in Acts, the breaking of the bread is linked with certain specific prayers—*the* prayers of thanksgiving, adoration, perhaps even consecration of the bread, the cup, and the congregation! I have supplied parallel arrows in my schema above, indicating that just as the "teaching" and "communion" are defined by the words "of the apostles," so the "breaking" and the "prayers" might be defined by the words "of the bread." The parallelism in the Greek wording is an interesting syntactical feature, though it is not possible to positively assert that it is significant in terms of ecclesiology. Is Luke signaling an early understanding of the Church and their practice in liturgy, or are these issues to which we are sensitive after a time of development? This much can be said: virtually every commentator believes that "of the apostles" refers to the two nouns that surround it—the teaching *of the apostles*; the fellowship *of the apostles*. What if both "the breaking" and "the prayers" similarly refer to "the bread"? In this case, the early believers would be understood as devoting themselves "to the breaking *of the bread* and the prayers (of the bread)," that is, to the prayers over or concerning the bread. Such a reading would render Acts 2:42 the first written record of key elements (actions and prayers) later seen fully developed in the liturgy of the Lord's Supper, earlier than the Eucharist described in the ancient Christian work known as the *Didache*.

Even if I am wrong here, it is surely significant that bread and prayers are mentioned in a single phrase. Like us, the early Church recognized not only the importance of visual actions (the breaking of the bread) but also of words to contextualize and interpret these before the face of God (the prayers). Together, these two phrases, "the teaching and communion of the apostles" with "the breaking and prayers of the bread," display those two elements of the Christian worship gathering that at some point become formalized into a liturgical shape that we can readily recognize today:

The service of the Word (a *synaxis* or "coming together" for teaching)

The service of the Sacrament (involving bread and prayers)

It is not necessary to make claims that Luke or his readers would understand these elements as we do. Good historical practice will heed the cautionary note of Paul Bradshaw, who warns us against "panliturgical" impulses that find liturgy everywhere in the New Testament, or that read back later practices and liturgical moves into these earliest texts.[3] It is enough to notice that the teaching and the bread-with-prayers are present and that they are associated with the community gathered around the apostles. Indeed, not very much later, we find that the worship service described in *Didache* 9:3–4 included two prayers over the bread. Without nailing down the precise shape or understanding of liturgy at the time when Luke was writing Acts, we see that, in his understanding, entry into worship was associated with the apostles, with teaching, with prayer, and with the sharing of blessed or "eucharized" (thanked-for) bread. It was entry into God's presence and into communion together, in the company of those who had been taught by Jesus and who had witnessed the resurrection.

The description of the earliest community goes beyond its basic commitments to explain more about its common life:

And fear came upon every soul; and many wonders and signs were done through the apostles. And all who believed were together and had all things in common; and they sold their possessions and goods and distributed them to all, as any had need. And day by day, attending the temple together and breaking bread in their homes, they partook of food with glad and generous hearts, praising God and having favor with all the people. And the Lord added to their number day by day those who were being saved. (Acts 2:43–47)

This earliest Christian body's life together was attended by an atmosphere of awe (the community was a surprising thing) and by surprising works done through the apostles. They actually lived together, sharing everything and demonstrating an unparalleled generosity or liberality of life. Notice also that there is a steadfast worship and coming together, both in "formal" ways (as they continue to be in temple) and informally, as they break bread together on a daily basis. (Here it is probably significant that the definite article, seen earlier in "breaking *the* bread," is missing.) Joy, thanksgiving, and praise for God characterize their mind-set, and their single-mindedness is contagious. A serendipitous growth occurs, not by their effort, but because the Lord does the work. Mission is not a separate department in this earliest Church, nor a special endeavor; rather, it flows naturally from the believers' common life in Christ.

Let us back up and consider more carefully the adherence to the apostles' teaching and fellowship. What was the teaching? What was this communion? Why is the identification of the Church with the LORD interconnected with their adherence to the apostles, so that the apostles themselves have become the touchstones or "hinges" for the community? We should note that the principle of direct apostolic contact is acknowledged not only in Acts, and in the community in Jerusalem, but in the gentile context as well. Thus, Paul challenges the Corinthians to accept his authority, launching the rhetorical questions: "Am I not an apostle? Have I not seen Jesus our Lord?" (1 Cor. 9:1). Here, as in 1 Corinthians 15:37, Paul presents his encounter(s) with the risen Christ as the equivalent of the close connection of the Twelve, who had lived with Jesus, shared his life, and witnessed his resurrection. So, then, it would seem that this recognized apostolic contact is not merely a formal prerequisite, as though the apostles had received authority from Jesus and then were to carry on as leaders in their own right. This is not like the passing on of the torch, or the mantle from Elijah to Elisha, since the person of Jesus is never superseded—nor can it be, because the gospel is not a principle or a process but is Jesus himself.

This is manifest in Peter's sermon, as construed by Luke in Acts 2. Peter does not pass on "information," "a lifestyle," or "doctrine" that he had learned from a former heroic teacher. Instead, the apostle's good news is nothing other than the proclamation of Jesus' life and actions, the proclamation of Jesus as LORD:

> Jesus of Nazareth, a man attested to you by God with mighty works and wonders and signs that God did through him in your midst, as you yourselves know—this Jesus, delivered up according to the definite plan and foreknowledge of God, you crucified and killed by the hands of lawless men. God raised him up, loosing the pangs of death, because it was not possible for him to be held by it. For David says concerning him, "I saw the Lord always before me, for he is at my right hand that I may not be shaken; therefore my heart was glad, and my tongue rejoiced; my flesh also will dwell in hope. For you will not abandon my soul to Hades, or let your Holy One see corruption. You have made known to me the paths of life; you will make me full of gladness with your presence." Brothers, I may say to you with confidence about the patriarch David that . . . he foresaw and spoke about the resurrection of the Christ, that he was not abandoned to Hades, nor did his flesh see corruption. This Jesus God raised up, and of that we all are witnesses. Being therefore exalted at the right hand of God, and having

received from the Father the promise of the Holy Spirit, he has poured out this that you yourselves are seeing and hearing. For David did not ascend into the heavens, but he himself says, "The Lord said to my Lord, Sit at my right hand, until I make your enemies your footstool." Let all the house of Israel therefore know for certain that God has made him both Lord and Christ, this Jesus whom you crucified. (Acts 2:22–36 ESV)

Notice how Peter's sermon effectively moves from the signs that the crowd has witnessed, back to Jesus, who is himself the center of it all. The marvels of that Pentecost gathering are seen merely as pointers to the One who is the center. Peter also describes the Old Testament Scriptures, specifically the person of David and the words of the Psalms, as pointing to Jesus. He works out his argument by means of an interest in the holy history and in the culture of the Jewish people, which both builds a bridge to his audience and issues a challenge to them. The speech describes Jesus as the One who vanquishes sin and death in his death and resurrection; next it goes on to talk about the ascension, by which Jesus entered into glory; and then it refers to the giving of the Spirit as the fruit of God's promises. The closing of the speech issues a tender appeal to the house of Israel, coupled with a mandate to them (and their families): repent and be baptized into the name of the Lord Jesus Christ. The proper response to the apostolic witness is to go through the door, to make an entry where God has provided one, being baptized, as St. Paul puts it, "into the death of Christ."

The apostolic teaching is both personal and corporate. Peter speaks with authority and yet points to the One alone who is the author of all. The content, means of argument, and manner are specific, focusing upon Jesus, reading the Old Testament in a particular way, and vocalizing God's invitation to his people to come into his presence. Coming into the presence of the Lord entails also joining with the communion of those who witness to him and who are now sharing in the new life. There is no sense of dissonance between the immediate presence of God and the sibling presence of the other believers gathered around the apostles. To join the Lord means to enter into a bigger company and to join the Church.

Indeed, the preaching of the apostles, represented in Peter's sermon, follows the pattern of Jesus himself, whom Luke has described in his Gospel as proclaiming "liberty," "sight," and "the acceptable year of the Lord" (Luke 4:18–19). Peter's sermon reiterates these very actions and words of Jesus, speaking explicitly of "Jesus of Nazareth, a man attested to you by God with mighty works and wonders and signs that God did through him in your midst." So, then, it is Jesus' own pattern of works, wonders, and signs that is being now expressed in the community. The apostles are producing wonders and signs; the whole community is speaking good news to the pilgrims in Jerusalem and pointing to Jesus, the true liberator and eye-opener. The year of the Lord's favor has finally arrived, so that many will enter into the company of Jesus and thus into the company of the apostles and other believers. God has acted decisively in his Holy One and now is acting in the same way through those who have been made holy by him. Through them, through history, through his Word, through signs and wonders, through the remarkable unity of this new community, he is showing what he has done, is doing, and will do in the world.

Already in Peter's first sermon, then, we catch a glimpse of the "apostles' teaching." But what is this "apostles' communion" of which Luke speaks? Why does Luke identify the Church as adhering to these specific men? We are driven here to consider the being and the unity of the Church as something that is substantial and interconnected with all of life. It is not simply a club of like-minded individuals who agree about a specific doctrine or way of life. The persons of the apostles were key, for not only had they been instructed by Jesus but they also had lived with him. He shared time and space with them, spoke with them, touched them, fed them, commissioned them, died in their place, and vivified them, breathing upon them after his resurrection. Just as the gospel is a Person, so the communication of that Person comes through persons; moreover, the purpose of God's forgiveness and healing is that we might be reconciled both to himself and to others, incorporated into the body of the Church.

Following the blessed Augustine of Hippo, Fr. Patrick Reardon points out that throughout the Acts of the Apostles there is a remarkable feature, "the Lord's reluctance—if that is the word we want—to deal with people one-to-one, bypassing the normal forms of human mediation."[4] In this helpful article, Fr. Reardon articulates a principle that we could label mediated immediacy. He demonstrates that even when the Lord speaks directly in the Acts, it is in order to call that person to be a means of mediation for others: Philip is told by the Spirit to mount the chariot of the Ethiopian so that he can interpret Isaiah to him; Peter's rooftop vision directs him to be a human instrument in calling the first gentiles in the household of Cornelius; Saul is stopped by a *Christophany on his way to Damascus, but Jesus refuses to tell him directly what he should do—rather, Saul is packed off to consult the Christians whom he had persecuted and from whom he will hear the gospel! So it is that the ministry of the apostles, and by extension the Church, is inextricably tied up with entry into God's presence. Fr. Reardon considers the pattern that we find in Acts to be a good corrective to the "'low ecclesiology'—rather popular these days—in which the believer is related to Jesus first, and to the Church second."[5] Instead, Acts shows us that communion with the LORD involves communion with the apostles and the Church. We enter into worship and into life together with them.

Entrance into worship, then, is bound up with entrance into the communion of the apostles. We worship amidst a large company, a *physical* company, a company that goes back to the first apostles. Moreover, the life that we share, enlivened by the Holy Spirit, also involves physical things—hearing, speaking, baptism, eating, healing, sharing in material goods. There is, as well, a tangible continuity with the religious past. The early believers continued to spend time in the temple, until it was destroyed, because the Lord Jesus was the fulfillment of Israel's history, not simply the intrusion of something new. As Peter proclaims, Jesus is the head of "all the house of Israel" (Acts 2:36), while also providing a way in for the gentiles, "all who are far away" (Acts 2:39 NRSV). And these many who are added come into the Church as its members focus upon Jesus and worship together.

Indeed, it is as a result of their worship that the fruit of the Church is borne.

Together, they devote themselves to the apostles' teaching and communion, to the blessing of bread and the prayers; that is, their worship revolves around the LORD, with the two poles of the Word and the Eucharist. As they worship, these fruits emerge:

- Life together (2:44, cf. "the ways of life," 2:28)
- Signs and wonders (2:43)
- Growth in love (2:44–45)
- The growth of the Church in report (2:47) and numerically (2:47b)

They were earnest in this pursuit of true worship, informed by the Word and their shared life with the apostles, nourished by the bread and the prayers. And as they deliberately gave themselves to these "first things," God gave the increase! It is difficult to hold together an earnestness in pursuing God's ways with a conviction that it is God who does the work. We tend to get it wrong in one direction (carelessness, presumption on God's mercy) or another (worry, drivenness, human pride). Yet, gathering together—in deliberate continuity with the apostles, in deliberate life with the community of believers, in concentration upon the LORD who is worshiped—affords the balanced intensity that is meant to characterize the Church.

Entering with Integrity (1 Cor. 11 and 14)

A number of scholars believe that Acts represents a stage of the early Christian movement subsequent to the time of Paul, so that the book reflects Luke's own context more than that of the first Christians. Such scholars contrast Acts with Paul's own letters and view Paul's words of instruction on worship to the church in Corinth as an indication that the earliest Christians approached their worship with a completely blank slate, feeling their way toward the liturgical and therapeutic ingredients that were most helpful in their mid-first-century venue. Then, they suppose, in Acts we encounter the understanding of an author who is part of the still young, but slightly later Christian movement on its way to institutionalization. Hypotheses of church development mounted by scholars such as F. C. Baur have left an impressive (but not always helpful) legacy, not only within the world of New Testament scholarship, but among nonspecialists as well. This percolating down effect means that contemporary Christians in the West now believe first-century Christians such as Paul's church in Corinth freely composed their worship moments, along with their manner of composition, but that after this golden age, there was a declension into "early Catholicism," ritualism, and authoritarianism. It is helpful for us to look at the pertinent passages in 1 Corinthians with close attention, to see what Paul actually says about worship.

First Corinthians 11 and 14 are particularly useful in giving us insight into Paul's teaching on "ortho-doxy." Here, I use the term orthodoxy, breaking it down into its constituent parts, so that *doxa is translated, as it can be, as "praise" or "worship" (over against the more common translation of doxa as "doctrine" or "opinion"). Orthodoxy is not simply "correct doctrine." Consider the English term *doxology, an *anthem or prayer by which Christians offer praise to the Triune God. Orthodoxy thus also involves the authentic Christian perspective and practice of giving glory, or "upright praise" to the Lord. The Corinthians passages present particular difficulties in interpretation for the twenty-first century but are worth reading with care. We will begin with the second part of 1 Corinthians 11, where Paul tackles problems in the Lord's Supper, then move back to his discussion of specific roles in worship in the first part of chapter 11, and finally look forward to chapter 14, which is sometimes taken today as a template for casually organized worship. Both chapters will help to fill in, from different angles, what is involved in full and honest worship, a worship that has "integrity" in every sense of the word.

In 1 Corinthians 11:17–33, Paul emerges in full troubleshooting mode. He brackets his comments by lamenting that the Corinthians' gathering together for worship has actually weakened them rather than strengthening them or nurturing them as a community (11:17, 29–30). This judgment indicates Paul's underlying conviction that the *synaxis* of Christians to worship and to share in the Supper is a solemn matter that changes the community—if not for good, then for ill! Consonant with this judgment is his indictment that they are not really keeping the Lord's Supper when they meet: "when you gather it is not to eat the Lord's Supper" (11:20 EH). Here, it is not clear whether Paul is detailing their intent—"when you come together, it is not *with the intent of* eating the Lord's Supper" or whether he is speaking of the result—"when you think and behave this way, it is not *in actuality* the Lord's Supper that takes place." Perhaps both meanings are carried by the phrase. The result of sharing is negative for some of the Corinthians, in terms of body as well as spirit, which would not likely be the case if only intent were in view. Paul fills in his judgment that their worship is in danger of becoming a pseudo-gathering and a pseudo-sacrament by specifically mentioning several ironic conundrums:

- Though they "come together" as those "called out," there are factions.
- In a situation of reverence, some show contempt for others and for the meal.
- The humble are being humiliated in a meal that remembers Jesus' humiliation.
- Some are unworthy of the table because they consider themselves worthy.
- In a meal focused upon "the body of the Lord" some do not "discern the body."

Paul guides his flock by using very strong language, leading them first to recognize the tragedy of the situation: what is meant to strengthen them has become a weakness and a reproach. In verses 17–22, he points out to them their scandalous attitudes and behaviors and what they are doing to the congregation:

> But in the following instructions I do not commend you, because when you come together it is not for the better but for the worse. For, in the first place, when you come together as a church, I hear that there are divisions among you. And I believe it in part, for there must be factions among you in order that those who are genuine among you may be recognized. When you come together, it is not the Lord's supper that you eat. For in eating, each one goes ahead with his own meal. One goes hungry, another gets drunk. What! Do you not have houses to eat and drink in? Or do you despise the church of God and humiliate those who have nothing? What shall I say to you? Shall I commend you in this? No, I will not. (ESV)

He also calls upon them in verses 31–32 to judge themselves and to accept the reproof of the LORD, so that the situation can be remedied:

> But if we judged ourselves truly, we would not be judged. But when we are judged by the Lord, we are disciplined so that we may not be condemned along with the world. (ESV)

In both cases, he directs the Corinthians away from isolation and self-centeredness, saying, in effect, "you are trying to treat the church as though it is your own private playground, so stop it! If you must turn inward, do so in self-examination, and then hear the disciplining words of the Lord, who has taken you out of the world and joined you with each other."

A renewed focus on their meaning and purpose as the body of Christ also provides the remedy. So, in verses 23–26, sandwiched between the two sections of verses 17–22 and verses 31–32, Paul trains their minds on the tradition concerning the Supper, a tradition that goes back to the Lord himself. Remembering this "passed-on" event, complete with its meaning and its healing, moves them out of self-absorption. What *is* the Supper? It is about Jesus' betrayal; it is about giving thanks; it is about sacrifice for others; it is about a new covenant; it is about eating and drinking *together* (the plural "you" is used throughout); it is about remembrance; it is about proclamation of this enacted love; it is about an unseen present solidarity with Jesus, and an assured future fulfillment of this life. These four verses, 1 Corinthians 11:23–26, are bookended by reference to tradition—what has been passed on through Paul to the Corinthians (1 Cor. 11:23) and what the Corinthians will pass on to others by keeping the tradition of the meal (1 Cor. 11:26).

Over this entire section hangs the question of verse 19—Who is genuine among them? (This question emerges with a certain amount of irony: only by means of "chosen factions" will the genuine believers emerge.) Paul hopes, of course, that all of them will be found genuine. He detests the divisions, which seem to be catalyzed not only by matters of personality but also by diverse theological opinions. (First Cor. 1 deals not only with personality cults, for in verse 10 he urges them "to say the same thing," *to auto legēte*, though the NRSV softens this, inadequately rendering it as "to be in agreement.") Paul does not simply call them to put differences aside so that they can have a surface peacefulness. Rather, peace comes, implies Paul, by concentrating upon Jesus and by holding to his truth. Moreover, though the gathering must have appeared as a free-for-all, Paul does not concentrate upon the atmospherics in his correction. Peace is not achieved by human will to be calm, nor by attention to ambiance. It comes by means of the Prince of Peace, who joins his own as they worship, and in the living Tradition that he has passed to them. So the apostle does not tell them to cultivate a certain feeling during worship by the use of music or by means of any other orchestration. The specific instructions that he gives them in summary are simple and highlight the reality of what they are doing as the body of Christ: they are to "wait for one another" and to remember that the Lord's Supper is more than a meal ("if anyone is hungry, let him eat at home" 1 Cor. 11:34).

This section in 1 Corinthians reminds Christians of every age, including our own, to be vigilant concerning any tensions that arise, both because of belief and human conflict. It warns against carelessness in the Eucharist. For, St. Paul asserts, when we gather together for the purpose of the sacred meal we are being incorporated into one body, and the Church should thus practice discernment and examination during this solemn occasion. (This principle issues a great challenge for ecclesial groups that practice "open communion.") Most of all, our hearts and minds are to be trained upon Jesus: as a result of this focus, the gathering will do what it needs to do to build up the body of Christ. The gathering is an entry, together, into the action and life of Christ, a receiving of his sacrificial love, and a putting on of this love, as we are joined together. Such authentic worship calls for preparation, repentance, memory, continuity, integrity, and a deliberate resolve to make room for each other.

It is clear that the Lord's Supper is crucial for St. Paul. Earlier in this same chapter (1 Cor. 11:1–16) we find other tantalizing teaching on worship in general. This passage is often wholly ignored or rendered mute when twenty-first-century readers assume that it speaks only to the context of the first century, since its presenting issue is about the appropriate attire or the appearance of women during worship. It is of course true that the length of women's hair or their use of head-coverings is not a live issue for us, for our culture attaches no symbolic importance to hats and does not consider cropped hair on a woman to be irregular or a rejection of her gender. (Most interpreters believe that the original debate was about veils specifically, rather than hair length.) However, we are not at liberty to consider this passage only in terms of first-century culture, because Paul gives theological reasons for his argument. These at least must be honored, even if the matter of head-coverings is judged to be a cultural question limited to his day. The underlying questions for those of us who read the Epistles as Scripture is, what in the teaching has ongoing value, and what is directed only to Paul's day? Moreover, what does this passage tell us about worship?

As we begin, we must acknowledge that the passage is full of tensions and complexities, since St. Paul's picture of reality and of upright worship is not simplistic. We must begin by noticing what this passage is *not* about. It does not set up:

- A "chain of being" from God through angels through man through woman, and on down
- A merely cultural habit of dress
- The repression of women
- The exaltation of men

What Paul aims to do is to refocus their worship (as we have already seen him do in the second part of chap. 11) by calling them to remember their "head" (Gk., *kephalē*, 11:3 *et passim*). He insists, then, that worship is about God, not about human beings. Those who think that Paul is establishing a multistoried hierarchy, from God, through angels, through men, through women, and on down, have not noticed the subtleties involved in his picture. Notice that in his presentation, both God the Son and woman have a "head," by nature. Should women be scandalized or offended to acknowledge that they come under a human head when God the Son willingly recognizes the Father as his?[6] Notice, too, that along with order and headship St. Paul also recognizes mutuality: "Nevertheless, in the Lord woman is not independent of man or man independent of woman. For just as woman came from man, so man comes through woman; but all things come from God" (11:11–12 NRSV). Notice, further, that woman is described as man's "glory"—and glory is a positive thing, after all, not a negative or dismissive term. The "glory" of the Father is seen in the Son, or in the moving of the Holy Spirit, as we have seen in our discussion about worship in the Old Testament.

Worship, however, is about God's glory, not about the glory of man in particular, or of humanity in general. Because of this role built into their natures—displaying the glory of Adam—women are told "to cover." For worship is not intended to display the glory of Adam, but to display the glory of God. This goes beyond the explanation that the beauty of women might be an erotic temptation or distraction for the men, though that acknowledgment of human frailty might be implied in the argument. Certainly worshipers do not want to be distracted from their worship; however, this imperative focuses on actively directing our attention toward the LORD, who is the head of all, rather than toward any human excellence, freedom, or beauty.

Paul gives another theological reason for head-covering—"because of the angels." This tantalizing throw-away remark has been the cause of great speculation. Is Paul thinking of the fallen angels mentioned in Genesis 6, those "sons of God" who were enticed by women in days gone by, with disastrous results, according to the Jewish legends about the angelic *"Watchers" and their progeny? This seems unlikely, since elsewhere Paul uses more explicit language when he is referring to hostile angels or spirits (e.g., "the principalities and powers of the cosmos"). It is more likely that he is thinking of the position of angels in the heavenly realms, who guard the mysterious presence of God (Rev. 4:6–8), who lead worship (Rev. 4:9; 5:14), and who all the while cover their faces and feet in humility (Isa. 6:2). If these glorious beings cover themselves when they are so near to God's presence and unencumbered by sin, and if their role is to orchestrate the praises offered by all of creation, then women should not be ashamed to take on a stance of humility as well. Indeed, men and women are given, it would seem, to *act* antiphonally, just as the angels sing antiphonally in Isaiah 6, showing God's holiness and *immanence among us. The man's head is uncovered, reminding us that Christ has made us worthy and lifted the veil so that all of God's people may see God's glory; the woman's head is covered to remind us before God that all of us are creatures and that our worship is for the One who is all-glorious.

The uncovered head of male worshipers in the Christian tradition is a strong statement when juxtaposed with the Jewish tradition of covering the head (whenever this started) and is consonant with the idea that Christ has raised up humanity, giving them the boldness to say, "Our Father." But the two traditions suggested by Paul (heads covered; heads uncovered) may be likened to the rhythm observed in liturgical eucharists, where there is both kneeling (or even prostrations) and standing—we kneel in abject worship; we stand, liberated and forgiven. Both actions are appropriate before the glorious God who calls us into his presence. There is a difference and a mutual giving in the roles that women and men play in worship, according to Paul.

And, by the way, women are not silenced here. Paul assumes that they will both pray and prophesy—with power or authority over, or upon, the head. Their spiritual service is ordered, as also is the service of the man and of the angels. It is not that Paul pictures only man as made after the likeness of God, and woman as made after the likeness of man—that denigration of women is not found in 1 Corinthians 11. Such a graded and unnuanced hierarchy may be poetically useful[7] but reality (whether we are speaking about humanity or about God) is much more complicated, as pictured by St. Paul and in the Scriptures in general. There is an *order* complemented by a *mutuality*. God is the head of Christ (1 Cor. 11:3) and yet Jesus is LORD and co-creator (1 Cor. 8:6). Man is the head of woman, and yet both are interdependent. When we worship, our gender is not erased but plays a role before the mysterious LORD who calls us together. (Thus the phrase "there is no male and female," Gal. 3:28 [EH], should not be used to neutralize 1 Cor. 11. Galatians 3 is about reconciliation, not role; it is about baptism, not balance of power. Our bodies and our genders matter to God, who created us male and female *before* the complications of the Fall!) Worship is not for the establishing of human rights but for honoring God.

One final word might be said, though it may provoke allergic reaction among some who are unnerved by tradition. Paul has offered two theological reasons for his teaching: the relationship between men and women, and the presence and role of the angels. He also has offered a reason from nature (vv. 14–15 speak about the long hair of women as something natural), which we have not discussed. All these *reasons* call attention to the larger picture, reminding us that worship is acknowledgment and entry into a larger reality. But his *conclusion* in verse 16 is just as remarkable. If one is not convinced yet, he argues, then the Corinthians must heed the "practice" or common "custom" ("what we are accustomed to *together*" is the meaning of the Greek word *synētheia*)—a custom found among "us" (the apostles) and among the "churches of God." Again, Paul appeals to what we do together. As with the second part of the chapter, St. Paul's appeal to custom in verse 16 forms a bookend with his prior appeal to tradition in 1 Corinthians 11:2: "I commend you because you . . . maintain the traditions just as I handed them on to you" (EH). His entire discussion about women and worship is surrounded by references to common custom and holy Tradition. Worship is bound up with what has been passed on, from Paul, from the apostles, from the Lord. Worship is not a place for eccentric actions but the time in which we enter *together* with the whole Church (and with the angels too!) into God's presence to give him glory.

Certainly there are social and cultural aspects to this passage—today women with heads uncovered (or cropped hair) do not evoke the idea of prostitutes or pagan mystical priestesses, as in the gentile world to which Paul was ministering. And so there is no pressing cultural reason to reject the actual practice of women uncovering their heads in worship today. It would, perhaps, be antiquarian to reinstate the wearing of hats in church when hats are not normally worn indoors by women any more, or if they are, this may call *attention* to women, rather than rendering them less distracting. But this does not mean that there is not something for us to learn in this section of the letter. The reasons that Paul gives challenge us to rethink our radical egalitarianism and to consider a more complex picture where order and mutuality together find a home because of the crucified and risen Lord of glory. If we are not quite ready to do this, then surely we can grasp that other clear message that sounds forth in this passage—worship is for the LORD, not for the showcasing of our gifts.

The admonition to worship *the* LORD comes even more strongly to the fore in 1 Corinthians 14:12b–40, to which we now turn. This passage should be comforting as we seek a way to understand worship together, for it shows us that the "worship wars" are nothing new. It also consoles us by suggesting that maturity in Christ helps to solve such problems: "do not be children in your thinking" (1 Cor. 14:20). The weight given to the role of the prophet, who speaks for God, adds a dimension to the understanding of worship. Worship is for praising God—yet we must also consider the "building up" of the Church (14:5, 12, 26). Thus, "tongues" may offer thanks or may bless the Lord, but they are better when interpreted, because then they both speak to God and minister to those gathered. There is a notable tension between this chapter and chapter 11—here Paul makes reference to women's silence (14:34), whereas in chapter 11 it is assumed that women both pray and prophesy in the gathering. We do not have time to work toward a solution here, since our purpose is to trace the theme of entry into worship.[8] It is helpful to notice that silence is not a matter of default but an integral part of worship. It is enjoined also of those who speak in tongues and those who are speaking when someone else receives a revelation. Paul here includes the women in his expectation of a maturity that will enable them to promote the "order" and "peace" of the assembly, which sometimes requires silence. His injunction, whatever it means, is not foreign to the rest of his discussion. Entry together into the presence of God, and listening to the Holy Spirit, is enhanced by silence—indeed, sometimes silence is required.

Again, our contemporary discomfort over this command to silence has led us to miss the obvious way that Paul frames his teaching—worship is about praising God and listening to God, and it is characterized by peace rather than irrationality and chaos. Worship is about communion with God, and concern for each other, not about exercising our gifts or demonstrating who is the most important. Worship, because it comes from those who are created, will involve not only words but also silence—the most profound sign of peace that human beings can perform in the presence of the God who speaks and acts. It may be that Paul separates out his discussion of worship into two sections in this letter, because in 1 Corinthians 14 he is speaking about the service of the Word, a service more like that of the synagogue, whereas in 1 Corinthians 11 he has had to troubleshoot regarding the service of the table (or altar), a service more reminiscent of the temple, since it involves the idea of the Lord's great sacrifice and the Passover celebration. However we picture the difference in context, both chapters agree:

- The "we" is as important as the "I."
- Anything that distracts from God is not helpful.
- Meeting together involves recognition of and sensitivity to others.
- Not everyone has the same role, but all roles are for the service of all.
- Spirit, mind, and body come together.
- Some things have been given to us to be retained.

Moreover, because worship is a coming together of the body of Christ, because the celebration of the Lord's Supper (with its words and prayers) actually is an entry into something bigger than we are, there is no place for attention to atmospherics or the attempt to "feel holy." To work for effect would be faithless. It would be to forget that worship *is* about the Holy One, and that we *are* meeting with God. There is, however, an effect, a serendipitous result of this kind of upright worship. Worship is directed toward God, to be sure. It serves to build up the body of Christ, since that also gives glory to the LORD. But it may also cause an unbeliever's heart to be unveiled, so that he or she will join in the worship and cry, "God is really among you." Our entry into worship enables others to enter. In worship, we together become more fully what we are meant to be, and so God is revealed. In this way, we take on the role, collectively, of ushers into the presence of the Lord. Paradoxically, this effect of worship comes as we concentrate not upon the "result" but upon the primary purpose of worship—the glory of the LORD. We must give ourselves to worship—and so the Church will be built up, and so others will marvel at the glory. Like David dancing, we are to give ourselves to rejoicing and praise. When we do so, we become a living sign of God's presence among his people, a means by which others hear his call to come, as C. S. Lewis puts it, "further up and further in."[9]

Entering in Fear and into Awe: Hebrews 10–12 and Revelation 4–5

But what are we entering when we worship, and to what are we inviting others? The veil is pulled back for us in the books of Hebrews and Revelation.

> For you have not come to what may be touched, a blazing fire, and darkness, and gloom, and a tempest, and the sound of a trumpet, and a voice whose words made the hearers entreat that no further messages be spoken to them.

For they could not endure the order that was given, "If even a beast touches the mountain, it shall be stoned." Indeed, so terrifying was the sight that Moses said, "I tremble with fear." *But you have come to Mount Zion and to the city of the living God, the heavenly Jerusalem, and to innumerable angels* in festal gathering, and to the assembly of the first-born who are enrolled in heaven, and to a judge who is God of all, and to the spirits of just men made perfect, and to Jesus, the mediator of a new covenant, and to the sprinkled blood that speaks more graciously than the blood of Abel. See that you do not refuse him who is speaking. For if they did not escape when they refused him who warned them on earth, much less shall we escape if we reject him who warns from heaven. His voice then shook the earth; but now he has promised, "Yet once more I will shake not only the earth but also the heaven." This phrase, "Yet once more," indicates the removal of what is shaken, as of what has been made, in order that what cannot be shaken may remain. Therefore let us be grateful for receiving a kingdom that cannot be shaken, and thus let us offer to God acceptable worship, with reverence and awe; for our God is a consuming fire. (Heb. 12:18–29)

The discourse to the Hebrews (which is, it seems, a bracing sermon rather than a "letter") challenges us to rephrase our question. It is not a matter of "to what are we inviting others" but "to whom" and "to Whom!" As we read this section of Hebrews, we might be tempted to understand the contrast between the old and new covenants in terms of physical over against nonmaterial realities. This is only partly true. The gathering at Mount Sinai involved an earthly mountain that could be, but was not to be, touched. At Sinai, there was a voice that could be heard, but from which the people shrank. The revelation resulted in a set of commands written on stone, tablets that could be broken and that the people would reject. The vision of Hebrews describes a reality not *less* solid, but even more permanent than these things: it cannot be shaken. It includes the material, but this material has been, is being, and will be transformed so that it is joined to the spiritual world. We hear of the blood of Christ (*real* blood that becomes our life); we picture the gathered assembly of God's people (*body*, soul, and spirit made perfect before God).

Consider the contrasts between the situation in Exodus and the one envisioned here. Mount Sinai was off limits, except by the LORD's invitation. Only the seventy went "up" to the feast that God hosted, and only Moses communed with God at the very pinnacle: the people needed, and were content, to use their representatives as a kind of human shield between them and the God who caused thunder, shaking, and burning. In the old covenant story, we do not hear about the Almighty being surrounded by a host: perhaps that is part of what Moses saw in his privileged vision, but we do not know. In Hebrews, to be gathered to God means to gather collectively, surrounded by others who know him and who now shine with perfection, as well as by the strange angelic host.

Above all, it means to be gathered to Jesus, *the* mediator of the new covenant, by means of the blood of the cross. Jesus is not simply a human shield, but actually joins us to God, for his blood speaks of reconciliation. Through him we are gathered to God and to each other, in contrast with the spilt blood that separated brother from brother in the primal story of Cain's first murder and Abel's first sacrifice (Gen. 4:4–15). Whereas the manifestations at Sinai marked a separation between good and evil, between the sacred and the common, the presence of the Son allows for a true approach and rapprochement—approach to God and inclusion in a huge company of worshipers. Indeed, it means to come before God as part of the "first born who have been enrolled" (Heb. 12:23); we are, because of the Son, Jesus (Heb. 2:22; 3:6), adopted "elder sons" (*huioi*) of the majestic Father, with the right to inherit.

Sonship language is, of course, difficult in our gender-inclusive age. However, it is pervasive not only in Hebrews but also throughout the New Testament, for example in Romans 8:19 and Galatians 4:6, where the very term "adoption" means literally "established as a son." Throughout their discussion of sonship, these passages also speak of children (*tekna*; *paidia*), and detail daughters as well as sons, so it is clear that no exclusion of women is intended. But biblical language for divine Sonship and human "sonship" cannot be ignored, because the term "Son of God" was a specific way of speaking about the Messiah, or Christ. When we simply translate as "children" we may well miss the wonderful implication that we, in Christ, have been made little "christs" (lowercase *s* sons of God) and inheritors within God's household.

Despite this privilege in the new covenant to gather and to approach as members of God's household, and even remembering the efforts of our mediator who makes the righteous perfect so that we may enjoy the holy Presence, Christian entrance never becomes something casual. With all its contrasts to the event at Sinai, the tableau depicted in Hebrews retains—even accentuates—a sense of awe and reverence: "For if they did not escape when they refused him who warned them on earth, how much less will we escape if we reject him who warns from heaven" (12:25b). To enter into worship, to offer "acceptable" or "pleasing" worship (12:28), is to be thankful and reverent. In both the Old Testament and the New Testament, there is a gathering and there is a warning. God draws near and speaks; God shakes and burns. "*Once more* I will shake" (12:26), says the Lord; "Our God *is* a consuming fire" (12:29), comments the biblical writer. The difference between Exodus and Hebrews seems, in the first place, to be found in the kind of mediation. Jesus brings to us a mediation that actually allows God's people, all of them, to enter together, rather than to approach, as the old covenant people did, at certain graded stages and at various distances, depending on one's formalized status. God's Word speaks to all and the vision of God's Holy City is for everyone together. In the new covenant, when God shakes, something solid remains. Burning brings purity, not destruction; shaking does not remove us from the Presence, and yet it is an indication that worship is to be reverent.

When we glance back to an earlier passage in Hebrews, we are reminded not only of our fragility but also of the mighty and effective provision that has been made for our astonishing entry into God's presence:

> And before him no creature is hidden, but all are open and laid bare to the eyes of him with whom we have to do. Since then we have a great high priest who has passed through the heavens, Jesus, the Son of God, let us hold fast our confession. (Heb. 4:13–14)

Our entry comes about by means of the physical (the "curtain" that Jesus opened for us was his own flesh, Heb. 10:19). Indeed, not only our spirits but also our bodies have been washed (10:22). To enter means to meet together as one body (10:25) and to confess our hope together (10:23) because we are "surrounded by a cloud of witnesses" (12:1) who have waited for us to be made glorious together with them (11:38). Through the work of Jesus in time and space, and through the ongoing work of the Holy Spirit, God uses our physical and temporal condition to bring us good, and to join us, across time and space, together:

> But you have come to Mount Zion and to the city of the living God, the heavenly Jerusalem, and to innumerable angels in festal gathering, and to the assembly of the first-born who are enrolled in heaven, and to a judge who is God of all, and to the spirits of just men made perfect, and to Jesus, the mediator of a new covenant, and to the sprinkled blood that speaks more graciously than the blood of Abel. (Heb. 12:22–24)

One writer comments that these verses place "Christ's heavenly liturgy squarely in the midst of the liturgical gathering of the humble, suffering community."[10] We could as easily say that they place the liturgical gathering squarely in the midst of the heavenly liturgy! When we worship, all that we are, all of us together, are being taken into the household, the realm, the city of God—and being transformed into something with integrity, something that is "unshakable" (12:27). Entry of this magnitude and depth calls for awe. Consider that the greatest One of all has assumed our humanity in order to make something solid of his fragile, flawed, rebellious, fearful, created ones. Consider how his sacrifice, even to the point of death on the cross, has forged a way for us to be healed and to become what God intends for us to be.

In the absolute sense, Jesus' atoning death is God's very own initiative on our behalf: John's Gospel tells the story of Good Friday by stressing that Jesus carried his own cross (19:17). It is by his death alone, and by the water and blood that flowed from *his* side, that we are forgiven, restored, granted new life, and now may "approach th'eternal throne" to worship freely. Only the

God-Man is the priest and the offering; only his cross is the true Tree of Life; only he tramples down death by death; only he is the reconciler and reconciliation for our sin. On the other hand, the New Testament is replete with injunctions that each person in Christ must carry his or her cross. Not one of us can atone for sin; but we *are* called to offer ourselves to God, in Christ, as a living sacrifice (Rom. 12:1). He is our substitute and our representative. Because of him we will never die; in him, even when we die, we shall live!

Here is a wonderful paradox: we are the house that is owned by the Son, the temple where the LORD is worshiped. Because of what Jesus has done, "the promise of entering his rest remains" (Heb. 4:1), and it is to this that God invites us: "there remains a sabbath rest for the people of God" (Heb. 4:9). How remarkable that we are being called to enter into God's own activity of rest, his eighth-day joy. (Because of the resurrection of Jesus, all Christians now participate in the dawning of God's new creation and look forward to it with solid hope.) However, since we follow in the train of Jesus, we are also sons and daughters who are being disciplined and who are admonished, "*Strive to enter* that rest, that no one may fall by . . . disobedience" (Heb. 4:11). This resting and striving are both activities that we perform together, enjoying God's presence and trusting his initiative, while also encouraging each other day by day to be vigilant. We enjoy a creaturely rest in God's own deep peace; we work together, helping one another. All this takes place at the will of the Holy Spirit, by whom we are being changed. In our "in between" condition both a brisk confidence and a careful attentiveness are appropriate. Neither are we to be obsessive nor are we to be careless. God works first, and so we work, together, with him. In the end, we learn this mystery: God's presence not only requires change (our repentance) but also brings about change: we are transformed!

As I write these paragraphs, the Eastern Church is remembering the notorious St. Mary of Egypt (fifth or sixth century), whose retold life story is interlaced with the motifs of entrance and transformation. According to tradition, this saint, prior to her conversion, seems to have been beset by something like nymphomania. Seeking ravenously for sexual partners even during the annual holy pilgrimage to Jerusalem, she is blocked by a divine force from entering the Church of the Holy Sepulcher. In praying before the *icon of the *Theotokos ("God-bearer") Mary, the mother of Jesus, who in Eastern Tradition is frequently called the Gate of Heaven, this woman repents and so is allowed to enter. Within she venerates the relic of the cross and, on leaving the church, pauses by the icon of the Virgin again to give thanks. At this point she hears the invitation: "Cross the Jordan, and you will find glorious rest." The new convert obeys the voice, pausing at the Church of the Baptist to be baptized and to receive communion: the rest of her days are spent in the wilderness as an ascetic, giving glory to God. Interestingly, though Mary was notorious for her sexual activity, she is numbered among the holy *virgins* in the Orthodox

Church. Her story and her memorial among the virgins indicate that a life of repentance, entrance into God's presence, reception of the eucharistic mysteries, and cultivation of rest from earthly care bring about a complete transformation of body and soul. Prior to entry, change is demanded; because of entry, change takes place.

We see the dynamic of change as a prerequisite to worship and as a fruit of worship most dramatically in the final book of the Bible, the Apocalypse of Jesus to John. The entire sequence of the Revelation moves from an urgent call for the Church to repent, to the solid and envisioned hope of transformation. Human integrity can refer both to an honest fear before the LORD and to fullness or wholeness, to our being what God has called us to be. Both types of integrity are pictured in the Apocalypse with a vividness that is striking among the books of the Bible. The visionary St. John, though in the Spirit on the LORD's Day (and so "prepared"), falls before the Son of Man as one dead (Rev. 1:17). His response is an apt and honest one before the Holy LORD. The proclamations to the seven churches involve six calls to repentance (2:5 [twice], 16, 22; 3:3, 19), and so it is impossible for anyone with an ear to hear "what the Spirit says to the churches" (Rev. 2:29) to miss this call. Only after we have noted St. John's abject humility, and this repeated call to repentance, do we then hear about how John is taken, by means of a disorienting rapture, into the heavenly realm.

The visionary, who acts as our human stand-in, encounters that which is utterly real, that which has both integrity and wholeness: the glorious One upon the throne; the burning seven spirits before the throne; four "creatures" who possess angelic aspects but who together represent the four elements of our world; twenty-four elders who are crowned yet cast their glorious garlands in honesty before the great Glory; and hymns that recall the whole cosmos that God has created. Even the numbers associated with the vision stress the solidity of God and his good creation. Here are perfect numbers, numbers of wholeness: one speaks of unity; seven implies perfection; four points to every aspect of creation; twenty-four sums up the people of God, that is, those associated with the twelve tribes and the twelve apostles. In this scene of fullness, all is ordered; there is purity, awe, light. All is balanced and centered upon God, moving by means of complementary roles taken by the worshipers. Indeed, Revelation 4 includes a representation of the entire creation and of history, all of this space and time under God's care. He is the One "who was, and is, and is to come" (Rev. 4:8) as well as the One who created all things (Rev. 4:11).

But John, human and fallen as he is, does not enter easily into the scene. Though "in the Spirit" (Rev. 4:2) he is faced with the concern of the unsealed scroll, the scroll that, as we will see on its opening, is the meaning and fulfillment of human history. And so, he weeps bitterly. Is our human problem a blot on the perfection of heaven? Are the heavenly worshipers jealous of their own peace? No, for immediately John is given an answer from one of the twenty-four who represent God's own humanity. The answer is the Lion-Lamb, the One who is both "in the midst of the throne and . . . in the midst of the elders" (5:6 KJV). Contemporary versions of the New Testament prefer to translate the phrase *en mesō tou thronou kai . . . en mesō tōn presbyterōn* as "between the throne and the elders" (instead of "in the midst of the throne and . . . in the midst of the elders"), probably because it is difficult to picture the Lion-Lamb in two places at once. Yet Jesus *is* in two places at once, just as he is both a Lion and a Lamb, and he is both slaughtered and standing. He is the living One who died, the exalted One who remains among his own, as we see in the song that the worshipers sing to the One who is "in the midst of the throne" (7:17 KJV). He alone is worthy to open the scroll—for he has brought about a change from death to life for the people with whom he utterly identifies. His manifestation as the Lion-Lamb reveals that he is conquering victor over sin and death, as well as the sacrificed lamb. He is also the high king and sympathetic priest, interceding on our behalf from the midst of the throne.

As we move from chapter 4 to the sight of Jesus in chapter 5, the worship scene is transformed, reflecting the change that Jesus has brought about. With us still are the worshipers from chapter 4—the One on the throne, the four, the seven, the twenty-four. But there is more detail and dynamism. With the One upon the throne appears the Lion-Lamb, while the twenty-four sing of saints "from every tribe and tongue and people and nation" (Rev. 5:9). We now see a complete people of God, no longer slaves, because they have been redeemed and transformed into kings and priests to reign and serve. Their worship takes earth up into heaven, for human prayers are described as held in the elders' bowls of incense, offered before the LORD. All of creation is rendered present, as this kingdom of human priests worships before the heavenly throne.

St. Gregory of Nazianzen is known for his saying "that which He has not assumed, He has not healed."[11] The converse is true, of course—what God the Son has "assumed" or *taken upon* himself in his Incarnation, all of that which is truly human, is healed, and so transformed. This includes our worship. Toward the end of chapter 5, the worship song itself changes, so that not only the creating power of God is celebrated but also his redeeming might and love: "To the One who sits upon the throne and to the Lamb be blessing!" (EH). True creaturely reality, especially true human reality, is expressed and brought to perfection in Jesus, the God-Man. Our human worship of God reflects this, for Jesus, himself God, honors and gives glory to the Father. And so our truest actions involve a turning, a change, as we learn to worship "in Christ." Thus it is that our worship becomes "unshakable." Indeed, worship will be found in earth as in heaven, as the two realms become one, joined by the One who is the God-Man.

So we have a "sure" or "certain" hope in Jesus' work to make us into kings and priests. The final chapters of the Apocalypse unveil this vision. After hearing the plea from God, "Come out of her, my people" (18:4; that is, out from the unreal and blasphemous Prostitute-Queen who is trying to usurp the place of God), the ransomed at last enter into the new Jerusalem. As they enter, they assume their role, to "serve" and "worship" (cf. 22:3) the LORD with integrity. They are his bride and they are also the inhabitants who enter the city, clothed with the Lamb's own glory. The "clothing" speaks of repentance (for they have made their robes clean), of awe in meeting the Lord, and of adornment (21:2) or transformation ("the former things have passed away," 21:4). New Jerusalem appears as a fertile and replete garden, a perfectly balanced and beautifully appointed city with physical and cultural aspects (21:26) as well as spiritual graces. It is a domain of integrity that requires no guarding (21:25), that houses a company of people who have taken on the character and attributes of the One whom they worship. And so we touch upon the deepest mystery of worship—our communion with the LORD himself.

Entering into the Mystery of the Holy Trinity

Now in reverence and awe
We gather round your word,
In wonder we draw near
To mysteries that Angels strain to hear,
That prophets dimly saw:
So let your Spirit
Shine upon the page and

Teach [us], Open up [our] eyes
With truth to free [us],
Light to chase the lies—
Lord Jesus let [us] meet you in your Word
Lord Jesus let [us] meet you in your Word.

Lord, your truth cannot be chained
It searches everything—
My secrets, my desires.
Your word is like a hammer and a fire—
It breaks, it purifies,
So let your Spirit
Shine into my heart and

Teach me, open up my eyes,
With truth to free me
Light to chase the lies—
Lord Jesus let me meet you in your Word
Lord Jesus let me meet you in your Word

Graham Kendrick,
"Jesus Let Me Meet You in Your Word"[12]

Graham Kendrick's contemporary worship song, intended as a preparation to hear the preaching of the Word, speaks of the wonder of being gathered to the LORD in worship. It is because of the One who is the Word that we can understand the written Word and come to understand the Father of whom that Word speaks. As John 1:18 puts it, "The Son . . . who is in the bosom of the Father, has *interpreted* him" (EH).[13] Entry into worship involves our inhabiting a mystery even greater than the community of the apostles, to which we have been called—it is participating in the very life of Christ. It therefore means being joined to the Father and to the Spirit through our life in the Son.

In speaking of our "entrance" into the life of the Holy Trinity, we must, however, tread very carefully. There is a good deal of loose talk these days about humanity joining in the egalitarian "perichoretic dance" of the Godhead: language like this has been used among theologians and has percolated down into popular Christian literature, song, and newer liturgies, so that one hears it routinely among Christians in general. It is helpful to remember that *perichōresis* (the technical term used by theologians for the inner life of the Father, Son, and Holy Spirit) does *not* mean "a movement that is dancelike," though many scholars and liturgists have said so. It refers to the deep indwelling and loving movement toward each other of Father, Son, and Holy Spirit, a mutual but ordered communion in which the Father retains headship, even while Father, Son, and Holy Spirit share each other's attributes, glory, and power. Their love is not the kind of undifferentiated love-fest that is pictured by some who are today co-opting the Holy Trinity as a kind of mascot for their own idea of what reality should be like. I recall, for example, the words placed in the mouth of Jesus in the recently popular novel *The Shack*:

> That's the beauty of what you see in my relationship with Abba [the Father] and Sarayu [The Holy Spirit]. We are indeed submitted to one another and have always been so and always will be. Papa is as much submitted to me as I to him, or Sarayu to me, or Papa to her. Submission is not about authority and it is not obedience; it is all about relationships of love and respect. In fact, we are submitted to you in the same way![14]

The elasticity with which the word *submission* is being used here (and elsewhere) voids it of all meaning.

It is important to realize that entry into the mystery of the Trinity, because we are in Christ, does not negate all the wonder about God that we have learned from the Hebrew Bible. No, our fuller entrance is *built upon* entry into apt repentance—upon human awe, creaturely worship, and a new grasp of reality. While the Godhead proves to be hospitable to those who seek God's face, God remains the host, and we the guests. The "union" is true, and involves—by God's great condescension!—some reciprocity, but it is in no way symmetrical. To state it in a self-evident way: God does not worship us.

If we build our understanding of transformation and communion fully upon the foundation of our creaturely awe of God, and upon the reverence of the Son for the Father, then we will not go far wrong. Let us listen in, as the Church has done for centuries, to Jesus' words in John's Gospel concerning the unity into which we are invited. Jesus has, by the time that he talks to his apostles on that last night, already spoken of the Father's search for those who will "worship him in Spirit and in truth" (John 4:24) and has promised that those who are in him will discover that "living water" (John 4:10) will come from them to others, just as living water springs from him. The basis of this transformation is seen as he speaks to his disciples about the One whom they will worship in chapters 14 through 17. Here we will consider only the beginning and the end of this long discourse, two paragraphs in chapter 14 and a paragraph from chapter 17.

> Jesus said to him, "I am the way, and the truth, and the life; no one comes to the Father, but by me. If you had known me, you would have known my Father also; henceforth you know him and have seen him." Philip said to him, "Lord, show us the Father, and we shall be satisfied." Jesus said to him, "Have I been with you so long, and yet you do not know me, Philip? He who has seen me has seen the Father; how can you say, 'Show us the Father'? Do you not believe that I am in the Father and the Father in me? The words that I say to you I do not speak on my own authority; but the Father who dwells in me does his works. Believe me that I am in the Father and the Father in me; or else believe me for the sake of the works themselves. Truly, truly, I say to you, he who believes in me will also do the works that I do; and greater works than these will he do, because I go to the Father. Whatever you ask in my name, I will do it, that the Father may be glorified in the Son; if you ask anything in my name, I will do it. If you love me, you will keep my commandments." (John 14:6–15)

These words are about Jesus, the Father, and us; but they are, first of all, about the Son and the Father. If we look carefully at Jesus' description, several things emerge:

- The Son is "in the Father" and the Father is "in the Son."
- God's being and God's works match.
- Jesus' being and Jesus' works match.
- The Father is glorified in the Son.
- The glorification of the Son (going to the Father) means glory for God's children too (I go to the Father: you will do greater works).
- God's love is expressed when he grants us power; human love is expressed in obedience.

Notice that there is an utter identity and mutuality between the Son and the Father, so that Jesus can say that when we see him we truly see the Father. Yet there remains a distinction—the Son speaks on the authority of the Father, the Son goes to the Father, and the Father is glorified in the Son. So, while the Father and the Son are *one*, they are distinguishable. (If this is the case with the Father and the Son, how much more in the case of our union with God?) By Jesus, we will be enabled to do great things, yet we are distinguished from God in our essence, and we will obey in our human form of love. God is truly hospitable, making room for us to have fellowship by means of our union with Christ. We take on, by his grace, divine characteristics—yet God remains God.

A similar paradoxical dynamic is seen in the subsequent words, where Jesus speaks of the Holy Spirit:

> And I will pray the Father, and he will give you another Counselor, to be with you for ever, even the Spirit of truth, whom the world cannot receive, because it neither sees him nor knows him; you know him, for he dwells with you, and will be in you. I will not leave you desolate; I will come to you. Yet a little while, and the world will see me no more, but you will see me; because I live, you will live also. In that day you will know that I am in my Father, and you in me, and I in you. He who has my commandments and keeps them, he it is who loves me; and he who loves me will be loved by my Father, and I will love him and manifest myself to him. (John 14:16–21)

The life of the Holy Spirit is bound up with that of the Father and the Son. Because of the Spirit we can "know" that the Son is in the Father. We can also know—and here is the astonishing thing—that we are in the Son and the Son is in us. But love involves more than knowing something; it is seen in obedience. Our responsibility is to show our love through our human action of keeping the words of Jesus, obeying him. At the same time, love is mutual between Father and Son, between Father and believer, between Son and believer. This means that love is shown in divine action as well: we receive the Holy Spirit; God the Son shows us the Father.

This staggering unity is developed with even more drama in Jesus' closing "high priestly prayer":

> I am coming to thee. Holy Father. . . . Sanctify them in the truth; thy word is truth. . . . I do not pray for these only, but also for those who believe in me through their word, that they may all be one; even as thou, Father, art in me, and I in thee, that they also may be in us, so that the world may believe that thou hast sent me. The glory which thou hast given me I have given to them, that they may be one even as we are one, I in them and thou in me, that they may become perfectly one, so that the world may know that thou hast sent me and hast loved them even as thou hast loved me. (John 17:11–23)

"That they also may be in us!" "That they may be one even as we are one!" Here a double unity is envisioned—our unity with the Godhead through Christ, our unity with each other. Such a unity amounts to glory for the followers of Jesus. This is such a staggering human glory that the ancient Christian theologians dared to call it "deification." But these Church fathers never let us forget, nor does Jesus in this prayer let us forget, that this glory comes at the initiative of the Father and because of what the Son and the Spirit have done, are doing, and will do for us. The unity of the Holy Trinity is to be wonderfully mirrored in his people, who are to become "perfectly one," even as they feed upon Christ and gaze upon the Three-in-One who is/are unity personified. It is as if John the evangelist anticipated the poignant words of St. Irenaeus, who, as we have already seen, would picture the Son and the Holy Spirit as the two hands of the Father, drawing us into God's love.

If we are bold enough to think of ourselves as actually joining into the inner-relation of Father, Son, and Holy Spirit, this may be said to occur when we worship, when we give glory to the Triune God, honoring the Father through the Son and in the Holy Spirit. The Spirit's delight is to glorify the Son, to "recall" him to us, and to help redeemed humanity to remember his teachings. The Son's delight is to glorify the Father, declaring or exegeting the divine mystery to us, so far as we can bear it. And our delight is to join in this giving of glory, all the while in awe that God wants us to bless him at all. Moreover, one sign of our union with God in Christ is that our love for each other (and for all things) grows as we worship—we enter more deeply into the communion of the Trinity as we grow into communion with each other, a love upon which the world can remark with wonder.

Yet we must "keep it real." Even the most perfect love of the Church is but a pale reflection of the One who is Love: Father, Son, and Holy Spirit. Never will we exhaust the wonders of that fellowship by which every communion comes into being. There is that between Father, Son, and Holy Spirit that belongs to them, to the Triune God, alone—yet God is not jealous of this love, but draws us into it, so far as we can bear it. Jesus said to St. Mary Magdalene, "I am ascending to my Father and to your Father" (John 20:17 EH). It is significant that our Lord did not simply use the first-person plural pronoun *our* Father as he spoke to Mary: for the communion that he has with Father and Spirit is unique. God is our Father because Jesus truly is the Son of the Father. And yet, by God's mercy and grace, we have received the true Light. Because he has ascended to the Father, taking our human nature with him, the Spirit has been poured out on the Church. Hebrews reminds us that he is pleading in the heavens before us, leading our worship; the Apocalypse pictures our prayers as an offering before the LORD that joins heaven and earth together in worship; and John's Gospel gives the assurance that by the Spirit we can truly enter, worshiping the One who will grant us more glory than we can imagine. Thus, in gratitude and reverence, we are bold to say "Our Father, who art in heaven, hallowed be thy name, thy kingdom come, thy will be done on earth, as in heaven."

Almighty God, your Son, our Saviour Jesus Christ
is the light of the world.
May your people, illumined by your word and sacraments,
shine with the radiance of his glory,
that he may be known, worshiped and obeyed
to the ends of the earth. . . .
Accept all we offer you this day
and make us new in him,
who is Lord forever . . .
and lives and reigns with you and the Holy Spirit.
One God, now and forever. Amen.[15]

Questions for Discussion

1. If, like the apostles at the Transfiguration, Christians are called to be "portable tabernacles" of God's glory, what conclusions can we draw about the theme of *entrance* in worship? Is entrance, perhaps, two-sided? In what ways is God's entrance into us different from our entrance in to his glory?

2. Why does Peter's speech in Acts 2 refer to the Ascension (which comes *after* Jesus' death and resurrection) when he talks about Christ's "entrance into glory," rather than referring *back* to the Transfiguration?

3. In what ways does communal worship enable the believer to maintain both a reliance on God and continual fervor in seeking him?

4. Is the practice of "closed communion" (for example, in the Roman Catholic, Orthodox, and Missouri Synod Lutheran churches) merely a return to the Corinthian factious behavior, or is "open communion" a failure to "discern the body"? Which practice (if either) is more in line with St. Paul's teaching to the church at Corinth?

5. Is the acceptance of a common practice, custom, or tradition in worship (with respect to head coverings, for instance) mere conformism? Why or why not?

6. Why does current North American culture have an allergy to the idea of submission? Has the idea of submission been misused or abused in previous centuries, or has submission as a value and humility as a virtue simply been forgotten? Are there positive ways in which submission might be understood in our current cultural climate?

7. Were it even possible, should we desire an entirely symmetrical, reciprocal relationship with God in our worship? Why or why not?

4

"From You Comes . . . Praise"

Traditional Liturgies of the East

From you comes my praise in the great congregation.

Psalm 22:25 NRSV

So far we have seen the importance of common prayer in the Scriptures and in the Christian Tradition, and we have attended to God's invitation, issued in both the Old and New Testaments, that we enter into worship. Worship involves entrance into a larger action, company, and space, by which we give glory to the Triune God. This idea is deeply embedded in the tabernacle/temple worship of the Old Testament and in its underlying view of God's heaven and earth as mysteriously interconnected. In particular, the Psalms, Chronicles, and Isaiah picture the boundary between heaven and earth as startlingly permeable and invite God's people to join in a *synaxis* ("gathering together") not confined to the inhabitants of the human realm. This perspective is amplified in the New Testament, when the Incarnation of the Son and the descent of the Holy Spirit set into play the idea of a whole cosmos joined together for the praises of the creating and redeeming Lord. We shall see that this great gathering into worship is a major theme that is sustained in the early formative writings of the period immediately following that of the apostles, and that it comes to full flower in the more mature ancient liturgies of the Church.

The connection between early Christian liturgy and the Jewish synagogue and temple cult is complex, as is demonstrated by debates between such liturgical historians as Oesterley, Dix, Bouyer, Kavanagh, Senn, and, more recently, those influenced by Paul Bradshaw.[1] Surely this new Messianic expression of the faith, Christianity, to which "a great many priests" became "obedient" (Acts 6:7), would have lines of continuity as well as marks of distinction from the Jewish ways of worship that formed its matrix. It is not my aim here, however, to put forward any theory as to the precise lines of connection between the Jewish and early Christian forms of worship (though this is an important area of investigation). Nor will I attempt to trace the whole development of Christian liturgy from the subapostolic era (that is, the generation that immediately followed the original apostles) up to today. Even the little history that I offer cannot go into much detail. I have selected important ancient Christian texts and actual ancient liturgies specifically to show how the idea of "entrance into worship" is both continued and amplified beyond the biblical period, especially in the Eastern liturgical tradition but also in Western forms of worship.

In some cases we will also notice the continued importance of the celestial liturgy of Isaiah 6 (and Rev. 4–5). Even where Isaiah 6 is not explicitly present, the general themes of holiness and entrance seen in both Testaments are found in the East from the earliest references (the *Didache) through to the mature liturgies associated with Saints Basil of Caesarea and John Chrysostom. The evidence for liturgical development in the West is considerably more complex, but we can see these same themes in the earliest references to liturgy in Justin Martyr and the (supposed) Western *Apostolic Tradition, in the *Gallican (prominent early Western) rites, in the *Sarum rite (the early Roman British rite that influenced Cranmer's Anglican prayer book), and finally in the mature Latin *Mass that became the norm after Trent. In this chapter we will investigate the Eastern tradition, which is a little more easily traced, and then follow with the Western developments in the next chapter.[2]

Entrance in the *Didache*

The *Didache* is a very early Christian book, lost for some time but rediscovered in the nineteenth century. Its precise origin, dating, and even original shape (is it a composite?) continue to be debated. By all counts, however, it is very early, with dates given for its first appearance ranging from the late first to mid-second century. Various venues of origin, including Antioch and Egypt, have been suggested. Frequently, however, the book is associated with Jewish Christianity and the Gospel of Matthew because it uses the same kind of "two way" language (blessings and woes) found in that Gospel and in wisdom books in the Jewish tradition. Whatever its exact origin, it is an important example of early Christian worship because it describes (or prescribes) some key elements of liturgy that persisted into subsequent centuries. Since it also comments briefly on the theology that lies behind its described liturgy, it is (to a certain extent) self-interpreting. Chapters 9 and 10 are the most pertinent for our study:

> Now concerning the Thanksgiving [Gk., *eucharistia*], thus give thanks. First, concerning the cup: We thank you, our Father, for the holy vine of David Your servant, which You made known to us through Jesus Your Servant; to You be the glory for ever. And concerning the broken bread: We thank You, our Father, for the life and knowledge which You made known to us through Jesus Your Servant; to You be the glory for ever. *Even as this broken bread was scattered over the hills, and was gathered together and became one, so let Your Church be gathered together from the ends of the earth into Your kingdom*; for Yours is the glory and the power through Jesus Christ for ever. But let no one eat or drink of your Thanksgiving (Eucharist), but they who have been baptized into the name of the Lord; for concerning this also the Lord has said, Give not that which is holy to the dogs [cf. Matt. 7:6].[3]

Didache 9:4 especially describes the mystery of the entrance into the kingdom. As the people worship, they are gathered together and thus become themselves the sign of that final age when the whole Church will at last be collected and live together in Christ's presence: "Even as this broken bread was scattered over the hills, and was gathered together and became one, so let Your Church be *gathered together* from the ends of the earth *into Your kingdom*." (The Greek verb associated with the noun *synaxis* is used here. Though this may simply be a natural use of the Greek verb, this term will eventually take on a technical meaning among theologians, so that *synaxis* becomes the label for the worship assembly in discussions of liturgy.)

The language used in the Eucharist that the *Didache* describes seems to have adapted themes found in various Jewish blessings and prayers. Featured are the images of the vine, bread, and the ingathering of exiles, all of which were well-known images in Jewish worship. The spreading vine speaks of the incorporation of the people of God—first in Israel and ultimately in Christ. We see this in the thanksgiving over the cup, which refers to the "holy vine of your servant David," into which members of the community are, as branches, engrafted (cf. Rom. 11:16–24). The broken bread recalls the "life and knowledge" made available in Christ. More than this, bread gathered into one basket is reminiscent of Jesus' miracles of the multiplication of the loaves, after which the remnants are collected—details that refer symbolically to the scattered tribes and the gentiles. These echoes of the Old and New Testaments, coupled with overt references to ingathering, are poignant symbols that speak of the entrance of God's people into a company and life that is bigger than the individual or the local community alone. Alongside the theme of being gathered, the *Didache* sets down the prerequisite for sharing in the bread: only the "holy ones" who are baptized into the name of Jesus, and thus have entered into a new reality, may do so.

The next chapter, *Didache* 10, details the prayers to be offered after the bread has been eaten:

> But after you are filled, thus give thanks: We thank You, holy Father, for Your holy name which *You caused to tabernacle in our hearts*, and for the knowledge and faith and immortality, which You made known to us through Jesus Your Servant; to You be the glory for ever. You, Master almighty, created all things for Your name's sake; You gave food and drink to men for enjoyment, that they might give thanks to You; but to us You freely gave spiritual food and drink and life eternal through Your Servant. Before all things we thank You that You are mighty; to You be the glory for ever. Remember, Lord, Your Church, to deliver it from all evil and to make it perfect in Your love, *and gather it from the four winds, sanctified for Your kingdom which You have prepared for it*; for Yours is the power and the glory for ever. Let grace come, and let this world pass away. Hosanna to the God (Son) of David! If any one is holy, let him come; if any one is not so, let him repent. *Maran atha.* Amen. But permit the prophets to make Thanksgiving as much as they desire.

The passage makes it clear that thanksgiving is offered because of the larger reality that has come to the faithful, a reality made present through the dwelling of Christ and the Spirit among them. Because of God's presence, the worshipers have been gathered as they worship, and thus they look forward to a complete gathering at the second coming of the LORD. Among them is the dwelling of the "holy Name" (Jesus, the power of God), who is the cause of this larger reality, by which even ordinary things such as food and drink are transformed into "spiritual food and drink."

This meal is described in terms of holiness and is understood as a foretaste of the kingdom, for which the believers have been "sanctified," or set aside. In their worship, Christians positively fulfill the cry of God's historic people, who called out *"Hosanna!"* on Palm Sunday but who did not persist in their welcome. An invitation to those who are "holy" is issued, and a call to repentance is sounded for those who are not sanctified. (Though there is no explicit echo of Isaiah 6 in this prescription for early worship, the emphasis upon holiness, found in both chapters of the *Didache*, is shared with the prophet, who saw the utter transcendence as well as the deep *immanence of the LORD. In the *Didache*, too, the Holy Lord is seen as "tabernacling" among his people; yet he is acknowledged to have all the power and glory.) Finally, the closing comment of *Didache* 10, that the prophets may offer Thanksgiving at liberty, is an indication of the larger space into which the people of God have been gathered—lavish thanksgiving matches the large expanse into which they have been brought and to which they will be brought by God.

The themes of gathering, bread, vine, and holiness had staying power in the Church. They are found again in later Syrian and Egyptian works, including what we can reconstruct of the early third-century Syrian *Didascalia Apostolorum* (Section 7),[4] as well as in the late fourth-century Syrian compilation known as *Apostolic Constitutions* (chapter 9),[5] in the Egyptian, late-second-century(?)[6] *Dêr Balizeh* papyrus, and in the fourth-century Egyptian liturgy of Serapion.[7] In one influential Eastern liturgy, the Syrian *Addai and Mari* (perhaps as old as the third century), we see also that the well-known language of Isaiah 6 was ready to hand and used to interpret both the mystery of entrance into God's presence and the astonishing healing that comes upon entering.

Anaphora of Addai and Mari

The *Anaphora (or "lifting up") is that portion of a liturgy where the people, with the priest, direct themselves deliberately to the LORD. It occurs, in full liturgies, after the reading and exposition of the Word and at the beginning of the actual Eucharist, as the people prepare to consecrate and receive the gifts. We do not have the whole of the Addai and Mari liturgy, but the Anaphora sounds our theme of entrance into mystery:

> Let your minds be on high . . .
> . . . A thousand thousand [sic] of those on high, Lord, worship thy majesty and ten thousand thousands of the armies of ministers of fire and spirit praise it in fear, together with the cherubim and seraphim that cry one to another and say: Holy, holy, holy, Lord God of Hosts. Heaven and earth are full of thy glory. Glory be to thee, O Lord Most High.
> *We too*, Lord, thy sinful servants, give thee thanks because thou hast wrought in us thy favor that cannot be repaid; thou hast put on our humanity so as to give us life by thy divinity, *thou hast exalted our low estate, raised up our prostration* and given life to our mortality . . .
> . . . *[M]ay our prayers be lifted up to thee* and may thy mercies descend on our petitions . . .
> We offer, Lord, this oblation before thee for the commemoration of all the righteous and just fathers, the prophets, apostles, martyrs, confessors, bishops, priests, ministers, and of all the children of holy Church that are signed with the signing of holy baptism; and *us too, Lord, thy humble servants that are gathered together and are standing before thee and have received by tradition the example* [literally, *tupsa*, *type] *that has come from thee.* . . . We celebrate . . . this great sacrament [alternate translation: "we perform this great *mystery"].[8]

This very early Eastern prayer pictures entrance into the heavenly realms, immersion into the historical Tradition, and solidarity with the action of the whole people of God. From this passage we can see that the language of the liturgy is not understood as simply a human attempt to understand the ineffable; rather, the liturgy is something passed down, worship that truly corresponds to the mysterious world of God. The liturgy is secure because it has been given to the congregation by means of the great Tradition, a tradition based on the *type* (the pattern or model) given to the Church by Jesus himself, presumably at his Passover with the apostles. This reference to *type* may well imply that the worshipers considered that what they did in the liturgy (the "type") corresponded to the spiritual reality (which would be the *"antitype," Jesus himself) in a direct way. The ancient worshiper would agree quite literally with the psalmist (Ps. 22:25 NRSV), who declared, "From you comes my praise in the great congregation." Jesus himself, the God-Man, establishes the pattern by which Christians are to offer thanksgiving and praise to the Father.

The Anaphora also links the human performance of the eucharistic mystery to the Incarnation, by which life has been given to those who are mortal. It is because God has put on human flesh that prayers may be confidently lifted up to the Lord of lords. Authentic worship is also made possible because of the cosmic *Divine Liturgy that continues always in God's heavenly presence, to which Christian worship corresponds, and with which the human liturgy is joined. God performs all this . . . yet human worshipers are called, in concert with God, to "lift . . . minds on high."

The Liturgy of St. James

We move on to the Liturgy of St. James, which is most likely our oldest surviving complete service of worship. It is believed by most scholars in its original form to have been developed for use by the Church in the fourth century, though it is associated with traditions going back to James the Just, the brother of Jesus. Though the *Jacobite (the adjective for "Jamesian") liturgy is even more exotic than the *Anaphora of Addai and Mari*, it has made its marks on both the East and the West. It comes into the Western consciousness through the English tradition of hymnody:

> Let all mortal flesh keep silence, and with fear and trembling stand.
> Ponder nothing earthly-minded, for with blessing in his hand,
> Christ our God to earth descendeth, our full homage to demand.
>
> King of kings, yet born of Mary, as of old on earth he stood,
> Lord of lords, in human vesture, in the Body and the Blood,
> He will give to all the faithful his own Self for heavenly food.[9]

This English hymn, which adapts the Anaphora found in the Liturgy of St. James, is sung to a French melody that is evocative of both God's greatness and his heartbreaking nearness to us. The liturgy itself, after a call to silence and awe similar to the hymn, proceeds to make a pointed connection of Isaiah's vision with the eucharistic sacrifice:

> for the King of kings and Lord of lords advances to be slain and given as food to the faithful. Before him go the choirs of Angels, with every rule and authority, the many-eyed Cherubim and the six-winged Seraphim, veiling their sight and crying out the hymn: Alleluia, Alleluia, Alleluia.[10]

In this "lifting up" prayer, the worshipers have already, so to speak, entered, trembling before the presence of the Lord of lords and singing the mysterious *Trisagion* ("thrice-holy" hymn) with the angels. These poignant words continue to be prayed today by Christians in the Indian and Syrian traditions of the Church. Moreover, those of the Orthodox traditions will recognize this hymn as the one still sung on Holy Saturday (in the Liturgy of St. Basil), while also discerning its continuing general influence upon the better known Liturgies of St. Chrysostom and St. Basil. Let us look more closely at this early liturgy and at its general structure, which developed around the movements of procession toward and entrance into the presence of the Lord.

Entrance in Eastern Christian worship is something done with the entire person, body and soul, and by the whole congregation. We will see that the entire structure of the Eastern rite revolves around two major points of "entrance." In both cases the priest and deacon approach the altar of God on behalf of the people, physically entering that space, and the people "enter" more fully into God's presence by means of the prayers and solemn hymns of the liturgy. The entrances involve processions around the church (in early days, we shall see, even *toward* the church), and for centuries those not actually processing often have changed postures, kneeling or reverencing the Bible or the chalice as they move by. We see this double dynamic of entrance in the Liturgy of St. James beginning with its "little entrance" (associated with the service of the Word) and the "great entrance" (associated with the Eucharist). In contrast to the later Eastern liturgies, the "little entrance" in the Liturgy of St. James occurs quite early in the service, though it is adorned by several prayers said by both the priest and the people. Frank Senn speaks about the development of the West Syrian Church and the precursors to the Liturgy of St. James, explaining that the idea of entrance was so central that it attracted development: after all, the entrances were expressed by the movement of the priest and the people and therefore were obvious "high" points of the liturgy.[11] Dramatic movement naturally attracts fervent prayer and hymnody.

A word is in order concerning the "entrances." A visitor to the liturgy, unaware of the meaning of the term *entrance*, might see the heading of this part of the liturgy in the service booklet and believe that the word actually signifies the grand processions made at these points, as the priest and other servers enter the congregational area first with the Gospelbook and then the chalice. However, the entrance primarily means that the priest and the people themselves draw near to God by the Word or the Sacrament, rather than referring to the appearance of the Scriptures in procession, or the chalice in procession, from behind the *iconostasis (the stand and gate that hold the *icons, situated between the people and the altar). The processions are associated with these actions because it is by means of the Word and Sacrament that we come into the divine presence.[12] Because Christ the Word (seen in the Gospel) has come among us and because the Holy Spirit is among us to sanctify the Eucharist (which itself is Christ's body and blood) and those receiving it, the company of the faithful is enabled to enter God's presence.

Entry into God's presence is a bold act. We should therefore not be surprised to discover in the entrances of the Liturgy of St. James recurring images from Isaiah 6 and prayers for purification:

Defiled as I am by many sins, do not utterly reject me, Master, Lord, our God.
. . . Sovereign Lord Jesus Christ, O Word of God, who freely offered Yourself a blameless sacrifice upon the cross to God even the Father, *the coal of double nature, that touched the lips of the* prophet *with the tongs, and took away his* sins, touch also the hearts of us sinners, and purify us from every stain, and *present us* holy *beside Your* holy *altar*, that we may offer You a sacrifice of praise.
. . . *lead all to perfection*, and make us perfectly worthy of the grace of Your sanctification, gathering us together within Your holy Church . . .
. . . God Almighty, Lord great in glory, *who hast given to us an entrance into the Holy of Holies*, through the sojourning among men of Your only-begotten Son, our Lord, and God, and Saviour Jesus Christ, we supplicate and invoke Your goodness, since *we are fearful and trembling* when about to stand at Your holy altar . . .
Let all mortal flesh keep silent, and with fear and trembling stand . . .
. . . Master and Lord, who visit us in mercy and compassion and *have granted us, humble sinners and your unworthy servants the grace to stand at your holy Altar* and to offer to you this dread sacrifice without shedding of blood for our own sins and those committed in ignorance by the people, look on me, your unprofitable servant and wipe away my transgressions through your compassion and purify my lips and my heart from every defilement of flesh and spirit . . .
We thank you, Lord our God, that *you have given us the freedom of entry into the holy place by the blood of Jesus*, inaugurating for us a new and living way through the veil of his flesh. *Having therefore been counted worthy to enter the place where your glory dwells*, and to be within the veil, and to look upon the Holy of Holies, we fall down before your goodness, Master. . . . And having uncovered the veils of the mysteries that symbolically surround this sacred rite, show us clearly, and *fill our spiritual vision with your boundless light*; and having cleansed our poverty from all defilement of flesh and spirit, *make it worthy of this dread and fearful presence*.[13]

Here, in first flower, we find an Eastern liturgy that celebrates the opening of the mystery vouchsafed to the prophet Isaiah, expressed fully in Christ. Here is the central focus of the proclamation and worship of the early Church— Jesus the Christ, who has come to be for God's people the divine provision, indeed, the gate, for entrance into his presence. References to holiness in contrast with human sinfulness, to being gathered together with the saints, to the ministering angels and all of creation for worship, and to God's transcendence and immanence in the Incarnation all find their place in this context. The Gospel reading is a poignant sign of Christ's presence among his people, and the mysterious Eucharist is seen as a poignant foretaste of the final entrance into his kingdom. To be touched by the divine should be to risk death, as the prophet acknowledged in his cry, "woe is me!" Yet, with Isaiah, those worshiping in the Liturgy of St. James hear the voice of grace promising, "I will heal." God's promise is heard in the Gospel; God's touch is extended in the Eucharist.

The Liturgy of St. John Chrysostom

All these elements are also incorporated into the most common liturgy of the Orthodox Church, that associated with *St. John Chrysostom ("the golden-mouthed"), AD 347–407.[14] Fr. Alexander Schmemann depicts the entire liturgy (which contains, like the Liturgy of St. James, both the "little" and "great" entrance) as a *graduated* entrance up into the divine Presence: "this rhythm of ascent—from 'this world' to the gates of the temple, from the gates of the temple to the altar, from the altar to the high place . . . to the heights to which the Son of God has lifted us."[15] Indeed, in the ancient tradition of Orthodox worship, the first reference to "entrance" is marked not merely in the Sunday Divine Liturgy, but during the Great *Vespers[16] of Saturday sun-down. (The liturgical day begins with the evening of the previous day, so that Saturday evening marks the commencement of the Lord's Day for those who understand "the evening and the morning" as the "first day" [cf. Gen. 1:5].)

As soon as night falls during the vesperal service, the deacon (whose voice represents the people) requests the priest to bless the people's entrance into the Lord's Day, saying "Bless, Master, the Holy Entrance. . . ." The priest responds declaring, "Blessed is the entrance of the holy people of God, now and always and for ever and ever. Amen." Only at this point do the people sing the song of Christ's radiant light and so begin their entrance into holy time, the time of the Lord's Day. So, then, on Sunday, the people come already prepared by the vesperal entrance (and frequently Vespers has been a time for confession as well, so that the preparation may be personal as well as corporate).

The tradition has developed so that the whole theme of movement toward the presence of God is sustained into Sunday, when the way is paved for Divine Liturgy by earlier services. There are three: *Kairon (the "Entrance Prayers"); *Orthros (this term for Morning Prayer comes from the Greek "Arise!"); and *Prothesis, the advance preparation of the *elements said by the priest, often during Orthros. The term Kairon is related to the Greek word *kairos, a term that indicates a specific "time" of some importance, over against the other Greek word for time, chronos, which refers to the ongoing flow of time and from which we get our word "chronology." By its very name, Kairon indicates the deep significance of the Divine Liturgy that is about to be celebrated, and that is, according to St. John Chrysostom, the very work of God ("Everything is brought to pass by the Father, the Son, and the Holy Spirit"[17]), even while the people work by their prayers. The Kairon prayers begin as the priest blesses God, and then with a beloved invocation of the Holy Spirit, a prayer that is said by Orthodox, whether lay or ordained, at the start of most worship times, both personal and corporate:

> O heavenly King, O Comforter, Spirit of Truth,
> Who are present in all places and fill all things;
> Treasury of blessings and Giver of life:
> Come and dwell [literally, "tabernacle"] in us and cleanse us from every
>   stain
> And save our souls, O good One.

The invocation of the Holy Spirit during Kairon implies that all the praise that will be given by the gathered people in the liturgy is inspired by God himself, whose Holy Spirit delights to give glory to the Father and to the Son—"from You comes my praise in the great congregation!"

The priest prays for God's mercy throughout this time of preparation, asking that "the door of compassion," personified in the willing and humble holy Mary, be opened for the worshipers. (Mary the mother of Jesus is not understood by Orthodox as a detraction from Christ who is the door to the sheepfold. We will deal with the *Theotokos and mediation later in our study.) Acknowledging with awe the liturgical time that is approaching, the priest then prays: "O Lord, stretch forth Thy hand . . . and strengthen me for this Thine appointed service; so that, standing without condemnation before Thy dread altar, I may offer unto Thee the holy and bloodless sacrifice." After bowing to the people, and as he enters the *sanctuary (behind the iconostasis), the priest declares his intent to worship: "I will enter into thy house: I will worship toward thy holy Temple in fear of thee." His priestly garb, which he now dons, is seen as a preparation for worship, and he also washes his hands so that he may "compass the altar" of God, loving the beauty of the Lord's house (see Ps. 26:6). Though these are quiet prayers said by the priest, he concludes by saying, "in the congregation will I bless Thee, O Lord."[18] Similarly, during the *Prothesis*, as the priest prepares the vessels and bread that will be used in the Eucharist, he remembers the mighty acts of Christ, especially his passion, the angelic hosts, and the heroes of the past, both from the Bible and from those who have led the Church. Praying personally, he is in the company of all the saints and remembers that Christ is with us at all times: "In the grave with the body, but in Hades with the soul as God, in Paradise with the Thief, and on the Throne with the Father and the Spirit wast thou, O Christ, filling all things, thyself uncircumscribed."[19]

It is this Christ who was truly present in local and historical situations, yet "uncircumscribed," who is present by the Holy Spirit. He it is who gives grace to his people to enter into that larger realm, company, and action that he has himself accomplished. In Christ, and by the Spirit, his people may bless the "kingdom of the Father" and pray "in peace to the Lord." Orthodox worshipers who come to participate in Divine Liturgy on Sunday literally find themselves entering into praises that have been going on long before they all arrive—*Kairon, Orthros, Prothesis*—and that began, indeed, the night before at Great Vespers. The human action of joining praises with those who are already worshiping mirrors the reality that, as human beings, we are joining the ranks of heaven who always worship the Lord, and the creation that glorifies God, each creature offering "peculiar honors to our King."[20] The worship is not their own, not of human devising; it is entry into that which is enormous, intersecting and spanning time and space. At the end of *Prothesis*, the deacon acknowledges both God's initiative and this specific, holy time (*kairos*) of worship, which redeems ongoing time (*chronos*). He cues the priest (or bishop, if he is celebrating), saying: "It is *time (kairos)* for the *Lord* to act!" (cf. Ps. 119:126). And so, the Divine Liturgy begins. The priest declares "Blessed is the Kingdom of the Father, and of the Son, and of the Holy Spirit: now and ever, and unto ages of ages"; the people respond, "Amen!"

The rhythm of this main service, the Divine Liturgy, with its waves of repeated prayers, refrains, and circular-but-forward movement, mirrors the complexities of human reality, which knows beginning and end in time, but which is also caught up, by the grace of God, in eternity. Those unaccustomed to formal liturgy, whether Eastern or Western, are sometimes put off by the comings and goings, the ethereal chanting of the liturgy, and the separate though linked prayers of priest and people. These features take their natural place, however, in a service that is understood as entrance into something *larger*—not everyone needs to know explicitly about everything that is transpiring. Guests to Orthodox services are sometimes concerned, for example, about the iconostasis—the stand between the place where the congregation worships and the altar. The iconostasis holds many icons and has three doors, one to the left, one to the right, and a double set of *Royal Doors in the middle, which are opened as the service begins. Its purpose is not to separate the people from what the priest and deacons are doing "in secret"; rather, the structure of the entire worship space communicates holiness. When processions come from behind the iconostasis, with the Gospelbook and with the chalice, they speak of Christ's coming to the entire Church, including those ancient faithful who are "asleep in Christ," and who are seen by means of their iconic representations on the iconostasis, the walls, and the ceiling. In the same way, the censing of the icons, the altar, the people, the eucharistic gifts, is not done simply to lend an air of mystery. Rather, the incense signals that all these are gifts to God, offered to him along with the prayers of the people, just as incense is offered in the celestial worship glimpsed by means of Isaiah 6 and Revelation 4–5. The incense is a sign of God's presence ("the smoke filled the temple") and of the prayers that are constantly ascending to the LORD. ("Let my prayer arise in thy sight as incense," Ps. 141:2 EH.) There is a mutual honor given between the priest and the people as they are censed, for both congregation and priest recognize God's presence among them.

Similarly, when the priest prays quietly, his prayers do not supplant but *complement* the praises of the people who are singing—all the worshipers do not serve identically, but with one voice and in harmony. *Dom. Gregory Dix suggests, in fact, that in the early days the high point of the liturgy—the thankful offering that the people make of themselves and of the eucharistic gifts of bread and wine, through which God will heal them—was performed in reverent silence. Later, when prayers of the priest came to be added to the most solemn points of the service, they were to be done quietly. This was not to keep the laity in the dark, nor to exclude them, but because "the real offering was the *act* of the people through the deacons, from which nothing should distract attention."[21] This sense of the liturgy as the thanksgiving of all the people is in continuity with the earliest descriptions of Christian worship, when the "Amen!" of the congregation was essential.

The Divine Liturgy is composed of two major parts: the Liturgy of the Word (also known as the Liturgy of the *Catechumens) and the Liturgy of the Eucharist (also known as the Liturgy of the Faithful). Originally, the services seem to have been more separate, and indeed, sometimes performed separately. As the Liturgy stands in its mature form, this classical division underscores the action of entrance—those who are not yet initiated approach God to hear the proclamation of the Word and to pray; those who are baptized are beckoned further up and in, to pray for those who are not yet fully initiated and to give thanks for the holy and mysterious presence of Christ among them, nourishing them in the sacrament. The keynote for the entire Liturgy of St. Chrysostom, especially when celebrated on the Lord's Day, is that "the Son of God" is "risen from the dead." The resurrection becomes the very catalyst of Sunday worship: "O Son of God, who has risen from the dead, save us, who sing unto you, Alleluia!" This resurrection theme is joined to that of the Incarnation and the reign of the merciful and holy Triune God, whose action in history and in the present encourages those gathered to seek the divine presence. The little entrance, as in the Liturgy of St. James, comes toward the beginning of the service of the Word. Just prior to this entrance the priest prays quietly while the people sing the entrance hymn that recalls the angels and archangels who wait before God, and asks that "with our entrance there may be an entrance of holy Angels serving with us and glorifying your goodness." Aloud, the priest declares, "Blessed is the Entrance of your Saints: always, now and ever, and unto ages of ages." The liturgy then proceeds to a series of threefold prayers that prepare for the higher or deeper points of the service. These prayers take the form of a litany between the worshipers, with deacon and priest taking the lead, and the people punctuating the prayers with cries—"Lord have mercy! (*Kyrie eleison)," "To You, O Lord!" and "Amen!"

In his study on the "little" entrance, Fr. Schmemann[22] describes how this procession (which like the Liturgy of St. James once took its place at the very commencement of the Divine Liturgy) came to be preceded by the triple cycle of antiphons and prayers now common to Eastern liturgies. These prayers that now come at the beginning of the Orthodox liturgy (whether that of St. Chrysostom or St. Basil) were first offered during the processions made from the Hagia Sophia to the specific church named for the saint or the feast to be honored, with an actual *entrance* occurring at the door of that church. Once the preliminary prayers were well established in usage, they persisted even when there was no procession, so that the first "little" entrance was delayed. Eventually, the entrance was transformed into a formal component of the liturgy and attached to the carrying out of the Gospelbook from behind the iconostasis into the midst of the people. The entrance of God's people into the heavenly presence is particularly emphasized at the reading of the Gospel: by deed and word they acclaim the presence of Jesus in the read (actually, chanted!) Word, for which and for whom they stand, and to whom they cry a formal *"Alleluia!" both before and after the Gospel is heard. Accompanying this spiritual entrance of the whole congregation is the deliberate action of the priest and other servers. At the climax of the "little entrance," they go through the Royal Doors from the congregational side into the sanctuary, and the deacon places the Bible upon the holy table, with deep respect. Their physical entrance maps out the entrance of the entire congregation into God's presence.

After the service of the Word comes the Eucharist itself, and here it is a matter of "further up and further in," as Reepicheep, the mouse of fame from *The Chronicles of Narnia, describes the creaturely approach to the "high places" of God's domain. In the words of Fr. Schmemann, "the eschatological meaning of entrance, as drawing near to the altar and ascent to the kingdom, is best of all expressed in the prayer and singing of the *Trisagion* [the angelic "holy, holy, holy!"]."[23] Interestingly, in the Liturgy of St. James, the *Trisagion* preceded the liturgy of the Word, while the consecration of the holy mysteries was preceded by the chant, "Let all mortal flesh keep silence

. . . for the King of kings . . . advances to be slain and given as food to the faithful. Before him go the choirs of Angels . . . veiling their sight and crying out the hymn: *Alleluia, Alleluia, Alleluia.*" In the Liturgy of St. Chrysostom, the *Trisagion* is both sung at the service of the Word and recalled at the Eucharist. It is the people's role, once they have "laid aside earthly care," to "represent the cherubim" and so "to sing the thrice-holy hymn" as the Lord approaches in the sacrament.

Both the older Liturgy of St. James and that of St. Chrysostom preserve the awe of entrance into God's presence: the first by enjoining silence and the second by accentuating the wonder that humans are enabled to enter into the *Trisagion*, in the place of the angels. As the priest declares in the Liturgy of St. Chrysostom, "We give thanks unto you also for this ministry which you do vouchsafe to receive at our hand, even though there stand beside you thousands of Archangels and ten thousands of Angels, the Cherubim and the Seraphim, six-winged, many-eyed, soaring aloft, borne on their pinions, singing the triumphal Hymn, shouting, proclaiming and saying. . . ." How astonishing that it is the whole congregation of those humans made holy by Christ who can now sing what the angels proclaim! "Holy, holy, holy, Lord of Sabaoth, heaven and earth are full of your glory!" And they can sing this because there is a Lord Jesus to whom they can shout, *"Hosanna!" (literally, "Lord, save!"). It is this Jesus who has come and who is coming to them as they worship in the name of the Lord. Christ's own people enter into an action larger than human action. As they have already reminded each other in a formal greeting, toward the beginning of the Eucharist, "Christ is among us! He is and ever shall be!"

The preparation and consecration of the elements of the Eucharist, in the same way, recall the whole of God's people—from the Theotokos Mary and John the Forerunner to the entire congregation there present. The central portion of the bread has been stamped with a seal that includes the cross and words "Jesus Christ" and "Victory." This portion of the loaf, specially consecrated, is called the "Lamb," and is broken with these words: "Broken and distributed is the Lamb of God, broken yet not divided, ever eaten yet never consumed, but *sanctifying those who partake of Him.*" A prayer is also made over the remaining bread that is not considered mysterious but that is intended to be shared as the *"antidoron" (literally, "in place of the gift") with those who are present but outside the fellowship: "Be mindful, O Lord, of this city, and of every city . . . of those who travel . . . of the sick . . . of those who . . . do good works in thy holy churches, and who remember the poor; and upon us all send forth your mercies." All these things look forward to the time that "with one mouth and one heart" God's entire people may "glorify and praise" the Triune God. Time itself is seen as filled up with the presence of God when, after the communion, the people pray, "that all day long we may meditate upon your righteousness." Finally, the dismissal recalls

Christ's holy Mother, the angels, John the Baptist, the Apostles, the Martyrs, the Fathers, the "ancestors of God" (incarnate!) Joachim and Anna,[24] and the particular saints of the day, "forasmuch as God is good and loves mankind."

The entire liturgy with its knit-together quality, its prayers, its songs, and its actions, joins the people of Christ together, causing them to enter into the cosmic action of praise as they enter the immense space of the heavens and as they intercede on behalf of the world, even while they remain aware of the hosts, human saints, and angels that surround them. Besides the written prayers of the liturgy, there are a number of prayers that have become available through the development of tradition for the personal use of communicants, many of which remind them of the "unceasing festival" to which they have been called, of "all the good things" of which God has made them partakers, of the Holy Trinity, of the numerous holy ones who surround them in prayer, and of the whole scope of the divine drama in which they have become living actors by means of the liturgy.[25]

The Liturgy of St. Basil

St. Basil was bishop of Caesarea (Cappadocia) from AD 370–79. We know from ancient sources that he developed a liturgy, probably by modifying and pastorally shortening an earlier Anaphora that came from Alexandria, perhaps a service that bore many resemblances to the earliest form of the Liturgy of St. James. Though St. Basil's name was very early associated with a liturgy, some scholars doubt that we can confidently move from these details to accept the attribution of his name to an Eastern liturgy now served ten times during the Orthodox year,[26] when it replaces the Liturgy of St. John Chrysostom. As with the Liturgy of St. John Chrysostom, what is now called the Liturgy of St. Basil was modified, shaped, elaborated, and so on, through centuries of use in the Church; and, of course, this is to be expected in a tradition that honors worship, not because it is the creation of one (albeit gifted) individual, but because it is offered by all the faithful, inspired by God's own Spirit. Nevertheless, it is not unlikely that St. Basil's prayers underlie the liturgy now used in Orthodoxy during the five Sundays of Great *Lent (prior to Palm Sunday), on Holy Thursday and Saturday, on the eves of Nativity and Theophany, and on his own feast day in January.

Though Basil's work preceded that of St. John Chrysostom, we have left it until this point because St. John's is better known and because the two liturgies bear a strong family resemblance. So close are the general similarities that for many years it was assumed that St. John had composed his Anaphora by shortening St. Basil's work. More recent studies suggest that the liturgies are related more as cousins rather than as mother and daughter: St. Basil appears to have modified an early form of worship used in Alexandria, whereas

St. John modified a liturgy used in Antioch, which he incorporated into the liturgical framework of St. Basil that was being used in Constantinople.[27] Mostly, the few differences between the Liturgies of St. Basil and St. John, as they are now celebrated, are seen in the particular (and quietly said) prayers of the priest. Here we will detail some of the points at which St. Basil's Liturgy diverges from that associated with St. John, specifically where the theme of entrance may be discerned.

So far as the people's corporate prayers are concerned, there is only one major difference. This involves the inclusion of the poignant song of praise that describes holy Mary, the bearer of God the Word ("Theotokos"), during the commendation of all God's holy people to the Lord and after the consecration of the elements. Some readers who are unaware of the resolution of earlier controversies in the Church may be astonished by this bold attribution of "God-bearer" to Jesus' mother. This title is associated with the Nicene and Constantinopolitan councils, when the Church recognized the complete divinity of Jesus and his unified person—truly and properly God and truly and properly man. Those who met at that time considered that it is insufficient to speak of holy Mary simply as "Christ-bearer," since that would imply a division of natures in God the Son. Mary might be understood as simply mother of the body, or "the human part" of the incarnate Word. But the mystery of the Incarnation demands that Christians use such surprising language as "God-bearer" in reference to Jesus' human mother. In the West, the parallel title has been "Mother of God"—never suggesting, of course, that Mary is mother to the Father or the Holy Spirit.

Since the eighth century, those worshiping in the form of St. John Chrysostom's Liturgy have sung a song about holy Mary at this climactic point of the service.[28] (Indeed, the song has been adopted also by the English hymn-writer Riley in "Ye *Watchers and Ye Holy Ones.") Here the language speaks of her as "more honourable beyond compare than the seraphim" because she gave birth to God, the Word. Probably in Chrysostom's own day, worshipers sang the earlier hymn found at this point in the Liturgy of St. Basil. It is just as striking, and it concentrates on the joy of the whole cosmos over Mary rather than on the angelic host alone:

> All of creation rejoices in you, O full of grace:
> the assembly of angels and the human race.
> You are a sanctified temple and a spiritual paradise,
> the glory [literally, "boasting"] of virgins
> from whom God was incarnate and became a little Child,
> Our God, existing before all ages.
> For he made your womb a throne,
> and your body more spacious than the heavens.
> All of creation rejoices in you, O full of grace.
> Glory to you.

At this point, may I plead with my readers who have Protestant sensibilities that they administer a quick antihistamine of charity against an anti-Marian allergic reaction? For in this song there is something important to see! The people are marveling at the wonder that the "uncircumscribable" God could be at home in a woman's womb. If God incarnate dwelled within the womb of Mary, then this was his throne, for he is King of kings. More than that, the one with whom God dwells is never left untouched: Moses' face shone simply by his being in proximity to God's glory (2 Cor. 3:13). If Mary's very body contained God, she herself must be spoken of as "more spacious than the heavens." This epithet also reminds us that in the Eastern Tradition, as well as in the West, holy Mary is seen as intimately connected with the Church. More than simply a beloved "elder sister," she is honored as its "mother," because of her motherhood of Christ. This is in harmony both with the imagery of Revelation 12 (where the mysterious queen is mother to both the Messiah and Christian believers) and with Jesus' commendation to the beloved (and deliberately unnamed) disciple: "Behold, your mother!" (John 19:27).

Those who are in Christ are part of that life of the Church that is "more spacious than the heavens," for the matrix in which the faithful live has been hallowed by the Lord of the universe. The honor given to the Theotokos takes seriously the mystery of the Incarnation and the power of the Holy Spirit utterly to change that which God inhabits. The glory attributed to holy Mary at this solemn point of the liturgy is glory that shines from the Lord and that returns back to give praise to the Source of all glory: God's power and love are not obscured, but are fulfilled and accomplished in this woman, his "handmaid" and handiwork.

Other prayers unique to the Liturgy of St. Basil are those said by the priest, mostly during the Liturgy of the Eucharist. However, at the close of the Liturgy of the Word, and serving as a kind of hinge to the Liturgy of the Eucharist, is a notable "second prayer of the faithful" (said *on behalf of* the faithful). In this prayer, there is a dynamic setup that is retained throughout the rest of the service: God has visited lowly humanity; God has raised up humanity before his glory to minister. God's descent enables humanity's ascent. Some specialists argue that the plural pronoun "us" ("You have set us . . . to serve at Your holy altar before Your holy glory") refers only to the clergy, both here and in the later prayers at the altar. However, it is important to remember that the traditional name of the second part of the liturgy (that is, the service of the Eucharist) was "The Liturgy of the Faithful," and that the Eucharist was made in ancient times from the gifts actually brought by the people, first-fruits of the gift of themselves as living sacrifices, united to the gift of Christ. Alexander Schmemann comments, "Who is serving . . . is not the clergy, and not even the clergy with the laity, but the Church, which is constituted and made manifest in all fullness by everyone together."[29] This "prayer of the faithful," said by the priest on behalf of the people, underscores the royal priesthood of believers, who are all entering, doing reverence, standing and serving, in various ways.

The prayers that ensue explicitly describe or implicitly assume the action of entering. There is entrance into a larger space: "Accept us who draw near to your holy Altar." Likewise, there is entrance into a larger action, with a sense of the historical offering of God's people: "accept [our service] as you accepted the gifts of Abel, the sacrifices of Noah, the burnt-offerings of Abraham, the priestly offices of Moses and Aaron, the peace-offerings of Samuel. Even as you accepted at the hands of the holy Apostles this true ministry, so . . . accept from the hands of us sinners these gifts." Similarly, in the prayer of the Anaphora ("the lifting up"), the reference to the host that surrounds God, and among whom the faithful enter, is amplified: "Who is sufficient to speak of thy mighty acts, to make all thy praises to be heard, or to tell of all thy wonders at every season?" There follows a doxological celebration of the Holy Trinity, ending with glorifying the Spirit "by whom enabled, every rational and intelligent creature does serve you, and send up perpetual praise, for all things are your servants. . . . Angels and Archangels, Thrones, dominions, Principalities, Authorities, Powers, . . . Cherubim . . . and Seraphim."

The recital of salvation history that takes place at the Anaphora lends itself to understanding worship as entrance into a larger space, action, and company. Whereas the rehearsal of St. Chrysostom focuses upon the death of Christ, that of St. Basil begins with primordial time, with the Creation itself, when God "ordered all things" for humanity. It stresses God's establishment of humanity "in the midst of a Paradise of plenty." Then, after detailing the Fall, it goes on to recall the many ways in which God nevertheless visited humanity and cared for them—by prophets, saints, the Law, guardian angels, and finally in the Son, who became "a dweller in this world" so that he could "make a way for all flesh." As Fr. Patrick Reardon reminds us,

> Generally speaking, in the West fallen man has been the starting point for most reflection on *soteriology for the past thousand years. For earlier Church History, however, this was not the case, nor has it ever been in the East. The older and more traditional approach begins, not with fallen man, but with man in his Christian fulfillment. It commences, not with man as sinner, but with man as sharer in the life of God. It gazes, first, at the goal of redemption, which is man's participation in the divine nature.[30]

The recitation of holy history in St. Basil's liturgy, going back to Creation, is in harmony with this perspective shared generally in the Eastern Church.

The prayer of consecration that follows is made to the Holy Trinity— "O Holy of Holies"—and actually names the holy presence of God as the inner shrine of the true temple. Along with other ancient writers like Irenaeus (before Basil) and Nectarios (afterward) the liturgy uses the language of "antitype" in reference to the mysterious elements—"presenting unto you the antitypes of the holy Body and Blood of thy Christ." This rings a little oddly—do these words suggest that the elements alone are "the antitype," "the *real* thing"? In the technical language of antitype over against type, as it is used in literary studies of the Bible, the type foreshadows the antitype, as, for example, the victor Joshua, who is the "type," foreshadows Jesus the Savior, who is the "antitype." Even in antiquity, scholars commented on the problem caused by this term and suggested explanations for it.[31] But surely we cannot think that the elements are the antitypes, the fulfillment of what was historically prior, that is, the body and blood of the Jesus who came into history. Christ's own body would then be relegated to merely the "type," the stamp corresponding to the real thing. If the elements truly are *antitypes*, that is, reality itself, then this is because they *partake in* Jesus' historic, resurrected, and eternal reality. And so, perhaps we can read the liturgy in this way: "We present unto you the antitypes [the *real* offering, over against the offerings of Abel, Noah, Abraham, etc. mentioned earlier in the liturgy, which were the types], the antitypes *that are* the holy Body and Blood of thy Christ."[32] Others have thought that the word *antitypes* here is only loosely used, so as to simply mean "something corresponding to" the holy body and blood of Christ. Whatever is meant precisely, the phrase is significant, as is seen by the context of the entire prayer. It brings the mystery of the Eucharist, the whole action including elements and congregation, into the larger dimension of history and the heavenlies. It would seem that St. Basil, of an earlier time and different tradition than St. Gregory of Nazianzen, would nevertheless have said "Amen" to St. Gregory's "offering up" address to Christ: "My actions are a copy of thy word [Word?] . . . it is thou who hast given me this mystic share in thy flesh in the bread and wine."[33]

The use of antitype language, then, fits perfectly with the ensuing prayer in St. Basil's liturgy, that both the people and the gifts presented before the Lord will be blessed, hallowed, and *shown* to belong to Christ by the descent of the Holy Spirit. It seems that in this ancient eucharistic service, the very act of worship has constituted the gathered people as holy, so that the prayer for the coming of the Holy Spirit ("the *epiclesis*") is not for a transformation, but a revelation of the sacred realm that is already there. Indeed, the worshipers pray that the Holy Spirit will change *them* and not merely the gifts, helping them, by the true light, to discern the body of Christ. The faithful and the gifts are shown, by the Holy Spirit, to be what God has made them.

Not only are all the company of the faithful remembered at this point (as in the Liturgy of St. John), but the prayer is explicitly made that the Lord "unite all to one another unto communion of the one Holy Spirit . . . that we may find mercy and grace with all the saints . . . and every righteous spirit made perfect in faith." The prayer is also made that worshipers "be made one with the holy Body and Blood" and that they "may become a temple of thy Holy

Spirit." So complete is this entrance that it becomes identification. God's people have *become* prayer, have *become* the temple, have *become* the body and blood of Christ. St. Basil's strong motif of entrance is sounded in the closing "prayer behind the ambon"[34] that is reserved for his feast day: "grant us at every time and season to meditate on your righteousness, that being led according to your will . . . *we may become worthy of a place* also at your right hand." The entrance of the liturgy is a foretaste of that grand entrance at the end of the ages, when the faithful will be like him and see him as he is.

In this very brief taste of ancient Christian worship in the East (and some of these services persist to this day), we have seen recurring themes that are conjoined with the theme of ongoing entrance. There is the constant sense that God's people join their worship to the whole household of the faithful and to the adoration offered by the cosmic powers of heaven. There is constant emphasis upon the holiness of God, a holiness that is transferred to all that comes into contact with the Lord through worship, and to all who enter into this holy act. Creaturely entrance into worship is seen as the complement or, indeed, the response made possible by God's entrance and indwelling of the human realm, his tabernacling among us. The major Old Testament text that expresses this is Isaiah 6, understood through the great visitation by God in the Incarnation. Those things that are set aside for God are done so with thanksgiving, so that the actions of sanctifying, blessing, and Eucharist ("giving thanks") come together. This means that, though God's actions are primary (especially the atonement and healing wrought by God the Son!), the elements of the Eucharist are identified with both the flesh and blood of Jesus and with the sacrifice of those who have a contrite heart, because they are "in Christ." To identify the Eucharist with human offering might seem presumptuous, as taking away from the uniqueness of Jesus' redeeming work. However, because the human element of offering comes after a protracted liturgy of humble entrance and preparation, and because it is surrounded by prayers that acknowledge the primacy of the Lord, worshipers are never allowed to forget that "One is Holy" in the absolute sense. Preparation, being gathered together in worship, cleansing by the Word, and healing in the Eucharist issue in the Church's transformation: entry into worship allows God's people to become what they are meant to be. As servants of God, they cleave to a hallowed time in which to honor the Holy One, "laying aside earthly care" and entering into a higher reality. Yet this does not mean a separation from the world, for which they pray, and which they carry as a holy priesthood into the presence of the Holy One, the healer and giver of life. The entire structure of the mature Eastern liturgies reinforces their action of entrance and joins human entry to a joyful celebration of God's deep visitation of his people in the God-Man, his presence with them in the Word and the Eucharist, and his ongoing tabernacling with them by the Holy Spirit:

O heavenly King, O Comforter, Spirit of Truth,
Who are present in all places and fill all things;
Treasury of blessings and Giver of life:
Come and dwell in us and cleanse us from every stain
And save our souls, O good One!

Questions for Discussion

1. How integral is the reverencing of the Theotokos Mary to Eastern worship? Is it possible for worshipers to distinguish readily between reverence, offered to human beings who have a special place in salvation history, and worship, offered to God alone?
2. Do you think that there is a vital difference between a Eucharist that asks explicitly for a change in the elements, through the invocation of the Holy Spirit, and one that repeats with solemnity, "This is my body. . . . This is my blood"?
3. How helpful is the language of type and antitype in reading the Old Testament today and in understanding what is happening in the Eucharist? What is the difference between this way of thinking and the use of the term *symbol* or *representation*?
4. The liturgies that we have looked at speak about not only the healing of the spirit in worship, but also of the body. How do Christians retain this physical dimension in worship without engaging in "magical" thinking about what God does for us in worship?

5

"In the Great Congregation"

Traditional Liturgies of the West

From you comes my praise *in the great congregation.*
Psalm 22:25 (NRSV)

As we turn from East to West, it is important to remember the warning of the famous Anglican specialist in liturgy, *Dom. Gregory Dix: "It would be misleading . . . rigidly to divide early eucharistic teaching into an Eastern or . . . a Western . . . doctrine."[1] This is true not only of doctrine but also of actual wording and practice in liturgy. There are, especially in the early years of the Church's life but continuing throughout the centuries, family resemblances between "Eastern" and "Western" prayers. Consider, for example, the similar language at the climax of the liturgy, where both East and West offer to God what is "his own."[2] The Western history is extremely complex, but we will reflect upon a few key early references to liturgy, as well as examples of very early Western worship, and then take into consideration several more mature worship service books. All the while we will notice where the theme of entrance makes its mark.

Clement I of Rome

We do not have full dates for Clement I. We do know that he wrote around AD 96, in the context of Rome, but with an eye to the larger Church beyond. Especially, he was concerned that the Church maintain its morality, its vitality, and its holy Tradition. There is no precise description in the places where he speaks about the Eucharist, though we can discern that even by his early day this was part of the worship gathering, rather than performed as a full meal. It is interesting that we derive from his works a general approach to worship that acknowledges the idea of entrance into God's presence: "Let us then draw near to him with holiness of spirit, lifting up pure and undefiled hands unto Him, loving our gracious and merciful Father, who has made us partakers in the blessings of His elect" (1 Clement 29).[3] The subsequent parts of this work, a letter to the Corinthian Christians, are replete with practical injunctions to holy living and urgent matters of order. Yet amidst this pragmatism, the bishop keeps before his readers the picture of an entire cosmos waiting upon the Lord in worship. It is into this joyful and awe-inspiring service that the gathered family of Christ has been called:

> Let us consider the whole multitude of His angels, how they stand ever ready to minister to His will. For the Scripture saith, "Ten thousand times ten thousand stood around Him, and thousands of thousands ministered unto Him, and cried, Holy, holy, holy, [is] the Lord of Sabaoth; the whole creation is full of His glory." And let us therefore, conscientiously gathering together in harmony, cry to Him earnestly, as with one mouth, that we may be made partakers of His great and glorious promises. For [the Scripture] saith, "Eye hath not seen, nor ear heard, neither have entered into the heart of man, the things which He hath prepared for them that wait for Him." (1 Clement 34)

> This is the way, beloved, in which we find our Saviour, even Jesus Christ, the High Priest of all our offerings, the defender and helper of our infirmity. By Him we look up to the heights of heaven. . . . By Him are the eyes of our hearts opened. By Him our foolish and darkened understanding blossoms up anew towards His marvellous light. By Him the Lord has willed that we should taste of immortal knowledge. (1 Clement 36)

Clement's great concern about the schisms in his day and his grief concerning the removal of godly leaders from their ecclesial positions are expressed in terms of a deep yearning for unity and *catholicity. By his letters, he hopes to foster a respect for the whole body of Christ.[4] A harmonious reconciliation in these matters is, he argues, "the gate of righteousness" provided by Christ for his followers to enter (1 Clement 38), so that they rightly may offer praise. Appropriately, the Epistle closes with reference to the "High Priest" Jesus (1 Clement 58), by whose intercessions the faithful may approach the Lord.

Justin the Martyr

Following close after Clement's letters is the work of Justin Martyr (AD 100–165), who had birth ties to Palestine (Samaria) but who lived as an adult in

Rome. His references to Christian worship are far more extensive, though also subsumed under his own pressing concern: to defend Christianity to a hostile culture. In the course of his first *Apology for Christianity, Justin finally gets around to describing the worship of the faithful, about which there was, in his day, much salacious gossip promulgated by nonbelievers. Since only Christians were allowed at the Eucharist, detractors of the faith were able to use general references to the eucharistic *elements ("body and blood") and to the kiss of peace as evidence that human sacrifice (of infants) and orgies took place at these secret meetings. Justin was aware of these charges of clandestine evil[5] and it is against this background that we must read his broad description of Christian worship, written primarily for the benefit of those outside the Church:

> On the day called Sunday, all who live in cities or in the country *gather together to one place*, and the memoires of the apostles or the writings of the prophets are read, as long as time permits; then, when the reader has ceased, the president verbally instructs, and exhorts to the imitation of these good things. Then we *all rise together* and pray, and, as we before said, when our prayer is ended, bread and wine and water are brought, and the president in like manner offers prayers and thanksgivings, according to his ability, and *the people assent, saying Amen*; and there is a distribution to each, and *a participation of that over which thanks have been given*, and to those who are absent a portion is sent by the deacons. . . . But Sunday is the day on which we all hold our common assembly, because it is the first day on which God, having wrought a change in the darkness and matter, made the world; and Jesus Christ our Saviour on the same day rose from the dead.[6]

In Justin's description of the meeting of these early Roman, that is, Western, Christians, we easily discern the same pattern that was established and continued in the worship of Eastern Christians: first, the reading and explanation of the Word, and then the Thanksgiving with bread and wine. This twofold service continued throughout the regions of the West, as in the East, and before long came to be known in the West as "The Mass of the *Catechumens" and "The Mass of the Faithful," since (as we have seen) the catechumens did not stay for the Eucharist proper. (Clear evidence for the term *Mass is seen by the third century when Ambrose speaks specifically about the eucharistic part of the service, in the fourth century when the pilgrim Egeria calls the entire twofold service by this name, and in sixth and seventh century manuscripts for various services, including the eucharistic "Mass" for those who are "chrismated."[7] *Chrismation is the anointing of holy oil that concludes the baptism service, indicating that the baptized are now anointed, as was Christ.) Justin himself does not give us a detailed description of the "prayers and thanksgivings," nor does he speak precisely about how the elements are "eucharized" (the actual word used to describe the "president's" action of giving thanks). Some of Justin's language (e.g., "president" or "presider") may be selected for the benefit of outsiders and not reflect how the Church itself spoke of its leaders. Clearly, he intends to proclaim the centrality of Jesus to those who are outside the faith and reading his work. He also aims to exonerate accused Christians: the Christians meet in order to be "exhorted to good things"; they remember the ill and those who are absent by sending them a portion of the gifts; they meet on Sunday not for some rebellious or evil purpose but in honor of God's good creation and the resurrection of Jesus.

Though Justin's apologetic purpose is a narrow one, even here we can see signs that the early Christians understood their meeting together not as that of merely a "voluntary association" or club, but as *entry* into a kind of worship that had been given to them by Tradition and divine revelation. Emphasis is put upon their gathering together, upon the holy ancestors (prophets and apostles) acknowledged as present in the reading of the Old Testament prophecies and in the new covenant "memoires," upon the rising together as a company to pray, upon the common assent of the people (Amen!), upon participation in the Eucharist (even with those faithful who are absent), and upon the solemn entrance into the Lord's Day when God began to create and when Jesus rose from the dead. The worshipers are joined with a holy company and enter into holy space and time.

This sense of corporate offering before the Lord is seen also in Justin's *Dialogue with Trypho*. There, in a polemical section concerning the superiority of Christian worship to anything that preceded it, Justin also speaks about the bread and cup as offered before the Lord by the Church together, throughout the world:

> God, anticipating all the sacrifices which we offer through this name, and which Jesus the Christ enjoined us to offer, i.e., in the Eucharist of the bread and the cup, and which are presented by Christians in all places throughout the world, bears witness that they are well-pleasing to Him.[8]

In this very brief note on the Eucharist (brief, because Justin has other fish to fry!), both the historical and spatial immensity of Christian worship is suggested. All the Jewish rites that went before are seen as looking forward to the worship into which Christians have been called by God. Some have questioned Justin's rhetoric in dealing with Old Testament sacrifice. It is helpful to remember Justin's context, when discussion with Judaism was still an inside debate between sister faiths that came out of the Hebrew past. In Justin's day, and indeed for several centuries following, there was the continuing worry that Christians would misunderstand the uniqueness of Jesus and be tempted to "return" to Judaism—yet, of course, Judaism itself had been radically altered, since there was no longer sacrifice after the temple fell in AD 70. Justin's concern, both theological and pastoral, is to encourage the faithful to offer before the Lord their gifts in concert. This entry is possible since the whole world has become God's temple, and its human priesthood, those who are in Christ, have been made pleasing to him in Jesus.

The Apostolic Tradition

Hippolytus of Rome lived a generation or so after Justin, about AD 170–235 (and should not be confused with the bishop of Portus of the same name who was martyred in AD 253). Debate continues concerning the original form of the *Apostolic Tradition*, a work now frequently associated with Hippolytus and found in various versions and languages. When it was first rediscovered in the nineteenth century, scholars believed that it was of Egyptian origin. In the twentieth century, it became common to attribute it to the Roman author Hippolytus, and now there are several theories about the work and how much of it goes back to that early date. Whatever its precise origin and development, the work is significant for us today because it was influential in the widespread twentieth-century "liturgical renewal" of both Roman Catholic and mainline Protestant churches. It is as a result of this work that the shape of contemporary Western liturgies is more in line with the classical liturgies (Saints Chrysostom and Basil) of the East, though some would argue that the demystifying spirit or atmosphere of those newer services lacks the reverence of an earlier age in the West.

In the case of the *Apostolic Tradition*, we see reasons for the warning heard earlier, that the liturgies of East and West should not be seen as "hermetically sealed" against each other, as though there was no influence from one Christian group to another. Even if Hippolytus is himself the Roman (and therefore Western) author or compiler of this work (as many have believed, and some continue to hold[9]), we should also remember that the *Apostolic Tradition* was authoritative in the Eastern (especially Syrian) Church, even more than in the West. If the work is a composite, as proposed most recently,[10] then it is still of great significance, for it offers collected materials from the second to fourth centuries that were evidently influential in the early churches. Some of these materials and the contours of the described liturgy have now again made their mark on Christian worship today.

Several passages in the piece have been believed by scholars to be important in illuminating what the early Eucharist was like for many Christians. We do not know the dating of all these passages, nor whether they describe what was going on in actual churches or whether they rather intend to prescribe an order of service. Thus, it is hazardous to make confident declarations about their influence or their value in recovering, say, third-century worship in Rome (or Egypt or Syria). But we do not need to settle these questions in order to observe that within this ancient work we see the pervasive theme of worship as entrance. Let us begin with the portion of the *Apostolic Tradition* that has

been most influential in twentieth-century worship, that is, the eucharistic
prayer offered by the bishop, described in *Apostolic Tradition* 4, following
the description of the bishop's consecration in chapter 3.[11] There are several
scholarly editions of the work,[12] but we will make use of the user-friendly
version offered as "a simple kindness" to the general reader on the Internet:[13]

> And [the bishop] shall give thanks, saying:
> The Lord be with you.
> And all reply:
> And with your spirit.
>
> The bishop says:
> Lift up your hearts.
> The people respond:
> *We have them with the Lord.*
>
> The bishop says:
> Let us give thanks to the Lord.
> The people respond:
> It is proper and just.
>
> The bishop then continues:
> We give thanks to you God,
> through your beloved son [[Child]] Jesus Christ,
> whom you sent to us in former times [or, "the last times"]
> as Savior, Redeemer, and Messenger of your Will,
> who is your inseparable Word,
> through whom you made all,
> and in whom you were well-pleased,
> whom you sent from heaven into the womb of a virgin,
> who, being conceived within her, was made flesh,
> and appeared as your Son,
> born of the Holy Spirit and the virgin.
> It is he who, fulfilling your will
> and acquiring for you a holy people,
> extended his hands in suffering,
> in order to liberate from sufferings
> those who believe in you.
> Who, when he was delivered [or "betrayed"] to voluntary suffering,
> in order to dissolve death,
> and break the chains of the devil,
> and tread down hell,
> and bring the just to the light,
> and set the limit,
> and manifest the resurrection,
>
> taking the bread, and giving thanks to you, said,
> "Take, eat, for this is my body which is broken for you."

Likewise the chalice, saying,
This is my blood which is shed for you.

Whenever you do this, do this (in) memory of me.

Therefore, remembering his death and resurrection,
we offer to you the bread and the chalice,
giving thanks to you, *who has made us worthy*
to stand before you and to serve as your priests.
And we pray that you would send your Holy Spirit
to the oblation of your Holy Church.
In their gathering together,
give to all those who partake of your holy mysteries the fullness of the
    Holy Spirit,
toward the strengthening of the faith in truth,
that we may praise you and glorify you,
through your son Jesus Christ,
through whom to you be glory and honor,
Father and Son,
with the Holy Spirit,
in your Holy Church,
now and throughout the ages of the ages.
Amen.

The thanksgiving begins: "Lift up your hearts"—a phrase well known in many Christian communities today. But in the literal wording of the Latin and Sahidic versions, the bishop's opening instruction is even more delightfully direct: "Up hearts!" or "Up your heart!" The orientation of the people toward the Lord and their entrance into his presence are established from the get-go. As they offer themselves and their gifts, they are to set their attention upon the Lord. The response given by the worshipers (our hearts are with the Lord) underscores the unusual situation of the faithful: they are *already in* Christ. The bishop thus reminds them to look to the Lord, so that they might become what they are. Here we see the same already-but-not-yet quality that New Testament scholars have remarked upon in the letters of St. Paul. God has done everything necessary to make himself present among his people; yet the Church's awareness of his presence is not automatic. All is sufficient; all is not yet perfected.

Though they must be reminded of their identity and purpose, it is the privilege of those gathered to worship that they are made "worthy to stand before you and to serve as your priests." There is some debate concerning whether the original (now lost) Greek used a word that referred specifically to the priesthood (*hierateuein*) or one that focused upon the action of liturgical service by all the worshipers (*leitourgein*). To decide this is unnecessary, for it is surely the case that, whichever word may be used, the ministerial actions are not performed solely by the newly consecrated bishop who is presiding. It is

the priestly people as a whole who are doing the work of worship, who offer
themselves and their gifts as tokens of their personal sacrifice. As they gather
together, they become sharers ("partakers") of the fullness of the Spirit. In
an expanded later version of our text, called the *Testamentum domini* (late
fourth century?), the sense of entry into God's presence is further accentuated: "Grant to all who partake of the holy things *to be united with you for
filling with the Holy Spirit.*"

Several of the versions speak here, as in other places of the *Apostolic Tradition* (including the description of the baptismal creed), of "the Holy Spirit *in*
the Holy Church." Numerous liturgists and theologians have seen this wording as very significant, for it is understood to declare that the Holy Spirit and
salvation are to be found *within* the Church.[14] However, we cannot be sure that
this is the original wording of the text, for it is not the wording of the Latin
translation, which is the most complete version that we possess. Whatever
may be the case, this phrase ("the Holy Spirit in the Holy Church"), whenever
it is found in the versions used by several communities, demonstrates that
early Christians of various places understood the Church, the gathering of
the faithful, to be that specific yet large arena of God's action and holiness.
The solidarity of the entire worshiping company is seen also in the people's
closing *Amen*. This "Amen" concludes the Eucharist with a corporate gesture,
as the worshipers began, acknowledging one another with the shared "kiss of
peace." From beginning to end, we see words and actions of those who believe
that they have been called as one body, reconciled in Christ.[15]

Other passages in this same work refer to worship services that may be either
the celebration of the Eucharist or some other service that included the blessing
and eating of food, especially wine and bread. Chapter 21, for example, speaks
of the sharing of bread, wine, milk, and honey with the newly baptized and is
replete with the pronoun "in": "I anoint you with holy oil *in* the name . . .";
"Heavenly bread *in* Christ Jesus"; "*In* God the Father almighty"; "And *in* the
Holy Spirit and [or "*in*"] the holy Church." As each newly baptized member
receives from the water, milk, and wine, they say "Amen" to the recited words,
agreeing that they find their being "in" the Holy Trinity. Their particular
presence within the larger realm of God and their special identity within the
Church are so important that some of the instructions about the baptism are
absolutely sacred. They are, in fact, to be passed on or given by tradition *only*
to those who will learn them from the bishop (21:40); they are not to be shared
with those who are outside the Church. (There is a mysterious reference here
concerning "anything else that should be said" during the worship. This may
well be a reference to the Lord's Prayer, that family prayer reserved in early
Christian traditions so that it was taught only at the end of the catechumen's
formation, or even during his or her very baptism.) In the baptism and in the
shared meal, both body and soul are understood as being taken into a new
kind of reality. The newly baptized, who can now, in Christ, boldly call upon

God as "Father," receives a mysterious new name, as suggested by the exalted Lord who in the Apocalypse promises a "white stone, with a new name" (Rev. 2:17) to those who receive "the hidden manna."

Here, then, in what may be one of the earliest existing descriptions of the Church's worship, and in a document associated with the West as well as influential in the East, we see awareness of entrance into a larger action, space, and company. The text reminds us, too, of the cross-fertilization of worship practices and forms between churches of the East and West, dynamics that did not stop even after these early years.

The Genius of Western Liturgy: Entrance, Theme, and Following Christ's Pattern

Though there is a family resemblance among all Christian liturgies, a generalization might be made regarding the developing tendency of Western liturgies, especially those found originally outside of Rome. These show special attention to thematic and variable prayers, responsive to the church year and suited to the particular feast or fast of the day. Eastern liturgy, though concerned also for various moments in the church year, tends to knit together the Christian story in the liturgy, always looking backward and forward so that the whole may be seen. The result is a complexity of references and a web of allusions that are sometimes difficult for the uninformed to follow. On the other hand, the preference for theme that has come into the West has sometimes given rise to an overemphasis upon creating the moment for the rest of the congregation. At its best, a stress upon theme may enable entrance into a bigger action: those worshiping pause to indwell and to reflect upon the specific moment celebrated in any one feast or celebration, and so they enter into salvation history by this route. A second point that we may observe in the mature Western rites is that they are very detailed in their "rubrics"—that is, the notations for the celebrant with regard to objects, actions, and gestures that are to accompany the words of the liturgy. Such detail may be interpreted, on the one hand, as an overconcern for actions that feed into atmospherics; on the other hand, the detailed instructions may well free those leading worship to enter fully into liturgical action, for (once the rubrics are internalized by the priest) there is no need to think about *how* one must perform the liturgy.

It would appear that liturgies in the West developed in two major streams: a first large grouping associated with Rome (and Africa), which originally seems to have been a rather sparse or reserved rite without much ornamentation,[16] and a group of more ornate Western liturgies that scholars call "Gallican." Until about the seventh century, the Roman liturgy and various *Gallican rites were followed in different places of the West; these had some influence, too, one upon the other. The Gregorian *Mass (associated with Pope Gregory I,

590–604), formally incorporated some Gallican traditions into the Roman rite, and this fuller rite made a strong mark throughout the medieval West, though there were also local options that followed. Pope Gregory was criticized for some of the changes that he made, on the grounds that they were "Eastern," but he argued that such moves as placing the "Our Father" before the Eucharist made sense and were not simply an Eastern tradition. By praying the "Our Father," worshipers identified with Jesus, entering into his pattern of petition. Many centuries later, as a result of the reforming *Council of Trent, Roman Catholic scholars were commissioned by the pope to restore the earlier *Gregorian rite and to remove many of the later embellishments that were seen as distracting or confusing to the people. By decree of Pope Pius V (1570), most Catholic communities adopted the corrected *Tridentine Mass (the Mass of Trent), the classical Roman Mass that aimed to reinstate the eucharistic prayers of Gregory's time, while retaining some local medieval traditions that had sprung up since then.

All these streams and cross-streams form a complex historical picture. Amidst all this, however, from the beginning, we see an emphasis upon *entrance* in Western liturgy, expressed somewhat differently from that seen in the East. St. Ambrose of Milan, writing among fourth century Western Christians (and so a contemporary of the Eastern St. John Chrysostom) leads the newly baptized in a reflection upon their baptism and first communion (called "mysteries"): "After the Holy of holies [referring to the baptismal font] was opened to you, you entered the sanctuary of regeneration; recall what you were asked, and remember what you answered" (*Mysteries* 2.5).[17] After reminding them of the wonder of their entrance into the waters, St. Ambrose speaks about how the worship service is linked to what God has done in history, and also to the unseen hosts of worshipers among them. Throughout, the people of God are described as a single entity: "the cleansed people, rich with these adornments, hastens to the altar of Christ, saying: 'I will go to the altar of God, to God Who maketh glad my youth'" (*Mysteries* 8.43). Because in baptism this corporate people of God has "laid aside the slough of ancient error, renewed with an eagle's youth," it now "hastens to approach that heavenly feast." The unified group of the newly baptized is led to the altar in solemn procession, and then, "as it comes, seeing the holy altar arranged, it cries out: 'Thou hast prepared a table in my sight'" (*Mysteries* 8.43). Though Ambrose insists that there is a mysterious change in the elements, he also declares that "it is . . . not bodily food but spiritual" (*Mysteries* 9.58). Scholars have made much of this teaching, which is found also in the eucharistic consecratory prayer described by Ambrose (or perhaps by one of his disciples) in another tractate called *The Sacraments*. In that prayer, the offering is depicted as "reasonable" and "unbloody" (*Sacraments* 4.6.27), words that will persist into the later rite of Trent.[18]

Even more of interest for our theme of entrance is the declaration ascribed to Ambrose that Jesus is "the author of the sacraments" (*Sacraments* 4.4.13).

Because the eucharistic blessing is so solemn, it is not said free-form by the bishop, as in earlier parts of the liturgy, but conforms specifically to "the words . . . of the Lord Jesus" (*Sacraments* 4.4.14), which are ratified by the people's "Amen." The eucharistic act takes place, too, while the whole congregation "is mindful of" the acts of Jesus (*Sacraments* 4.6.27). Here is purposeful entrance into Jesus' action—word and deed—as the celebrant and people follow in the pattern of their great high priest, Christ. Just after the time of Ambrose, St. Augustine of Hippo declared to the newly baptized: "there you are, on the table; there you are, in the cup!" (*Sermon 229* for Easter).[19] In their self-offering, God's people are joined with the sacrifice for all time, that of the God-Man, Jesus.

Entrance in the Liturgies of the Bobbio and Sarum Missals

The West remained hospitable to many local traditions in the lengthy period prior to the formation and legislated prominence of the Tridentine Mass. We will examine only two of these, looking for an awareness of worship as entrance: the eucharistic service from the *Bobbio missal (an early Gallican rite, though perhaps with influence from Rome in key parts) and the *Sarum rite, which is essentially the old sixth-century Roman rite associated with Gregory I, with local variations. The Gallican and Roman rites are both very ancient, but it was the Gregorian rite that would persist, almost in entirety, due to the efforts of the Council of Trent. Though the Sarum use is only one of the many liturgies based on the Gregorian rite that might have been found in the British Isles during the medieval period, it is particularly significant. This is because it became prominent in Britain beyond its origins in Salisbury and was eventually the foundation upon which the Anglican Cranmer based the composition of the Anglican prayer book.

The Bobbio missal[20] provides for us a fascinating glimpse into the seventh- or eighth-century Western world of worship, probably that of southeastern Gaul. It contains both a *lectionary (a schedule of Scripture readings) and other elements of what we would call a "sacramentary," that is, a book with instructions and resources for various services. Especially interesting in this work is the provision for numerous special services and variable prayers.

It is intriguing that we see several elements in common with the Eastern Church, including a love for the *Trisagion, which is here called the "Ajus" or *Agios*. This repetition of "Holy God, holy mighty, holy immortal" is sung at the beginning of the service of the Word, in agreement with Eastern liturgies. This is interesting, because the Roman rite from about the sixth century instead used the *Gloria in Excelsis*, that is, the hymn based upon the song of the Christmas angels. (The Bobbio manuscript actually prints out the *Gloria*, so it must also have been used; but the *Ajus* was so well known that it is simply indicated by name and not printed in full.) Following the processional psalm, sung antiphonally, the *Ajus* was sung in both Greek and Latin, followed by the *Kyrie eleison*, sung thrice, and the *Benedictus* (that is, the song of Zechariah). Though this beginning of the liturgy of the Word does not engage in as elaborate a preparation as that found in Eastern worship, we may observe a similar emphasis upon God's holiness, God's mercy, and the visitation of God to his people in darkness. All this is brought to a summation by a *"collect," a prayer that "collects" or gathers the petitions of the congregation, variable for the occasion.[21]

The Old Testament reading and the Epistle reading (sometimes supplanted by a life of the saint of the day) are rounded out by the *Benedicte es*, that is, the Song of the Three from Daniel's fiery furnace. (The song is found in the extended *Septuagint text, Dan. 3:51–90.) It is a litany of praise, folding the congregation into the praise of the entire cosmos, from the winds and rains to the persecuted faithful, epitomized in three young men called Shadrach, Meshach, and Abednego. (In Hebrew the names are Hananiah, Azariah, and Mishael.) So well-known was the song to these early worshipers that it is not printed out in full anywhere in the missal but simply indicated for use. One commentator thinks that the prominence of the Song of the Three must point to a time of persecution in the Western Church where the missal was used.[22] Such speculation is hardly necessary to explain why it was so beloved. Rather, it is an ideal song for God's people in any context, placing them within a lively cosmos of praise and thanksgiving, despite their humble station or circumstances. It was well known in ancient days as "the canticle of blessings" and is referred to by such preachers as the fifth-century St. Caesarius of Arles.[23] Because this song is less known today, coming as it does from the *apocryphal or "deuterocanonical" works[24] not often read in Protestant circles, I will quote at length. In this marvelous psalm, notice how God is especially glorified in the temple (for Christians, the temple is wherever Christians may be found!) and adored for his general mercy toward his creation:

> Blessed art thou, O Lord, God of our fathers, and to be praised and
>   highly exalted for ever;
> And blessed is thy glorious, holy name and to be highly praised and
>   highly exalted for ever;
> Blessed art thou in the temple of thy holy glory and to be extolled and
>   highly glorified for ever.
> Blessed art thou, who sittest upon cherubim and lookest upon the
>   deeps, and to be praised and highly exalted for ever. . . .
> Bless the Lord, all works of the Lord, sing praise to him and highly
>   exalt him for ever.
> Bless the Lord, you heavens, sing praise to him and highly exalt him for
>   ever.

Bless the Lord, you angels of the Lord, sing praise to him and highly exalt him for ever.

Bless the Lord, all waters above the heaven, sing praise to him and highly exalt him for ever.

Bless the Lord, all powers, sing praise to him and highly exalt him for ever.

Bless the Lord, sun and moon, sing praise to him and highly exalt him for ever.

Bless the Lord, stars of heaven, sing praise to him and highly exalt him for ever.

Bless the Lord, all rain and dew, sing praise to him and highly exalt him for ever.

Bless the Lord, all winds, sing praise to him and highly exalt him for ever. . . .

Bless the Lord, you sons of men, sing praise to him and highly exalt him for ever.

Bless the Lord, O Israel, sing praise to him and highly exalt him for ever.

Bless the Lord, you priests of the Lord, sing praise to him and highly exalt him for ever.

Bless the Lord, you servants of the Lord, sing praise to him and highly exalt him for ever.

Bless the Lord, spirits and souls of the righteous, sing praise to him and highly exalt him for ever.

Bless the Lord, you who are holy and humble in heart, sing praise to him and highly exalt him for ever.

Bless the Lord, Hananiah, Azariah, and Mishael, sing praise to him and highly exalt him for ever; for he has rescued us from Hades and saved us from the hand of death, and delivered us from the midst of the burning fiery furnace; from the midst of the fire he has delivered us.

Give thanks to the Lord, for he is good, for his mercy endures for ever.

Bless him, all who worship the Lord, the God of gods, sing praise to him and give thanks to him, for his mercy endures for ever.

This Song of the Three is a wonderful example in early worship of how the personal and contemporary are commingled with the historic and general: "Bless the Lord, *Hananiah, Azariah, and Mishael,* sing praise to him and highly exalt him for ever; for he has rescued *us* from Hades and saved *us* from the hand of death, and delivered *us.*" As the story of Daniel's three friends is recalled in its particularity, the praises of the three heroes merge with the praises of God's people, who see themselves also as rescued from death and from imprisonment by Christ. (The song is made even more poignant by the ancient Tradition of the Church, in which the mysterious figure "like a man" who joins them in the furnace is seen as a preincarnational appearance of God the Son. He is "God's enduring mercy" personified.) This stirring recital of God's care for the whole of creation, for particular servants, and for the worshiping congregation sets the keynote for corporate worship. Then, the Gospel reading (as with the Eastern Churches) is preceded by the Trisagion (Ajus), sung yet again, but only in Latin this time. The double singing of the Trisagion, coupled with the Song of the Three, demonstrates a strong notion that the worship was seen as *ongoing* or *intensifying* entrance into holy time and celestial worship. The congregants go further in and further up.

In the liturgies preserved in the Bobbio missal, there are alternate elements set out for use at various occasions. These variations are seen not only in the collects and special prayers, but also (surprisingly!) in the solemn *Anaphora ("Lift up your hearts . . ."), which in Western use begins with a variable prayer called the *Contestatio. On the feast-day of Peter and Paul, that Contestatio prayer continues as expected (and in consonance with the Eastern Church) with "It is very right and meet." However, it then goes on to speak of the glory of the omnipotent God in his holiness and wonder and "among his apostles" who have "preached throughout the world and to its ends." Peter is remembered for his passion and Paul for his preaching. Their special forms of witness to the Lord (martyrdom and preaching) are actually numbered among the works of the Lord, works that were seen also in the prophets and are continually adored by angels. With Peter, Paul, and all the heavenly hosts, the people offer their praises to the God who shows his love to them.[25] Some liturgists do not approve of this eucharistic prayer because it has such regard for saints, however holy, rather than looking upon the Lord alone. This criticism might be countered by noticing that Peter and Paul are remembered for how they glorify the Lord. As a pair, they point to the One who underwent the true passion, the One who is the Word; thus in this prayer, the highlighting of the apostles need not detract from the glory of the most Holy One.[26] Here, among other numerous examples of especially keyed beginnings to the eucharistic prayer, we see the Western penchant for thematics, which may be helpful or distracting to those who worship.

Entrance in the Sarum Rite

The Sarum rite was dominant in Britain during the eleventh century, though it has earlier roots in the Latin rite that came to Britain many centuries earlier.[27] Sarum use, let us remember, was an adaptation of the rite established in the time of Gregory I (d. 604) in Rome. The missal is replete with rubrics (or directions) regarding the actions that the priest and servers should use to accompany the words. These are given in very particular detail, including special instructions for the practice of processionals[28] to the church on Sundays and on special feast-days such as Christmas, Epiphany, Easter, Ascension, Corpus Christi, and All Saints. Even before the procession, special blessings were done with salt and water, with the sprinkling of the altar and the worshipers themselves. All of these actions and words serve to infuse the liturgies with a sense of mystery and awe. Salt and water, in harmony with the biblical meaning of this imagery, are used to separate out the people and their worship from that which is ordinary. As with the other Roman and Eastern rites, the Mass is in two parts, the Liturgy of the Word and the Liturgy of Communion. The entire Mass begins with a hymned invocation of the Spirit (*Veni Creator Spiritus* "Come, Spirit Creator . . ."), said (or sung) while the celebrants put on vestments. The first prayer acknowledges the presence of God and petitions him for purification in words that have persisted in Anglican and Catholic liturgies to this day:

> O God, to whom every heart is open and every desire known, and whom no secret escapes, purify by the infusion of the Holy Spirit the thoughts of our heart; that we may merit perfectly to love and worthily to praise you: through Christ our Lord, Amen.

These preparations are followed by a composite of psalm and prayers, interspersed with this antiphon (call-and-response of the congregation) of approach: "I will go to the altar of God, to God who makes glad my youth. Lord, have mercy. Christ, have mercy." (We pause to note that this is the very psalm cited by St. Ambrose in his description of the baptized approaching their first Eucharist.) After the congregation and priest immerse themselves in the Lord's Prayer and the praise of the Virgin (who is understood as personifying the Church), the entrance proper begins. The priests and other ministers next engage in a time of confession and forgiveness, which calls to remembrance the entire people of God. The priest acknowledges: "I confess to God, to blessed Mary, to all the saints and to you" and then the helping ministers do the same. Mutual absolution is given, and the entire sequence concludes with reference to the "helping Lord, who made heaven and earth" and who is blessed for all time. The people have entered into holy space and time. Their preparations complete, the priest and deacon exchange the kiss of peace, a potent sign of the human reconciliation for which Jesus called: be reconciled to your brother before you bring your gift to God's holy altar.

The service of the Word is heralded with this prayer of entrance, said prostrate by the priest: "Take away from us, O Lord, all our iniquities, *that we may be worthy to enter into the holy of holies* with pure minds, through Christ our Lord." Following the clergy's procession to the altar, the *Gloria in Excelsis* (the angelic "Glory in the Highest!") is sung, followed by other collects and prayers (seven in number). The gifts to be used in the Eucharist are taken up to the altar in the sight of all the people. Once the Epistle has been read, the Gospel is prepared by the *"Alleluia" song, the Gospel is read, and the creed follows: this Western pattern is completely consonant with the flow of the Eastern rite that we have already traced. The priest offers special prayers for holiness as the Eucharist proper ("the *Canon of the Mass") approaches:

> Receive, O Holy Trinity, this oblation, which I, an unworthy sinner, offer in honour of thee, of the blessed Virgin and all the saints, for my sins and offences, and for the salvation of the living, and the rest of all the faithful dead. In the name of the Father, and the Son, and the Holy Spirit. Let this new sacrifice be acceptable to the omnipotent God.

Notice that this prayer, though made by the priest on his own behalf, acknowledges the entire Church, living and dead. As a further antidote to priest-centered worship, the priest asks for the congregation to pray for him as well: "Pray, brothers and sisters,[29] that my sacrifice and likewise yours may be acceptable to our Lord God." Here, again, is the reference to an "acceptable" Eucharist, that is, one that matches the eternal sacrifice in the heavenlies, according to the pattern given by Jesus himself.

As with the Eastern liturgies, the notable faithful are named, both those living and those "asleep": "venerating the memory in the first place, of the glorious Virgin Mary, the mother of God and of our Lord Jesus Christ; But also of thy blessed Apostles and Martyrs, Peter and Paul, Andrew, James, John, Thomas, James, Philip, Bartholomew, Matthew, Simon and Thaddeus; Linus, Cletus, Clement, Sixtus, Cornelius, Cyprian, Laurentius, Crisogonus, John and Paul, Cosmas and Damian; and all thy saints." This list of saints in the Sarum use is likely identical with other masses current in the Middle Ages; derived from the earlier Gregorian Mass, the same list was preserved after Trent and has persisted into the liturgy revised by *Vatican II.

The consecration of the bread and wine takes place in the words of institution, that is, the word that Jesus spoke: "this is my body; this is my blood." This is typical of the Roman rite, which stresses the Lord's words as effective, rather than placing emphasis upon a special prayer (*epiclesis) asking that the Spirit change the elements, which is key to the Eastern rites.[30] The consecratory words are made first over the bread and then over the cup, raised so as to be seen by all the people. Even in medieval times, when many lay people did not routinely take Communion, it was important to the people that they witness what the priest was doing and offer their prayers in concert with him. So we have the anecdote repeated about a devout lay person complaining that he could not see the consecration, enjoining the officiant, "Heave it higher, Sir Priest!"[31] After the consecration, the priest requests that the gifts be accepted by God, as those of "thy righteous servant Abel, and the sacrifice of our Patriarch Abraham, and that which thy High Priest Melchisedech offered to thee, a holy sacrifice, an immaculate *host." Though we do not find here an explicit *epiclesis* (the prayer that calls down the Spirit upon the gifts) the offering is understood to ascend to the heavenly throne: "We humbly beseech thee, O Almighty God, to command these things to be borne by the hands of thy holy angel to the altar above in the presence of thy Divine Majesty." Does the "ascent" of the offering suggest also that the people are ascending in their worship, or is it simply the token of their praise that ascends?

Once again, the priest offers prayers for the recent dead, followed by prayers for the worshipers there present, with whom he identifies as "us sinners," while beating his breast. The priest beseeches that they might be granted "some part and fellowship" with "the holy Apostles and Martyrs; with John, Stephen, Matthias, Barnabas, Ignatius, Alexander, Marcellinus, Peter, Felicitas, Perpetua, Agatha, Lucy, Agnes, Cæcilia, Anastasia, with all thy saints." (Notice that this list includes female names, beyond that of the Virgin Mary.) Following this petition comes the "Our Father" (placed at this high point by Pope Gregory) and the *Agnus Dei*, based on the acclamation of John the Baptist ("Lamb of God, who takes away the sin of the world, have mercy on us . . . grant us thy peace"). This petition, says tradition, was added to the Roman rite a little after the time of Gregory, when Pope Sergius I of Rome introduced the *Agnus Dei* into the liturgy. This appeal to the Lamb of God, though not offered collectively in the Eastern liturgy, corresponds to the declaration in that tradition made over the breaking of bread, where the priest says, "The Lamb of God is broken and distributed. . . . *He sanctifies those who partake of Him.*" As in the Eastern usage, some of the bread (though not all of it) is mixed in the chalice. There will be communion in both kinds, but the commixture is considered important, for it speaks of eternal salvation, the gift by which those who "prepare" for "the embracing of eternal life."

The theme of entrance is seen again in the prayer offered by the priest as he receives the bread: "*Hail eternally*, O most holy flesh of Christ: to me before all things, and above all things, the greatest sweetness. The body of our Lord Jesus Christ be *to this sinner, the way and the life*, in the name of the Father, and of the Son, and of the Holy Ghost." Priest and deacons communicate, presumably sometimes followed by the people, and then after Communion there is prayer and a blessing.

My approach in this book has been to consider past liturgies and practice, as much as possible, with a sympathetic eye, looking to learn from our older siblings. It would be dishonest, however, not to pause at this point and to comment that in both the West and the East there have been times when the laity did not regularly receive communion but only attended the worship service. This unfortunate reserve came about through a sense of the awe of the mysteries and from feelings of unworthiness. It is not clear from the rubrics of the Sarum rite how often the people actually communicated—more instruction is given with regard to the clergy. During the time when it became prominent in Britain, Pope Innocent III called the fourth Council of the Lateran, which in its twenty-first canon required any Christian over the age of seven to receive Communion at least once a year—obviously, infrequency of communion was a problem in the twelfth century. However, the people were enjoined to participate through attendance and prayers, even when they did not receive the sacrament itself: this kind of reception was labeled "spiritual" reception. It may be that infrequent communion is more of a built-in problem for the West than for the East. Only in the West is a theological accommodation made, in the category of spiritual reception. Again, in the West, it is acceptable for a priest to celebrate a "private Mass," a practice that became common in the Middle Ages due to the great number of Requiem masses for the dead that were in demand at that time and also due, no doubt, to an exaggeration of the role of clergy in the "work of the people." In the East, there must be at least two people present, for the laity's "Amen" remains as important as the priestly words of institution and consecration. However, reluctance to receive communion regularly was quite common among laity in both East and West until recently.[32] The flip side of this reserve is, of course, a casual attitude toward Communion among those who do not take account of the mystery of the Eucharist. This stance is not limited to some Protestant congregations, or so it seems. After Vatican II, the well-known laywoman Anne Roche[33] critiqued Roman Catholic churches for passing out the *host like "chicklets" into the hands of unprepared children, in the atmosphere of the circus. Difficulties with Communion both in the East and the West have been critiqued, and corrected, in recent years. For a Roman admission and criticism of irregular communion see documents as early as the Catechism of the Council of Trent, which states, "let not the faithful imagine that it is enough to receive the body of the Lord once a year only, in obedience to the decree of the Church. They should approach oftener; but whether monthly, weekly, or daily, cannot be decided by any fixed universal rule. St. Augustine, however, lays down a most certain norm: 'Live in such a manner as to be able to receive every day.'"[34]

Let us return to our observation of the Sarum rite itself. Prior to the recession, the priest again does a prostration, while he prays to the Triune God that the Eucharist may have its effect on all those who have been worshiping. Then, as if by way of confirmation, the priest recites, as he and the other ministers process out, John 1:1–14[35]—that staggering passage about the Light that has shone in our darkness, and the glory "as of the only Son from the Father, full of grace and truth." This quotation from John 1 is one of the happy traditions that came into the Latin rite after the time of Gregory and was retained in the Mass laid down by Trent. This closing, a meditation upon the light of Christ come into the world, parallels the Eastern post-communion song of joy: "We have received the true light. . . . Let our mouths be filled with your praise, O God." In the Sarum usage, as well as among Eastern Christians, God's people reflect on the wonder that they have entered holy time and space and that they have truly been visited by God. Even at the time of the dismissal, they take with them the vision of divine glory as strength for their "ordinary" life, and so set out to meditate upon the radiant Son for the whole day. Blessed by God, they may (like Simeon) depart in peace, for their eyes together have *seen*, and as a company they have been changed by the majestic presence of the Lord. In summing up the strengths of the early Roman Mass, Theodor Klauser puts it this way:

> True liturgy should not be the expression in words of the individual's subjective thoughts and feelings . . . since it is the worship of a community. Now the Romans possessed a special gift which they used to create a liturgy of this kind. This gift consisted of their ability to compose ordered and well-constructed formularies.[36]

The Tridentine Mass[37]

Some of the practices that sprang up in the medieval period, however, detracted from the well-composed liturgy that was the early genius of Rome. Helpful additions had come into the Roman liturgy, such as the recital of the *Nicene Creed—a powerful way of transporting the worshipers into the midst of the universal and historic Church. Other traditions were not so beneficial. Many have complained that the continued universal use of Latin in countries where it was not understood by everyone was alienating for the common folk—even though it was a means of continuity or familiarity for those with education and the means to travel.

Moreover, the embellishments that had become common among the many different variations of the Western rite frequently obscured key points of the liturgy. Besides the complex number of variable prayers that were prescribed for use, other adornments that were aesthetically pleasing came into play, but they threatened to overshadow the prayers of the people. Among these were "tropes" added to the music (that is, the use of complex and extraneous musical cadenzas or whole compositions to the chants) and musical sequences added to various parts of the service, especially when the Alleluias were sung before the reading of the Gospel. Editorializing was also common during the reading of Scripture, so that it was difficult to determine which parts of the reading were Scripture and which parts were commentary. Even sober prayers such as the plain *Kyrie eleison* ("Lord, have mercy") were not spared but were "farced" (i.e., "stuffed") so that they lost their original purpose. The congregation's clear cry, modeled upon the humility of the publican who was intent for God's mercy on him, a sinner, was transmuted into a hodgepodge of a hymn: "*Lord*, splendid-king-of-heaven-and-arc-of-our-salvation-perpetually-saving-and-always-favorable-to-your-people, *have mercy*."[38]

The sixteenth-century Council of Trent in time responded to such problems, but of course there was also the galvanization of external criticism by the protesting Reformers of Germany, Geneva, Britain, and elsewhere. In their "counter-reforming" moves, the theologians of Trent addressed the past difficulties of the Mass as well as the doctrinal disputes of the day. It was decided that the common language of Latin would be retained in the liturgy but that the priests and people should be better instructed so as to understand their traditions of worship. In order to facilitate the instruction, the Mass itself was examined, and the Papal encyclical *Quo Primum* was written by Pope Pius V in 1570, commending a universal, revised, and restored Roman rite. Pope Pius explained the process and purpose in this way:

> These men [his commissioned scholars] consulted the works of ancient and approved authors concerning the same sacred rites; and thus they have restored the Missal itself to the original form and rite of the holy Fathers. . . . This work has been gone over numerous times and further emended, after serious study and reflection. . . . It is most becoming that there be in the Church only one appropriate manner of reciting the Psalms and only one rite for the celebration of Mass. . . . This new rite alone is to be used unless approval of the practice of saying Mass differently was given at the very time of the institution and confirmation of the church by Apostolic See at least 200 years ago, or unless there has prevailed a custom of a similar kind which has been continuously followed for a period of not less than 200 years.[39]

This Tridentine ("of Trent") Mass was not, then, new but was largely a restoration of the Gregorian Mass and was rendered virtually universal through the Pope's encyclical, becoming the Mass said almost everywhere in Roman Catholic churches until the time of Vatican II in the 1960s. The revisions of Trent included the removal of the numerous tropes and a reduction of the number of sequences that could be used at the point where the Alleluia was chanted. Remaining were only the well-known sequences, *Victimae paschali laudes* ("Praise the Paschal Victim!" for Easter); *Veni Santa Spiritus* ("Come, Holy Spirit!" Pentecost); *Lauda Sion* ("Praise, Zion!" Corpus Christi); and *Dies Irae* ("Day of Wrath," for All Souls and funeral liturgies). Later, the thirteenth-century traditional sequence called *Stabat Mater* ("The Mother was Standing") was restored for use during the Lenten *Stations of the Cross, as well as for the Feasts of Our Lady of Sorrows, observed on September 15 and during Passion week. However, these five sequences were used for special occasions only, and the medieval penchant for embroidering (and so possibly obscuring) the Gospel reading at every occasion was in this way controlled.

The Tridentine rite, then, refurbished many of the aspects of the older Gregorian rite, which (as we should remember) had itself incorporated "Gallican" elements from other rites in the West as well as practices from the East. The Liturgy of Trent also preserved some of the customs that had become widespread since the time of Gregory throughout the West—most notably, the use of the *Agnus Dei* ("Lamb of God . . . have mercy upon us"), a chant introduced by Pope Sergius in the century after Pope Gregory. Most of the practices that had come after the time of Gregory and were retained, however, are those that were confined to the quiet prayers and actions of the priest, not to the words said in interaction with the congregants. In the liturgy we see the same twofold structure, the Mass of the Catechumens (the Word) and that of the Faithful (the Eucharist). As in all the ancient rites, the priest faces the altar during the Eucharist, so emphasizing his offering to God, on behalf of and with the rest of the congregation. This feature has been roundly criticized in recent years—perhaps undeservedly—as alienating the people from God and was one of the substantial changes made during the reformation of the Mass in the 1960s council known as Vatican II. Certainly, the rotation of the priest toward the congregation, along with other modifications of the Roman Catholic Mass, has made for a less formal atmosphere in our day, for better and for worse. Theological arguments can be made for both postures, and this liturgical debate is ongoing between traditionalists and progressive liturgists in the West, and also between West and East, since Orthodox liturgies retain the orientation (literally, "toward the east") of the priest. It might be noted that the classical posture of the priest toward the altar better communicates to the congregation their own orientation, or entrance, into the presence of God. However, liturgies express truths in various ways and through different combinations of actions, words, sights, sounds, and even smells. I will not arbitrate here between the Tridentine and Vatican II practices; I will merely plead that Christians extend courtesy and understanding toward brothers and sisters who practice differently, noting strengths as well as weaknesses in actions that are foreign to their own experience but for which there is traditional and theological justification.

In the observations that follow, we will go sequentially through the Mass, without mentioning every detail, but with an eye to the theme of entrance. The following description is not full enough to give a sense of the entire structure of the liturgy but will show where the Tridentine Mass either introduced or restored elements that highlight the entrance of God's people into a larger action, place of worship, and company of worshipers.

From the very beginning of the service, even in its preliminaries, we see an attention to a careful "entrance" into God's presence that is very close to that which we have observed already in the Sarum rite. (And let us remember that the Sarum use was largely a variant of the Roman Gregorian rite.) For example, the sprinkling of water (*Asperges) is accompanied by the recitation of David's famous penitential Psalm 50 (in the Greek and Latin Bibles), which is known as Psalm 51 in the Hebrew and Protestant communities. Pope Pius V also required that during the entrance the priest recite Psalm 43 (or 42 in the Hebrew and Protestant Bible: "Vindicate me, O God and defend my cause") responsively with the server, so that there is a special emphasis upon verse 4: "I will go to the altar of God." The service, then, maintains the tradition seen even in the time of St. Ambrose when this psalm was part of the eucharistic approach of the newly baptized. During this entrance, the sense of reverent joy is undeniable: "Send forth Thy light and thy truth: they have conducted me, and brought me unto thy holy hill, into thy tabernacles" (Ps. 43/42, verse 2). Following this responsive approach to the altar comes the *Confiteor ("I confess")—an extended confession said by both the priest and the server, who speak on behalf of the people.

The kiss of peace that was exchanged in the Sarum use between priest and deacon is dropped, except for the High or Solemn Mass, where priest is joined by deacon and subdeacon. The confession itself, in the Mass of Trent, has become a very serious affair, to be accompanied by the beating of the breast. Yet even in the sober approach, we see a lively hope for communion with God: "We beseech you, O Lord, take away our iniquities, that we may merit to enter with pure minds into the Holy of Holies, through Christ our Lord." Along with this prayer for the Lord's clemency, there is a prayer that refers to the merits of the specific saints whose relics are kept in the place of worship where the liturgy is being said. This may seem foreign and even cause concern for some readers who understand the intercession of the saints as a means of separating the people from God and see the saints as intermediaries obscuring the grace of Christ. However, according to the theology of the communion of the saints (found in both East and West) the strong prayers of these sponsoring brothers and sisters, who behold the Lord in eternal worship, are actual helps to the present worshipers, enabling them to enter. Saints, like the "angels, help us to adore Him: ye behold him face-to-face."[40] The theologians of Trent thus make specific reference to the use of relics, naturalizing their presence within the service, and offer a theological response to Protestant criticism that these are being used simply "magically" or in superstition. The relics are understood as a tangible representation and connection with older siblings in the faith, and together the living and the dead represent one worshiping family.

In the same manner as the Sarum (and other medieval) uses, the Gloria in Excelsis is sung, but this is preceded by a preparatory chant: "Lord have mercy, Christ have mercy, Lord have mercy." The memorials of various saints and past heroes do not find a place here (as they had in the Sarum rite) prior to the reading of the Epistle. Presumably the reference to the relics has already made this connection, so that the reading of the Scriptures may now be placed directly after the Gloria. Those used to other rites may be surprised to hear the exchange "The Lord be with you; and with thy spirit" prior to the reading of the Epistle (and again before the congregational prayers that follow the gospel), rather than as a proper prelude to the reading of the Gospel. Immediately preceding the reading of the Gospel there is also a reference to the purifying experience of Isaiah, a motif of prayer found more usually at the time of the Eucharist in Eastern worship. The deacon who will proclaim the Gospel prays, "Cleanse my heart and my lips, O Almighty God, Who cleansed the lips of the Prophet Isaiah with a burning coal." In harmony with Jesus' own words that the Word makes his followers clean (John 15:3), the Gospel reading is thus presented as itself purifying, so that the servers and worshipers are prepared for the rest of the service: "Through the words of the gospel may our sins be wiped away." It is helpful to remember that the reading of the Gospel is connected in the liturgical imagination with the Incarnation, for it is the reading of the Word about the Word. The idea of cleansing is thus wholly appropriate, for the incarnate Son has come to cleanse and heal. So, too, is the prescribed physical action: the congregation stands to greet the One who is the Word during the reading of the Gospel, as they also will stand when the Incarnation is celebrated during the recital of the creed.

Though much has been simplified in the Tridentine service, the prayers that precede the Anaphora ("Lift up your heart") appear to be more extensive than some of the earlier rites, lending a sense of mystery and gradual approach to the climax of the service. God's creative and redemptive purposes are detailed in the priest's prayers, which place the Eucharist within the context of God's majestic actions in history:

> O God [the sign of the cross is made]
> who wondrously established the dignity of human nature,
> and still more wondrously restored it,
> grant that by the *mystery of this water and wine,
> we may be made sharers in His divinity,
> who deigned to become a partaker in our humanity,
> Jesus Christ, Your Son, our Lord:
> who lives and reigns with You
> in the unity of the Holy Spirit, God, forever and ever. Amen.

By the Eucharist, the redeemed human race is linked within the One who "deigned to become partaker of our humanity." Further, the movement of this prayer from the connection of humanity to Christ, to the communion of Father, Son, and Holy Spirit, suggests that there is even a link forged between redeemed humanity and the fellowship of the Holy Trinity, through the tangible connection of the faithful with the incarnate Son. Enshrined in this prayer is the ancient theological mystery: "God (the Word) became Man that humanity might become divine."[41] Our entrance into glory is dependent upon the entrance of the Word incarnate into our world and the mission of the Holy Spirit as well.

To this theological dimension are added other elements of holy history. The prayers are offered, while the altar is censed, through the intercessions of the "blessed archangel Michael who stands at the right hand of the altar of incense"—a tradition that goes back to the story in Luke's Gospel, where the father of John the Baptist meets this glorious angel as he presents his human offering before the Lord. What is going on in the human worship has always mirrored the celestial worship—now, by God's coming among his people in the flesh, human worship is more intimately joined with the worship in heaven.

Though the worship recalls all that God has done to provide an open door for his people, the entrance of the worshipers is not understood to be automatic or facile. Thus there is also an attentiveness to whatever might hinder the prayers. There is, in Psalm 141 (Greek and Latin, 140), a reference to the altar of incense followed by an acknowledgment of the human predilection for wandering and distraction (Ps. 141:1–4). Verses 3 and 4 are cited at this point in the liturgy: "Set a watch, O Lord, before my mouth, and a door round about my lips: that my heart may not incline to evil words to making excuses for my sins." This psalm has a long history of use in both West and East (see the *vesperal services) and is especially striking in its Greek and Latin wording, which speaks about the possibility of "making excuses for sins"—a phrase that is not found in the Hebrew text. (Let us recall that the early Church, guided by the Holy Spirit, read the Old Testament in the Greek, and that this version has continued to have an impact on the Church throughout the centuries, informing other translations, including the Latin. Specialists have recently discovered that in some cases the Greek version may be even closer to the original than the Hebrew texts that we possess today.) This psalm was significant in the formation of such great theologians as Saints Augustine and Cassiodorus (the late-fifth-century Roman Christian monk), who both quote it in their work: by way of the Mass, every officiating priest enters into this same salutary recognition of the human condition. Yet there is a way that has been prepared, by the high priest Jesus. So the priest goes on to pray, while washing his hands, words from Psalm 26 (LXX 25):3–12, while he offers the gifts to the Lord on behalf of the whole Church and then commends himself to the prayers of the people worshiping with him: "My foot hath stood in the direct way: in the churches I will bless You, O Lord. . . . Pray brethren, that my sacrifice and yours may be acceptable to God the Father Almighty."

The action of entering by the way of the Lord is complemented by the idea of God's entrance into the human realm, a dynamic we have seen everywhere in both Western and Eastern liturgies. Especially prominent in this regard is the prayer of humble welcome, said by both the priest and the faithful prior to the reception of communion. "Lord, I am not worthy that You should come under my roof: But only say the word and my soul will be healed." This prayer, based on the humility of the gentile centurion, may be considered as a Western cousin to the Eastern prayer of reception, which looks to the faith of the thief upon the cross: "Like the thief I will confess you, Remember me, O Lord." It is also paralleled, in both its reverence and its intent, by the Anglican "prayer of humble access," framed by Cranmer on the basis of several of the preparatory Sarum prayers: "We do not presume to come to this thy table, merciful Lord, trusting in our own goodness, but in thy manifold and great mercies." The people identify themselves, in these three related prayers, with examples of the faithful from history who have come from marginal backgrounds but who have been received by the deep love of Christ. The solemnity of the moment is expressed in yet another extensive confession (identical in wording to the priest's earlier *Confiteor*), this time repeated by the deacon, who confesses as a representative, giving voice to the entire people, while the priest is communicating.

Unlike the medieval rites, which are silent about the reception of Eucharist by the people, the Tridentine rite gives explicit instructions for the Communion of the faithful, who receive the host upon the tongue, with the prayer that the body of the Lord preserve their soul unto everlasting life. The connection of the material (the body of the Lord) and the spiritual is made through this priestly prayer. The Mass ends with a blessing and with the famous phrase of the deacon, *Ite* ("Go!"), *missa est*. There has been a great deal of controversy about the meaning of the second part of this phrase. For generations, theologians suggested that the phrase implied that *something* had been offered to God (e.g., "the offering has been *sent*" *missa*), but the tendency now is to see this as a simple dismissal: the service is over, the dis*missal* has now been made. It is, of course, from this phrase of dismissal, seen both at the end of the service of the catechumens, and here, at the end of the Eucharist, that the word *Mass* was derived—and very early, too. Whatever the origin and precise meaning,[42] the phrase is dependent upon the understanding that the people have entered, for now they are being sent out. The recessional, happily, retains the medieval practice of reciting the prologue of John's Gospel—not only the priest, but all present, have seen the true Light that has come into the world. Transformed by that Light while worshiping in the great congregation of the faithful, they are in their turn sent into the world as light.

Questions for Discussion

1. Where do we see historical problems in the Western tradition concerning the biblical ideal of "the priesthood of believers"? Does the office of "priest" in the Church, conferred upon particular individuals, necessarily detract from an appreciation of the priestly work of the whole congregation?

2. Could the provision of elaborate prescribed preparations for the celebration of the Mass lead to a fear on the part of the congregants of participating fully in the liturgy? How might this be avoided without rendering the worship wholly casual?

3. How important is it for congregants to be aware of the meaning of the priest's actions and the wording of the priest's own prayers in order to participate intelligently in the Mass?

4. What theological and practical problems do the reference to saints and their relics pose for those outside of the catholic Tradition? Is this a dividing issue that was understandable in the time of the Reformation

but might be solved in our day, or do insurmountable differences in theology and the doctrine of the Church remain?

5. If the Holy Spirit is spoken of as *in* the Church, are Christians restricting the power of God to work outside the bounds of those who call themselves Christian?

6. Is the Eucharist an appropriate time to celebrate the human dimension (heroes and heroines of the faith), or should the focus be solely on the atoning work of Christ?

6

"Your Church Unsleeping"

Expressions of Worship Today

The day Thou gavest, Lord, is ended,
The darkness falls at Thy behest;
To Thee our morning hymns ascended,
Thy praise shall sanctify our rest.

We thank Thee that Thy Church, unsleeping,
While earth rolls onward into light,
Through all the world her watch is keeping,
And rests not now by day or night.

As o'er each continent and island
The dawn leads on another day,
The voice of prayer is never silent,
Nor dies the strain of praise away.

The sun that bids us rest is waking
Our brethren 'neath the western sky,
And hour by hour fresh lips are making
Thy wondrous doings heard on high.

So be it, Lord; Thy throne shall never,
Like earth's proud empires, pass away:
Thy kingdom stands, and grows forever,
Till all Thy creatures own Thy sway.

"The Day Thou Gavest,"
John Ellerton, 1870

This hymn, sung to the confidently peaceful tune of St. Clement, is a trifle archaic in its wording; however, it remains beloved not only in the Anglican communion as a whole but in other English-speaking fellowships and congregations as well. My earliest memories of it go back to the evening meetings of my childhood Salvation Army *"corps" (parish) in Toronto, and to the Army's music camp in Jackson's Point, Ontario, when it was sung accompanied not by organ but by the mellow tones of the brass band, with euphonium and soprano cornet taking the lead. Its prominence may be due to its poignant use in the late nineteenth century for the Diamond Jubilee of Queen Victoria. This was a time when England was in the race with other major nations to annex huge areas of Africa. Yet the chosen hymn was not "triumphalistic" in tenor; rather, it expressed gratitude for the worldwide turn to Christ that was being witnessed at that time. Perhaps the poet Ellerton was sensible of the incipient dissolution of the British Empire and the strong likelihood of wars to come. At any rate, the lyrics place confidence not in the British Empire but in the Lord of the world and of the Church—the One whose kingdom stands, and who is praised everywhere and at all times, as is his due.

We have seen an insistence both in the Scriptures and in the ongoing Tradition that the worship of God's people is to be *"catholic"—that is, Christians praise God "according to the whole" (kat'holon). A palpable sense of this universality comes to me, as it must have to the nineteenth-century hymnist John Ellerton, each time that I hear the creed recited, knowing that it has been recited for generations and that it is still declared all across the globe on Sunday. My memory of the entire Church is also elicited whenever I join in the contemporary song, "I am the bread of life . . . and I will raise him up!" Perhaps my appreciation of the catholicity of the Church during the singing of Sister Suzanne Toolan's song is an idiosyncratic response, though the scriptural lyrics are so powerful that they have been translated into twenty-five languages. For me, they recall an early adult experience in liturgical worship: I can still hear Anglican bishop N. T. Wright (then the Reverend Doctor, my professor at McGill) singing in his strong baritone voice as I was immersed in the awe of a Eucharist celebrated in the chapel at Diocesan College in Montreal. I had no idea then that the song was the handiwork of a Catholic nun: yet it is remarkable that an American Roman Catholic celibate, a married English professor-priest, and a young Canadian Salvation Army woman officer should be joined in praise by means of this simple but poignant song—a song that recalls Jesus' words to the crowd in John's Gospel and also those to Martha concerning the resurrection.[1]

Whenever I hear or sing these lyrics, the scene of that first liturgical experience is juxtaposed with memories of many wonderful Christians that I have met over the years, whom I imagine are also at the same time singing Lord's Day praises wherever they are worshiping. Or they have given such praise several hours earlier, or will offer similar thanksgivings when I go off to sleep:

"and hour by hour fresh lips are making Thy wondrous doings heard on high." Moreover, the day is coming (and now is) when we will sing his praises all together, without any separation of time or space!

Andrew Lumbuye, a remarkable Kenyan music leader whom I met at an Anglican conference in Jerusalem, told me that his countrymen have an expression to describe their home place of worship—he "prays from" St. Francis Chapel at Makerere University, Kenya; I "pray from" St. George Antiochian Cathedral in Pennsylvania, United States. But when we pray, our prayers are joined together. We are gathered before the very throne of the Father, whose Son has taken to himself all of what is authentically human and whose Spirit is everywhere—especially where two or three are gathered together—teaching the Church how to commune with the Father.

In this study, we are considering how worship is something entered—an action, a place, and a company of worshipers that is larger than we might have imagined. We have seen how the theme of entrance into worship is prominent in the Old Testament, throughout the New Testament, in early Church writings, and in the mature liturgies of the Church, both East and West. Commonly, however, this entrance into worship is not a conscious perspective among Christians today, who are, at least in North America and other Western countries, involved in significant conflict over the style, form, and content of their worship gatherings. In this chapter we will "visit" various congregations in North America and a few abroad, observing and listening to our brothers and sisters in Christ, bringing our biblical and liturgical study of entrance into worship alongside actual "snapshots" of worship services. These congregations have been selected neither for excellence nor as cautionary tales. Rather, they are worshiping communities known to me, of various affiliations, geographical locations, and characteristics, whose members desire to be faithful to the Lord: Roman Catholic, Orthodox, Anglican, Presbyterian, Salvation Army, and *"emergent." At the close, I will also present two snapshots from Chinese churches, one Protestant and one Catholic, as a reminder that the question of worship form or style is not confined to our continent.

In presenting these worship situations, I have relied upon my own memory and careful notes as well as upon a questionnaire filled out by pastors, priests, and worship leaders. Yet it would be pretentious to call these "case studies." What I present here is wholly anecdotal (with a few checks and balances). Given these limitations, I trust that my vignettes will ring true to those who have worshiped in contexts similar to these, showing similarities and differences that are informative and worth consideration. My ears and eyes are trained, of course, upon the theme of entrance in particular, showing how it continues among Christians today. Since I am presenting congregations of various traditions, there will be points at which some of my readers may be alarmed, or at least stretched, for I have not shied away from describing the particularities of each gathering. In offering these pictures, I have deliberately adopted what can be termed "a hermeneutic of empathy," entering into every service wholeheartedly along with those who are worshiping. However, at times we will note an amnesia concerning the perspective of entrance, where this has been supplanted by a reimagining of worship in other human terms. In such cases we will glean some helpful warnings to carry into the next chapter, where we will "troubleshoot," responding to unhelpful attitudes and practices surrounding worship today. Because of this element, and so that I can give a candid (if sympathetic) analysis in every case, all the congregations will remain anonymous, though I will place them in as specific a context as possible.[2]

A Roman Catholic Parish on a Saturday Evening

This parish is a large one in a mature residential area, of mixed economic levels, and located in a middle-sized American city. It sponsors a school for elementary children and has a sizable staff, a choir, lay teachers, and a Wednesday night adult education program. The program and small groups reinforce the vision of the parish, proclaimed on its Web site, that "to be a disciple of Jesus is to be a student." Masses are offered several times during the week as well as on Saturday evening and twice on Sunday for the Lord's Day Eucharist. There was a downpour the evening that I attended, and it was a football night (with the team at home!), yet the attendance was over a hundred, including worshipers of all ages and several different racial backgrounds. Though the choir does not sing on Saturday night, there were two excellent soloists (members of the choir) and a fairly young but accomplished pianist/organist. These musicians lead the hymns, the responses, and the Psalms.

The *sanctuary is large, with soft beige and light blue coloring, and feels voluminous until the congregants gradually enter to fill it. Around the sides are statues (mostly of St. Mary and one of St. Joseph) and modest stained-glass windows in muted colors, with common emblems such as wheat, candle, cross, cornucopia, heart, anchor, sword; I am told later that these represent the Christian virtues. Indeed, the bulletin and Web page encourage meditation upon these, and we are reminded in the announcements of the regular opportunity for all-day Friday vigil over the sacraments, "spending time with Jesus." (There is a longstanding tradition in Roman Catholic and Anglo-Catholic parishes of meditation and prayer in the presence of the *"reserved" sacrament, that is, the remaining and carefully saved bread and wine from the previous Lord's Day Eucharist.) For those with an understanding of Jesus' real presence in the sacraments, this is time literally spent in the presence of the Savior—something that takes on great significance when it occurs on the fast-day of Friday, the day when the Lord was crucified. "Can you watch with me for one hour?" is taken as a challenge for Christian devotion today, offering the faithful the opportunity to be vigilant where even the disciples failed, leaving only the

women and the beloved disciple at the foot of the cross. This practice, along
with other weekly opportunities for worship in the parish, matches the sober
self-description on the Web site: "We celebrate the sacraments, our encounter
with Jesus, at moments in our lives defined by tradition, piety and necessity."
As we wait for the service to start, the pianist is playing a selection from
Gustav Holtz's "The Planets" (Jupiter), which turns out to be the tune for one
of the hymns to be sung ("O God Beyond All Praising"[3]). The rack in front of
my pew has two hymnals, a general Catholic hymnal entitled We Celebrate
(which contains a mixture of traditional, ecumenical, and charismatic pieces)
and another home-grown collection called "St. ____'s Favorites." I am intrigued
to see that We Celebrate includes a new setting of "Ein' Feste Burg" ("A Mighty
Fortress"), which includes two of Luther's original lines but then adapts the
Reformation hymn by means of lyrics from Omer Westendorf (1916–97).

Candles are lit as the service begins, and quiet reigns. Two young boys as-
sist the priest (one Caucasian, one African American—or African?), as well
as several "extraordinary ministers" who will act as lay servers of the Eucharist.[4] The celebrant is a priest from Africa who is working on his doctorate
in the local Catholic university; he is no mere visitor, however. His rapport
with the people is excellent, as they respond to him verbally as "Father" and
warm to his leadership. There are not only hymns but also a sung psalm (Ps.
19) and sung responses, which most of the people know. The service follows
the *Vatican II format,[5] including preparatory prayers, the *Kyrie (Lord, have
mercy), *Gloria, Scripture readings (with a formal *"Alleluia" accompanying
the Gospel), homily, prayers of the people, and Eucharist proper. I was intrigued
by the sung response to the Gospel reading: "Your word, O Lord, is truth;
consecrate us in the truth." The liturgy reinforces the cleansing effect of the
reception of the Scriptures, preparatory for the movement into Communion.

The homily is given without notes, making for a close connection between
the priest and the people. This is good, since the biblical texts have been challenging: Numbers 11, which articulates the hope that all God's people might
be prophets; James's discourse against the careless wealthy; and Mark 9:38–48,
about being prepared to respond to God's word even if it requires harsh discipline ("if your hand offends you, cut it off!"). From his Nigerian context,
the priest understands such rigors and tells the story of a Hutu candidate for
the priesthood who did not want to go and minister to the Tutsi (traditional
enemies of the Hutu). He makes a connection with this congregation, however,
when he follows up with the story of an American Marine who went out of
his way to show remarkable love to an elderly stranger. The challenge today,
we are told, is to go beyond the natural and human ability to love and to truly
show Christ's presence in the world. His sermon is followed by congregational
prayers, led by a layperson, and then by the Eucharist itself.

During the Eucharist there is a remarkably beautiful song called "In the Sight
of Angels" (1999) composed by Steven C. Warner: "In the sight of the angels,

O Lord, I will sing your praise; in the company of angels I bless you." The people sing it alternately with the male cantor as the *elements are received. This congregation, by their engagement and participation in a liturgy that stresses the *communion of saints and the adoration of all God's creation, enters into worship. The atmosphere is more casual, of course, than the pre-Vatican II service, which we observed in the previous chapter, and those used to the *Tridentine Mass would balk, no doubt, at the stance of the celebrant, facing the people rather than oriented toward the altar. Certainly the specter of "worship wars" is not absent in the Catholic community of this city, for its summer diocesan paper featured an article entitled "Two Rites Make a Wrong,"⁶ questioning the pope's recent decision to allow for more return to the pre-Vatican II liturgy. The changes since Vatican II have included music as well: one finds more congregational participation than previously, since the tunes are more "singable"; there is probably less awe in most services, however, since contemporary music tends to be "folksy" and Catholics have not inherited a tradition of congregational hymnody with which they are, as a whole, comfortable. In the service on this Saturday evening, the singing was varied and mostly kept the focus upon adoration. Perhaps the only questionable note was the intrusion of Sidney Carter's once-trendy "Lord of the Dance" (1967), which has always seemed to me to trivialize the sacred moment of Christ's passion: "I danced on a Friday when the sky turned black; It's hard to dance with the devil on your back." I think to myself, "It's hard to worship with sixties banality on our back!" This is, perhaps, one "ecumenical" song that might better have been omitted by the editorial board of *We Celebrate.*⁷ Its presence is a reminder of the relatively new status of the modifications that have come about in the Roman Catholic communion since Vatican II, some of which are now being reexamined.⁸ Amid the renovations and negotiations, the perception of entrance into worship remains intact—this parish enters worship with the hosts of heaven and the Church catholic, seeking the face of God.

Orthodox at the Dormition

In taking account of the worship of God's people it is not always helpful to concentrate upon large and long-established congregations; after all, this is not a typical setting for many Christians in North America.⁹ Our second snapshot takes us to a popular holiday town and to a worship service at an Orthodox mission parish only a decade old. It is observed on a weekday, the "Feast of the *Dormition of the Theotokos," and is celebrated, as is usual, on the evening prior to August 15. The Feast of the Dormition is known to Anglicans as "the Falling Asleep of the Virgin" (cf. the French verb *dormir*, "to sleep") and to Roman Catholics as "The Assumption." Orthodox call St. Mary the *Theotokos, which literally means the "God-bearer," a title given to her at least as early as the framing of the Nicene-Constantinopolitan Creed and designed to ensure that she is understood to be the mother of the *whole* united God-Man Jesus, not simply of a separate human part. Mary's death is celebrated as a great mystery, for she is believed immediately following it to have been taken directly into glory, first in the soul and soon after in the body. Her final story is taken as foreshadowing what will happen to the entire Church, which St. Mary represents in her person. This teaching has not been "dogmatized" by the Orthodox as it has been for Roman Catholics in the papal definition of the Assumption in 1950. Orthodox, however, affirm both Mary's death and her glorification as part of their "family teachings"—not part of the gospel to be preached outside the Church, but part of the mystery of holiness, passed down by Tradition, hymn, and prayer, and offering concrete hope for those who are in Christ.

I arrive slightly before the beginning of the service. The priest is already at prayer behind the *iconostasis, and the choir is singing quietly at the back, off to the side, raised slightly on a platform: evidently the music being sung is a quick rehearsal of a difficult part of the liturgy to come, for the leader gives a few quiet words of instruction, and the *troparion[10] is sung once more. It is startling to see an electric keyboard in a tradition that usually relies upon *a cappella singing, but one hardly notices it. It is being used not for atmosphere but with great care only to establish (or reestablish!) the key when necessary. The choir members, numbering about twelve, also lead in reading some of the psalms and prayers and are evidently rather new at their work; clearly some are converts to Christianity, not simply to Orthodoxy. As I glance through the prayers, which are provided in the photocopied parcel kindly offered to me by a man three rows up, I am struck that only a few of them focus upon the topic of the feast; others are prayers or psalms found in other Orthodox services. holy Mary is being honored, but the divine host of the feast (and the main object of worship) is clearly the Triune God, whose glory is named throughout.

Sunday service attendees in this parish usually number about 120: the congregation has grown rapidly enough in its decade-long existence to warrant the purchase of a building more suited to its needs. Though the church is in the Antiochian jurisdiction, there are only a few Syrian faces, and not a word of Arabic is spoken in the liturgy, which the priest intends to be "pan-Orthodox," spanning national distinctions in character. The building, once a Protestant chapel, has been refurbished—much rich brown wood, deep red carpeted floors, blue *"apse" (semicircular vault) with an *icon of the Theotokos (with infant Jesus in arms) facing the congregation, and stained-glass windows now fitted with Orthodox crosses in red on a background of white and textured clear glass. Icons take their usual places on the side of the worship space (in this case, between the windows) and on the iconostasis.

There are only about forty persons present for this mid-week summer service, but the congregation consists of people of various ages and different backgrounds. I discover, as the service proceeds, that the pan-Orthodox character of the parish is expressed throughout: Some stand while others sit during the preliminary chants. Some kneel for the great entrance while others stand, crossing themselves as the chalice proceeds past them. Some touch the priest's robe (cf. Acts 5:15; 19:11–12) in Old-World style when he goes by, while others kneel, waiting for the priest to place the chalice upon their heads.[11] It is Russia meets Antioch meets America.

As the service begins, I notice that there is no deacon to ask the priest for the initial blessing of the service; this is done by a subdeacon, a local member who holds a "minor order." A counterpoint of prayers is performed by priest, subdeacon, choir, and some others who join the choir from their seats. At the end of the service, the priest announces that a deacon will be ordained for service in the parish in the near future. This is a parish in the process of growth and change.

The entire service is comprised of an abbreviated vesperal service linked to the main part of the Divine Liturgy by some special hymns for *Dormition of the Theotokos, songs that celebrate the one who has been "brought into life by Him who dwelt in her virginal womb," thus giving hope to the faithful. Among the chants is a refrain that places the ascended Theotokos in honor above the angelic orders: "The dominions and the thrones, the rulers, the principalities and the powers, the cherubim and the fearful seraphim glorify thy Dormition" (*Vespers *Sticheron, *Tone 1).

For the Epistle reading we listen to Philippians 2:5–11, that ancient hymn about the humility and exaltation of Christ, whose name is the LORD (the One named *YHWH in Isa. 46:21–23). Hearing it read provides a helpful foundation for the keeping of the feast, since we are reminded of the true humanity of the LORD himself, who ascended with our human nature to the heavens, only after his submission to death on the cross. His mother and all Christians follow the same route to glory as they carry their own crosses: "let this mind be in you." Yet, he is the unique pioneer at whose name every knee bows, whether in heaven or on earth—especially the knee of the Theotokos, who is now with him in the heavenlies. Since the Feast of the Dormition comes close after the Feast of the Transfiguration of Jesus (on August 6), the Epistle teaches the congregation to understand the glorification of God's people as a fruit of Christ's own glory, shining on his people, beginning with the Theotokos.

The brief vesperal service has supplanted the usual cycle of prayers that normally make up the first part of *Divine Liturgy. We come to the little entrance, when the Gospel procession occurs and the vesperal service melds with the Liturgy of the Word. For me, the prescribed reading of the Gospel is unanticipated. It is made up of two readings conjoined, Luke 10:38–42 and Luke 11:27–28,[12] neither of which name Mary the mother of Jesus. Though there is no narrative of the Dormition in the Scriptures, these twinned readings prove apt:

And a certain woman named Martha welcomed Him into her house. And she had a sister called Mary, who also sat at Jesus' feet and heard His word. But Martha was distracted with much serving, and she approached Him and said, "Lord, do You not care that my sister has left me to serve alone? Therefore tell her to help me." And Jesus answered and said to her, "Martha, Martha, you are worried and troubled about many things. But one thing is needed, and Mary has chosen that good part, which will not be taken away from her."

And it happened, as He spoke these things, that a certain woman from the crowd raised her voice and said to Him, "Blessed is the womb that bore You, and the breasts which nursed You!" But He said, "More than that, blessed are those who hear the word of God and keep it!"

Juxtaposed in this way, the passages speak forcibly to the faithful about the "one thing necessary": devotion to God's Word (spoken/written and incarnate), to which we are all called, with Mary the sister of Martha. There is also an assurance that God aims to bless all the faithful along with the Theotokos Mary, as they hear the Word and obey it (him). Here we are cured of any sentimentality that might be fostered unwittingly by the exalted language of the festal hymns. Holy Mary, along with her namesake Mary of Bethany, chose the part of hearing Jesus' word; blessed are all those who follow their example to hear and "do whatever he tells you" (John 2:5).[13] Alongside the positive honor afforded the mother of the incarnate Word, there is an insistence that more is involved than a natural familial connection: those who do the will of God may also be brother and sister and mother (Mark 3:35)! It is not simply that Mary is the natural mother of Jesus, though the physical dimension is important in our salvation. It is also that we are connected to her, and to Jesus, in the mystery of salvation.

The push-and-pull of the readings and hymns for the day are a powerful illustration of the interplay between the *kataphatic and *apophatic tendencies of Orthodox theology. God and the mysteries of God are expressed both in positive (kataphatic), and in negative (apophatic) statements. These two approaches are self-correcting, so that the faithful do not devolve either into idolatry or a woolly agnosticism. The latter tendency, vagueness about doctrine, may be found commonly among "liberal" Christians who speak reverently about the inability of human language to adequately capture the mystery of God, thus freeing their liturgists to adopt pagan language—God our Mother—alongside other more traditional titles. The former tendency of literalism is well known in Christian history, and may be seen, for example, in unwarranted depictions of God the Father, in "noncanonical" iconography, as an old man with a gray beard.

In the case of this service, the use of negative and positive ways of speaking helps the worshipers to keep their equilibrium in honoring the Theotokos. The human girl Mary, with the entire universe, was transformed by being joined to God the Son in the Incarnation; yet her (and our) complete salvation is not automatic, since it requires human response and the ongoing work of the Holy Spirit. Holy Mary is, by virtue of her obedience and her union with the human Christ, "more honorable than the cherubim"; yet Christ alone is to be worshiped. The case of Mary's exaltation brings us near to the Orthodox teaching of *"divinization" or *"theosis": the Almighty means to make of us "gods," but only by his grace and not by our human nature. The Liturgy proclaims that "One alone is holy" in himself—that is, the Lord Jesus Christ. Mary is "blessed." But so too may be holy all those who are joined to Christ—and yet only God is the truly blessed One. As John Chryssavgis puts it, positive and negative ways of speaking the truth are "two sides of the same coin."[14]

In the homily that follows the Gospel, the priest seeks to lift the eyes of the congregation to the mystery of the Church itself by way of the readings and by way of thinking about Mary. He refers to a recorded sermon by *Metropolitan Kallistos Ware, in which that theologian-priest refers back to the patristic explanation of Moses' action in removing his shoes before the burning bush. The shoes are made of (dead) animal skins, and all that is dead or death-dealing must be doffed as worshipers approach God, as they approach worship, as they approach the mysteries of the faith. Holy Mary, too, was aware of the marvel of the Son, as we can see in the well-known icon of the "sweet-kissing Jesus," who is cheek-to-cheek with his contemplative Mother. In that icon, holy Mary's eyes are full of the wonder of her child. It is the wonder not simply of a new mother but a response to the One who is the God-Man, whose glory fills heaven yet has tabernacled within her womb. Pay attention like Mary, says the priest, to "where you are at"—in the holy Church of God. Only one thing is necessary—to sit at Jesus' feet among brothers and sisters. At the feast, let us take off our shoes, entering into the wonder of the Theotokos and observing the same devotion as Mary of Bethany.

With the reference to the Thrice-Holy Hymn sung by both the Cherubim and congregants, we are ushered into the high point of the Liturgy. The Liturgy of the Faithful follows the order of *St. John Chrysostom. There will be no more special highlighting of the Theotokos in honor of the day until the dismissing benediction.

Two features stand out during the Eucharist—the first is that almost everyone receives Communion; the second is that the same young woman who was blessed by the chalice in the Great Entrance goes forward, again is blessed (but does not receive) and returns to her seat. This is something quite unusual in an Orthodox church, going beyond the common offering of blessed bread (the *antidoron) to non-Orthodox by members of the congregation. It seems to approximate the kind of "blessing" practiced in other liturgical traditions, for example, in the Roman Catholic or Anglican contexts, when a visitor (or child) who cannot receive goes forward to be prayed with by the priest at the time of Communion. I wonder if this is a common practice in this parish or is due to a special circumstance, and I will soon learn the answer. The second outstanding feature is the family atmosphere that is apparent after the closing of the service. During the announcements we hear about the priest's enthusiasm that the fast preceding the Dormition is now over—though he says some purists may want to wait until the morning to break the fast. We also are informed with joy about the young woman who was blessed, that she is to be baptized on Sunday. All the guests present—four of us—are noticed, welcomed by name, and asked to give an update on our latest news. It is impossible to remain anonymous. This parish highlights, in its unique and unpretentious way, the observation of John Chryssavgis—that one finds in Orthodox liturgy a strange mixture of "homeliness and awe."[15] The closing announcements, along with the architecture, "emphasise and . . . embrace all the people" and "abolish the man-made distinction between sacred and profane."[16]

An Anglican Service of the Word

The difference between our last snapshot and this third vignette, also a parish situated near the ocean, is quite striking. This Anglican parish is rather large, composed of an imposing blond building with a tower (cross atop), a beautifully landscaped courtyard, a covered passageway adorned with foliage, and a parish hall with offices and large meeting spaces. It is situated in an affluent residential area in a large Canadian city and has clearly been in that area for decades. In the *narthex (lobby) is a welcome desk, with two young people offering information on small groups that might be of interest to newcomers (it looks as though there are more than a few).

Entrance into the sanctuary gives a sense of warmth, breadth, and height. Though it is contemporary-modern, with a parabola shape to the ceiling, the architecture follows the classical pattern for a Western church: the baptismal font is at the back central entrance, and the whole is shaped as a cross, with a small chapel on the south side of the crossbar and a congregational area on the other. Carpeted in burgundy, the central aisle brings the eye forward (eastward) to the chancel, slightly raised within a beige-white inset dome, spanned by a huge golden cross and illumined more brightly than the rest of the worship space. There are honey-brown pews, discrete skylights, colorful stained-glass biblical scenes high on the sides, and gleaming organ pipes over the extra space where the crossbar goes to the north. In the south chapel, which is toward the front of the sanctuary, there is a sizable memorial window, localized to speak of this Canadian milieu to which the gospel has come. (I hear later that this window as well as those in the chancel at the front were made from fragments of eleventh-century glass gleaned from Canterbury Cathedral, because those windows were shattered during the air-raids of World War II.)

The congregation is very large for a Sunday evening (about five hundred by the end of the evening) and made up largely of twenty- or thirty-somethings (single? mostly Caucasian, but some Asian), dressed casually for the most part. Those who have come early are singing along with the worship leader, accompanied variously by the organ or a praise band, with tuba, violin, keyboard, and other instruments. There is also a choir loft to the back, adorned with more organ pipes and stained-glass windows. The choir sings from that loft during the morning services, avoiding the atmosphere of a performance on stage. Instead, the music comes from behind, filling the place, rather than from a stage, with the imaginative spotlight upon it.

As we enter, we are handed a bulletin printed with a simplified liturgy and songs: overhead songs would be difficult in this environment, but perhaps that media is avoided for other reasons. The songs focus upon the majesty of God, using a mixture of language—"He" (descriptive of God), "you" (addressed to God), "I" (personal devotion), and "we" (corporate praise). The contemporary songs are not repeated more than two or perhaps three times, and one is an intriguing setting to old lyrics: "Praise my soul, the king of Heaven: Praise him! Praise him!" The atmosphere is friendly, but there is little chatting, since the worship has already begun, or at least the approach to it, in the singing.

Partway through the opening songs, the worship leader interjects and says that, contrary to usual practice, we are going to practice one of the songs to be sung later in the service. There is a recording team on site taping the congregational singing to be part of a new recording of a contemporary worship song newly written by the music-leader.[17] Most know the song already, he says, but some will not have heard it yet, and he wants the entire group to participate fully in this singing at the appropriate time in the service so that they can bless others who will listen to the recording. The song is lyrical, accompanied by organ and violin, and is a "conversation" between the LORD, who introduces himself as "the First and the Last" (cf. Rev. 1:11) and the worshipers, who respond "Glory! Glory! Glory to you!"[18] Though this is a "run-through," a sense of worship surrounds the moment, especially as we sing it the second time.

The singing "prelude" comes to a conclusion with a welcome from the worship leader, who is also the pastor in charge. He offers a prayer of confession, inviting everyone to join in. It would seem that the service is following a modified version of the 1962 Canadian *Book of Common Prayer (quite similar to Cranmer's 1662 version), where the confession is placed at the beginning of the entire liturgy, rather than before the Eucharist, with the purpose of preparing the people to worship without impediment.[19] A hymn is then sung (Wesley's "And Can It Be?") with a brisk upbeat, but also with organ, which enhances its classical style. We have begun the service proper. The hymn serves both as a commentary upon God's mercy and as an invitation to worship: "Bold, I approach th'eternal throne."

Indeed, the order follows that of BCP Evensong, but without all the prayers—there is a reading from the Epistles, followed by the *Apostles' Creed, said with gusto by most of those present, like a kind of manifesto. This corporate witness is supplemented by an "interview testimony": one of the leaders questions and so gives voice to a couple who have just returned from a mission overseas. Between the time of witness and the second reading (from the Gospel) there is another hymn, this one extolling the power of God's Word. The second reading is followed by a sermon, which is the high point of this Evensong, construed as a Service of the Word. The sermon is preached from a portable pulpit, centered in the nave more closely to the congregation than the raised preaching pulpit at the side. The pastor during his message stays close to the Gospel text, "I am the way, the truth and the life," but also refers to the Epistle: he deals with the difficulties of the claim that Jesus is unique, when proclaimed in today's environment, and urges confidence in the incarnate Son of God for the health of each believer and for the Church as a whole. It would seem that this question is a live one for the group. Indeed, I reflect, there has been some recent debate in this diocese concerning the place of Christianity among other world religions. The key to this problem, says the pastor, is to remember who Jesus is, rather than to think about Christianity as a system alongside others. Clearly, the exposition of the Word is a serious matter for these Christians; yet the homily is not heavyhanded but rather suited to a mixed group with nonbelievers (especially young adults), complete with humor and illustrations from popular media and literature.

When asked afterward about his general approach to worship, the pastor acknowledges the centrality of the Word for this congregation: in Ephesians 5:19, we are enjoined to speak among ourselves and to praise God, yet "our worship . . . [directed] to God and to one another may not be the most important thing we do." His understanding of the horizontal dimension of worship, including the possibility of outreach during a time of praise, matches that of another Anglican musician who comments:

> Oh that all singers could understand a collaboration of the *heart* and not *art* in worship even when striving to do their best to present with excellence hymn, psalms and spiritual songs in the House of the Lord! . . . [In] the account of Paul and friend [Acts 16:25] in the prison at midnight [they were] singing praise *and the prisoners were listening.* . . . In worship, prisoners of many different difficulties are present and they are listening when they hear dialogue through music with our Lord and Savior Jesus Christ! That's evangelism in a liturgical church service.[20]

However, in the view of the pastor of our selected parish, neither what we say to God or to others is the most significant thing in corporate worship. Rather, "what God says to us is more important at a gathered meeting." Mutual encouragement and praise of God, then, give way to instruction and evangelism in this specially designed service, which is attended by friends who are interested in Christianity.

The sermon is followed by the new song practiced earlier at the gathering—"Behold, I Am the First and the Last!" It functions as a confirmation and response to the sermon since it too announces the ultimacy of Jesus the Christ. But its singing is also conceived as a "service" to others who will hear this song, and so may be moved with the congregation to sing "Glory!" to Jesus. Those beyond this local congregation are thus kept in view, especially those who are not yet in the Church. The song is followed by the prayers of the people, offered by a member of the congregation. Here the focus outward is extended even as the needs of the world and those known in the parish, including the communicants at the morning services, are recognized. All the prayers are brought together in the *"collect" of the day that remembers, according to the church year, the lives of two apostles. The collect reiterates the burden of the sermon, that Jesus alone is the Way, Truth, and Life: "O ALMIGHTY God, to know you is to have eternal life, whom truly to know is everlasting life: Grant us perfectly to know your Son Jesus Christ to be the way, the truth, and the life; that, following the steps of your holy Apostles, Saint Philip and Saint James, we may steadfastly walk in the way that leads to eternal life; through your Son Jesus Christ our Lord. *Amen.*"

The collect is one of the three most ancient forms of prayer, along with the "litany" (a dialogue between priest and congregation) and the *Anaphora. This ancient form of prayer was brought into the Anglican communion by its earliest liturgist, Thomas Cranmer (1489–1556), and was commended by him because of its two qualities of brevity and variety. The form of the prayer is threefold: address, petition, and the ascription of power to the Lord, or to the Holy Trinity. Often the first or second of these parts is briefly enlarged in order to fit into the liturgical theme—for example, God is addressed according to his characteristics, or the petition is amplified by reference to the Scriptures or the feast day. Cranmer borrowed the form from the ancient Church by way of the Sarum missal and himself composed some of those better known collects (first published in the prayer book of 1549)[21] that are still in use in the Anglican Church (often in a contemporized form) today. The collect most celebrated among evangelical Anglicans such as those we are visiting in this study would be that composed for the second Sunday in Advent, but read at other times as well: "Blessed Lord, who hast caused all holy Scriptures to be written for our learning: Grant that we may so hear them, read, mark, learn and inwardly digest them, that by patience and comfort of your Holy Word, we may ever hold fast the blessed hope of everlasting life, which thou hast given us in our Saviour Jesus Christ, Amen." In this collect, the giver of the Scriptures and the power of the Bible are highlighted by means of the metaphor of food, for Christians live "by every word that comes from the mouth of God." As for the collect used in the service we are studying (that is, the collect for Saints Philip and James), it speaks aptly about the God "whom to truly know is life." Through its use in the closing prayer, we are reminded of Jesus' unique self-description as the Way, Truth, and Life, and are exhorted to follow steadfastly in this belief along with the apostles. This prayer shows real insight, reminding those praying of Philip's question that Jesus shows the way to the Father (John 14:8)—and he is himself the Way!—and of James's words that we must be "doers and not only hearers" of God's Word. The collect's special intent, to bring the congregation's prayers together in the context of the Scriptures, remains effective and vital to this day, as this younger congregation hears God's Word, sees the living Christ, and worships.

The service concludes with a final hymn of praise, accompanied by the organ, and a benediction. Those present mingle and talk, visit the information table, or go to the hall for refreshments. The conversation is lively, as one expects among students and young professionals. In one group a young man with a foot cast seems intent on debate or discussion with a slightly older woman and another young man, continuing to struggle with the questions evoked by the sermon.

A Presbyterian Confessing Church at Lent

This Presbyterian congregation in the southeastern United States is intent on fidelity to its Reformed tradition (it is a "confessing" church) and aims to give a "gracious witness" to Christ in a relatively hostile culture. Its weekly bulletin is informed by the liturgical structures given in the *PCUSA Book of Common Worship*, and describes the worship as "an intentional blend of ancient, traditional, and modern forms of liturgy, prayer, music, and communication." The varied congregation (different ages, social backgrounds, and races) and the number of those involved in the worship (pastor, choir, worship team, contemporary worship leader or vocalist, lay assistant) bear out the signaled intention to "gather as a family of believers of many ages and backgrounds, and so use all the means at our disposal to invite each worshiper into the presence of God." Entrance into worship is thus a central idea for this body of believers. As with many Protestant churches, musical expression occurs in the hymns and *anthem, but I am surprised to discover that it is not confined to these places. Prior to the beginning of the service, handbells are played—a lovely, yet brief fantasia on "Oh, the Deep, Deep Love of Jesus."[22] The chatter ceases, despite the conspicuous presence of youth and little ones. People pray or sit quietly as a lyrical piano prelude begins in a minor key suited to *Lent. Clearly, the congregation has received instruction regarding preparation for worship.

Looking around we see a good deal of warm wood, with large beams angled up from the corners to a center pointed window, a burnt-orange carpet, colorful

banners on the side walls, and hanging globe lighting. The well-filled sanctuary seats about two hundred, but there is a removable wall to one side that
will allow for more seating. The front has a slightly raised platform, with the
choir, piano, and organ on one side, a smaller worship team and instruments
on the other, and a pulpit with chairs for the leaders on the center under the
cross, which is on the front wall. In front of the pulpit is a table with communion elements on it: for non-Communion services it would accommodate
the Bible. The wood beams and angles remind one of a ski lodge, as does the
entrance room, which features sofas and a stone gas fireplace. Those gathered
are reverent but clearly at home in this intimate setting.

The music prelude comes to an end, and the pastor steps forward, offering
a welcome and a brief orientation for newcomers: "Welcome in the name of
our Lord and Savior Jesus Christ. We are glad each one of you is here today
and trust that God has brought you here for a reason. Visitors, welcome. We
invite you to sign the black books in the pews so that we can put names to
faces. . . . We believe that God meets us here as we gather in his name and in
Spirit and Truth." Following these words are some announcements regarding
"our common life together in this part of the body of Christ." The pastor
then enunciates the theme of the service—the importance of watchfulness
in prayer against temptation—which he explains will persist through to the
Communion service itself, and then invites all present to "tune in and listen
to God's Word." In conversation with the pastor later, I hear that the general
worship themes of praise, thanks, confession, petition, response, and sending
are found in every service, but that a specific theme, linked with the Scripture,
and (when possible) with the liturgical season, is very deliberately built into
every service, with preparation beginning months ahead.

The call to worship is from Psalm 32:6–7, led by a layperson: "let everyone
who is godly pray to the Lord in a time of trouble. . . . Come let us worship
the Lord!" The same man announces the song of preparation, which is accompanied by organ—two verses of "Go to Dark Gethsemane."[23] Over the
microphone we hear a pleasing, though not imposing, male voice, that of
the pastor, who is clearly also an accomplished musician: "learn from Jesus
Christ to pray!" The pastor then tells the congregation, "You are the family of
Christ," and invites them to greet each other. This "Call to community" lasts
about a minute, with the increasing volume of a piano reminding the people
to return to their places to sing. As the people reassemble, the contemporary
song group (piano, guitar, and singers) invites the Holy Spirit to "Dwell in
the Midst of Us!"[24] This song is not only an invocation but also reestablishes
the main theme, for its refrain repeats the Lord's words in the garden, "Not
my will but yours be done." The music at this point is entered into with a
little less confidence: perhaps it is a new song for the larger group. By the end
of the song, however, the refrain is being sung more robustly. After this, the
opening prayer is offered by a member of the band, who thanks the Lord for

the assembly, prays regarding trials, and asks that the congregation will be enabled to "want to do your will," even more than bringing their own desires before God.

The first reading comes from Luke's narrative of Jesus in the garden, to which people are instructed to listen because "this is the Word of the Lord." The reading is followed by the "important Word for the children," a mini-message about prayer. The young man speaking to the children calls their attention to prayers that take place even while we sing: "Dwell in the Midst of Us." "Who did we sing that to?" "To God, Jesus, and the Holy One," answers a young girl. "What bodily actions do we use when we pray?" The same young girl is very vocal with answers to his questions. The children then are told (with the parents listening in) about Jesus' prayer, "not my will but yours be done," linked to the song that asked the Lord to "come and change us." Receiving a blessing, they rejoin their parents. The entire church will stay together this morning for Communion: on non-Communion Sundays, children under seven proceed at this point to "children's church," where they will engage in worship and teaching with the same focus as the adults. I am told that they are also trained during this time for their future participation in the main service, which they will attend regularly when they enter second grade.

The second reading is also from the Gospels, this time from Jesus' instruction in Matthew about the Lord's Prayer. I learn that the pattern for readings more typically includes an Old Testament and New Testament reading but that this depends on the needs of the sermon, which sets the agenda for these services—though the church observes the church year, it does not follow the *lectionary. The people sit for both readings, rather than standing for the Gospel: the readings, then, are conceived as instruction, rather than as pieces in a liturgical drama, the impression given by standing to receive the presence of Christ in a Gospel with Alleluias.

The prayer before the sermon requests that the Lord would "open our ears." We are brought up-to-date concerning the teaching that has gone on in previous weeks, on Jesus' human nature and his ability to stand trial faithfully, as seen in Hebrews, and in the Gospels. This morning, the scene in Gethsemane should remind us of the creation of humankind in the garden: God will rescue, even when the disciples fail, as did the first couple. The pastor gives immediacy to this dramatic story of Jesus' passion, referring to the action in the present tense and speaking about what is happening to Jesus on "this very night." The people are enjoined to wake up.

In harmony with the Reformed approach to worship, everything in the service is centered around the Word. In the bulletin, congregational confession is entitled "Response to the Word," while the Communion service is entitled "Sealing the Word." There is no creed recited in this service. (In other liturgical contexts the recitation of a confession or creed is frequently understood to be a response to the preaching of the Word.) However, I discover later that the creed is a frequent component of this congregation's worship and usually occurs in non-Communion services toward the end of the service as an affirmation, just before the final "Sending-out" hymn. When the creed is said, the service bulletin indicates by means of footnotes where the creed has been informed by the Scriptures. This, too, focuses the attention of the worshipers upon the written Word.

This week, as seems appropriate for Lent, there is a more extended time of confession, one that is quite striking in its format: The pastor sings to the congregation as a call to confession, and they join him in song as a response. The confession is specific, articulating the human problem of lack of diligence in prayer (according to the day's theme). But there is silent time, as well, for the sake of personal meditation and confession.

Special instrumental music is played during the *offertory and introduced as one of the players indicates that the lyrics are printed in the bulletin. The congregants are asked not to be distracted by the performance but to understand the dramatic flair of the music, played by organ and piano, as indicating Jesus' agony and watchfulness in the garden. The traditional "Doxology" ("Praise God from whom all blessings flow") closes the offertory, and we move into the Communion service. The pastor invites the congregation to "believe that God's mercy is new" and to see this Communion as a remembrance of Christ's death as well as an anticipation of the heavenly table: would they please follow the outline in the bulletin? The Eucharist begins with the Great Thanksgiving ("the Lord be with You") and is followed by the pastor's extemporaneous prayers, as allowed for in both the *Book of Common Worship* (1993) and the *Book of Order* (2007–2009).[25] In the bulletin, these prayers are designated to the Father, to the Son, and to the Holy Spirit, but the Father is mostly addressed in them, with reference to the Son and the Holy Spirit. The pastor rather foreshortens the first prayer, which customarily remembers God's acts in creation and for Israel, but he stresses the second prayer, drawing from Galatians and Philippians 2, as he remembers Jesus' humility and faithfulness. The prayer focusing upon the Spirit is not exactly an *epiclesis*, but it does request that the Holy Spirit make the *elements the body and blood of Christ *for those who will receive.* This implicit tripartite structure, studded with congregational acclamations and ascriptions of praise, is completed by the recitation of the Lord's Prayer. Then, in the mode of historical narrative, Jesus' words of institution are recited as a holy story concerning Jesus and "his friends, the disciples," with a bridge made to the congregation: "These are the gifts of God for you, the people of God." The instruction is also given to wait for the bread to be served at the seats, and then, "we will eat and drink together." As bread is distributed, there is reverent quietness, and the solo music of an alto recorder playing the tune of "Go to Dark Gethsemane" and "Draw me Nearer, Nearer, Precious Lord."[26] Once all have been served, the pastor says: "This is the body of Christ broken for you: take it and eat."

The same quiet descends as the cups are distributed, and the recorder plays "I Lift My Eyes Up" followed by a reprise of "Go to Dark Gethsemane." The congregation is told: "This is the blood of Christ poured out for you for the forgiveness of sins. Take and drink."

Once the elements have been received, the pastor leads in an extended time of prayer, petitions, and intercessions, in which he retains the theme of watchfulness in prayer but moves specifically into the needs of the congregation and the world, praying for the children, youth, neighbors, troops, the president, and all of our needs and wants and desires, spoken and unspoken. He finishes with Jesus' own words, "Your will be done." The service closes with the old gospel hymn, "I Surrender All,"[27] which is surprisingly the only first-person-singular song that has been sung the entire morning. The benediction is given in the triune name, and the people are sent out "to love and serve the Lord." The quiet is broken, and people chat with abandon.

Though the Reformed tradition is strong in this church, we could hardly consider the worship here typical. For one thing, it has been very carefully framed, and I am not surprised to learn that the services are planned months in advance, with attention to detail and to every component. There is also a very special musical dimension in the church, with musicians who are both accomplished and fervent in their faith. There is an eclectic and intelligent approach to music, both contemporary and traditional, and the congregation is exposed to helpful and creative (but not self-advertising) arrangements of the music. For example, in leafing through a past bulletin, I discovered a wonderful musical medley perfectly suited to Lent, consisting of a contemporary song joined to a version of the *Kyrie*. The song was the well-known contemporary version of Charitie L. Bancroft's nineteenth-century lyrics "Before the Throne of God Above" (simply sung in the major key) interspliced with Shane Bernard's modal-sounding refrain, but adapted here to the ancient prayer, "Have mercy, have mercy, Kyrie Eleison!"[28] The interplay between verse and lyrics leads the worshipers helpfully to move between meditation upon God's grace available through Jesus Christ and prayer asking directly for that mercy from the Lord.

Though the effort that has gone on behind the scenes for these services is manifest, it is also clear that the worshipers in this Presbyterian congregation understand, along with the pastor, "Christ to be the primary/ultimate worship leader, with the Holy Spirit uniting our human worship to the ongoing and eternal worship of Heaven."[29] Human leaders in worship have the responsibility to "invite and facilitate worship by drawing people to the Word and Spirit of God." The use of the music also bears out the pastor's careful words, "I am cautious not to replace the spoken Word with music, but to supplement it." Conversation with the pastor confirms the impression that the Word is primary, although this Reformed congregation practices Communion more frequently (once a month, with other special Sundays) than most other churches in the PCUSA. All the services are centered, then, around both a specific theme and

around the Word in general: gathering around the Word, proclaiming the
Word, responding to the Word, sealing the Word (if there is Eucharist), and
bearing the Word into the world. The pastor takes his supervisory responsibility
seriously and gives careful guidance to those who are also leading in the worship, in order that the people may be helped to worship and not get stalled on
arguments over worship style. In this guidance, and indeed in congregational
teaching in general, the pastor has offered "regular and diligent explanation
of our worship style as Scripture and theme-driven rather than style-driven."
This vigilance and care has made for a unified congregation that knows why
they are gathering together.

Salvationists at Christmas

We enter into the meeting-hall, or "citadel," of a middle-sized *"corps" (congregation) of two hundred or so members located in a busy area of a major
city in Ontario, Canada. The congregation is well established, comprised of
both newcomers and of families that have attended for several generations.
It has been considerably larger in past years: many young "officers" (pastors)
and lay leaders have been nurtured in this congregation, and a generation ago
it had numerous musical programs, even sending a junior band comprised of
children and teens overseas for special performances and assemblies. The area
of town is less residential than it was in the past, and many of the members
have moved to the suburbs, as is the case in other major cities, so the make-
up of the congregation has changed. There is a preponderance of gray heads
but also younger members and children in the congregation, of various racial
backgrounds.

The atmosphere is rather casual, though subdued, prior to the beginning
of the "meeting." (This is the term typically used for a "service" in the Salvation Army congregations.) People greet each other and chat briefly (though
quietly) as they enter. Some are dressed up, others wear more casual clothing,
and still others wear a Salvation Army uniform—mostly of the contemporary
type, though there is an older woman still wearing the high-collared zipped
uniform and bonnet of the last century. Organist and pianist, situated off to
the front and side, play softly in duet, and the empty platform causes my eye
to fall upon the focal point—a large lit-up cross in the center of the wooden
panels that make up the back of the platform. The colors of the carpet, wall,
and chairs are in beige and off-pink tones, and there are contemporary stained-
glass windows (geometric mauve, pink, and beige, with no pictures) on the
side of the hall. It is the Sunday after Christmas, and a few Poinsettias are
placed at various strategic spots, especially at the base of the platform. To
the side at the front is the Salvation Army flag, with its red, yellow, and blue
colors proclaiming the reality of the Father, Son, and Holy Spirit. At the

front directly before the congregation is a bench and also a table covered by a maroon cloth with golden fringe and golden embroidery proclaiming, "Holiness unto the Lord." The table has a large Bible open upon it. Soon, the music becomes more stirring, and from the back of the platform emerge the choir (songsters) and band (made up of brass instruments), who take their seats on either side of the platform. They are followed by the officers (who are husband and wife) and corps sergeant major (a local officer, the equivalent of elder or subdeacon), who sit directly at the front of the platform, behind the pulpit, which is centrally situated on the platform. Any speaking on the part of the congregation has ceased, as the people listen to a brief word of welcome from the corps officer (pastor).

The pastor reminds the congregation that they are here to worship and that healing and transformation come through this action. There is a gradual warm-up to the worship through contemporary (and some not-so-contemporary) choruses, some of which seem particular to the Army but others that are more well known, such as Melody Green's "There is a Redeemer" (1982):

> Thank you O my [F]ather,
> For giving us Your Son,
> And leaving Your Spirit
> 'Til the work on earth is done.

A psalm is recited responsively to complete the entrance into worship, and the opening song is announced: Isaac Watts's "Joy to the World" (1719). The band plays, and the congregation stands to sing. Following this, the people sit for a second song, "Since Jesus Came into My Heart,"[30] led by the corps sergeant major, accompanied by clapping from many and interspersed by individual testimonies, solicited by him. The people are used to being asked to give testimonies and are reminded that the end of the year is an apt time to reflect upon what God has done for them. Their spoken testimonies are capped by the offering of the Songsters, who sing a Christmas carol in a more subdued mode.

The children then are invited up front where they are treated to a brief story and then return to their seats to the singing of "Go Tell It on the Mountain!"[31] The corps sergeant major apologizes that there is no "church school" downstairs today (where the children would normally go at this time), and gives the announcements, welcoming any guests.

The Scripture, from John 1, is then read by a member of the congregation, followed by the chorus, "Father in heaven, how we love you; We lift your name in all the earth." Though this is no *Trisagion*, it does reflect upon the God of the heavenly temple who may be praised by his people: "Blessed be the Lord God almighty, who reigns forevermore!"[32] This rings as a kind of commentary upon the Scripture reading, that famous passage from John's prologue proclaiming the mighty Creator who is sovereign over all his creation and who has taken on human flesh. Indeed, the corps sergeant major comments upon the connection between the Scriptures and the chorus. We can praise the Lord, he says, because of the birth of Jesus. During the chorus, which is sung a number of times, members of the songsters and band come down from the platform and sit with the congregation in anticipation of the sermon to follow.

The congregation is prepared to receive the sermon by means of an instrumental solo played by a younger member of the band and then by a lengthy petition offered by the corps officer, who presents the needs of the people and prays for them. Since the people are about to hear the Word expounded, the prayer is as much for them as for the one who will preach, or "give the message," in the terminology of this congregation.

The message, by "Mrs. Corps Officer," concentrates upon the theme of advent—God is near and has, in the Incarnation, closed the distance caused by sin. As with other evangelistic sermons, the emphasis is on challenge and upon an invitation to "each one" to respond. The response is formalized in a time of invitation at the close of the service, where each member is encouraged to ask, "Will I give myself to God?" The prayer chorus matches the moment: "He is here!" A few come forward to kneel at the "mercy seat" at the front and are joined by an older woman in uniform (not the corps officer-wife), who prays quietly with them. When these return to their seat, at the end of the time of invitation, the woman officer gives a brief prayer that emphasizes the love of Jesus, the truth of the Scriptures, and the importance of our response.

The quiet intensity of the appeal time swiftly modulates in the closing hymn, as the music offers a vibrant introduction to "Hark the Herald Angels!"[33] At the conclusion of this final song, the officer gives a benediction that closes with the name of the Holy Trinity. (Though there has not been as much explicit naming of the Trinity in the meeting as in liturgical worship, it is clear that this doctrine is foundational: even the songbook begins with a section devoted to each of the divine Persons.) The spoken benediction usually is doubled by the musical one, sung personally as the officers make their way to the back of the hall to greet the people: "O Father, let thy love remain; O Son, may I thy likeness gain; O Spirit, stay to comfort me: O Triune God, praise be to Thee!"[34] As soon as the music ends, people rise, meet and greet friends, chat, and go at leisure to the back of the hall and to the vestibule, where coffee and cookies await them.

One of the most noticeable things about the service is the swing of moods, from reflective to bouncy, from yearning to confident. There is also a mixture of modes of song, from the traditional carols (still called "songs") to contemporary. With the exception of the responsive psalm, there is little formal liturgy, and so the leader (whether officer or his helpers) provides continuity by offering commentary upon the song or whatever is transpiring, linking element with element in the worship. It would seem that a great deal of time is taken in preparation for the hearing of the Word: the people come down from the platform, the mood is set instrumentally, and prayers are offered. Though the theme of entrance is not explicit, certainly the presence of God is recognized, and the people are invited to be attentive. The reading and exposition of the Word, however, does not seem so solemn as the moment of invitation or dedication, to which the message seems to have been leading all along. Indeed, there is a theology of the mercy seat among Salvationists that they are "saved to serve," that each must offer himself or herself as a living sacrifice:

> My life must be Christ's broken bread,
> My love his outpour'd wine,
> A cup o'erfilled, a table spread,
> Beneath his name and sign.
> That other souls, refreshed and fed,
> May share his life through mine.[35]

The woman officer has spoken of God's nearness to each of those present, and so has invited each to respond. The intensity suggests that there has been an inner response even among those who have not physically come forward for prayer. Indeed, the final carol ("Hark the Herald Angels!"), in this context, intimates that the heavens are rejoicing for the human response seen during the appeal as well as for the Incarnation of the Son—like a closing "victory song." The angels are praising, and so too are the people who have dedicated themselves to God. Everything is capped by the musical benediction, this week framed as a salutation to the King of kings: "All Hail, King Jesus! All Hail, Emmanuel!"[36] Its final line sends each member of the congregation to "sound his praises" for the following week and "for eternity."

In conversation with one of the past officers of this corps (congregation), I heard him reflect upon the role of the worship leader "to provide opportunity for the people to respond *individually within community*." As an informed teacher, well aware of the differences and commonalities between Salvationist meetings and liturgical services of other traditions, he also commented:

> Music in our tradition . . . happens throughout the service, beginning, middle, end. As a means of calming, stirring, reflecting, committing, resting, waiting. It connects on several levels—to the eye (words and notes); to the ear; but significantly to the mind and heart. Instrumental music . . . sometimes remind[s] one of words and thoughts [and] at other times transcend[s] words [and] thoughts. Music engages the individual *and the individual in community*, allowing for harmony . . . the transcend[ing] of socioeconomic divides . . . the contribution of gifts, the hearing of our voice, the blending of our voice.

This emphasis upon the individual and the "individual in community" matches what we have seen in the meeting as a whole. There is certainly a sense of communion with each other in the Salvationists' sharing of testimony; the stronger quest in this movement, however, is for the meeting of the individual with God, expressed in the first-person singular songs, the altar call or appeal to each person, and the witness "since Jesus came into my heart." This emphasis upon the individual is found not only in the Salvation Army but in many other evangelical communities as well, in whose roots we may see a reaction to formalized and impersonal or "cold" religion. The downside to such an emphasis is a tendency to slide into sentimentality; the upside is that the Salvationist is frequently marked with joy. C. S. Lewis lamented, concerning the lost "gusto" of Christian exultation that can occur in mainline church situations: "It would be idle to pretend that we Anglicans are a striking example [of this joy]. The Romans, the Orthodox, and the Salvation Army all, I think, have retained more of it than we. We have a terrible concern about good taste."[37] As one who has worshiped in all four contexts, I think that I would agree.

Emergent

Just as the early Salvation Army was born out of William Booth's response to the sluggishness of the Methodist Church of its day, so today there are a number of worshiping communities that identify themselves as *"emergent,"[38] seeking a liveliness beyond the traditional confines of their mother denominations. Many of these retain ties and are led by those ordained in these mainline groups, but worship takes place in venues and forms that are, in some ways, unusual. Their hope is to reach the unchurched as well as to fire the imaginations of young people alienated by the normal practices of some churches. I met with one such group, young even by emergent standards, that had two part-time ordained leaders and was small enough to allow for flexibility in its meeting time and place. This particular Sunday evening in the early fall, the group joined with another ministry group several miles from its normal meeting place. The worship took place in the basement of an established urban church, and there were greeters at the door as I came in. Beginning with a meal served by the emergent congregation, we were joined by about thirty graduate students and teachers from abroad who had been invited to come to the meeting for a meal and to practice English conversation. We ate around the tables, chatted according to a suggested conversation pattern, and when this part was concluding, heard an invitation to stay for worship with the emergent group that had provided the meal. Many of those attending the meal and conversation were Asian or Middle Eastern, with religious backgrounds other than Christian, but a few expressed interest, and one actually remained behind with us.

Since the evening had already been long, the service was abbreviated but still composed of two parts—Word and Sacrament (which is practiced weekly in this congregation, an unusual practice for its "mother" denomination). Gathering and conversation have already taken place, and so as we come to silence around the large table, one of the members fits it with an earth-tone tablecloth, a candle, a loaf and chalice, and a bowl of water. The atmosphere is sober, yet not somber. The congregation numbers about sixteen this evening, mixed in gender and mostly under thirty. (One older man, who is not one of the leaders, is a well-known member of the group.)

The celebrant welcomes everyone and uses a laptop projection in order to engage the group in a call to worship, which is Psalm 19: "The heavens are telling the glory of God; and the firmament proclaims his handiwork. . . . Let the words of my mouth and the meditation of my heart be acceptable to you, O LORD, my rock and my redeemer" (vv. 1, 14 NRSV). Into this initial time of singing, accompanied by folk guitar ("Forever, God is faithful!"[39]), are interwoven prayers of adoration, confession (with assurance), pardon, and preparation for hearing the Word. There are two readings of Scripture, one from James 3:1–12, followed by the sermon, given by the second leader. Finally, the major theme of the service (discipline in using words) emerges clearly, a subject that has been latent from the first song by Matt Redman: "You are God in heaven, and here am I on earth, so I'll let my words be few."[40] The "stewardship" and disciplining of the tongue is part of a teaching series, we are reminded, about the stewardship of what God has given us.

Another song responds to the sermon and helps to prepare for the Eucharist, which follows. The Anaphora and Communion prayers approximate the free-form pattern of the PCUSA, with some influences also from Anglican or Methodist wording. Communion is practiced simply, around the table, with each person serving the next. Before we receive, instructions are given, including the words to repeat: "The body of Christ, broken for you." A hospitable suggestion is made for any who may not feel free to communicate: they may instead ask for a prayer from the person beside them, as two around the table now do. Clearly, the group is expected to act as a "priesthood of believers" and to be prepared for such a modification.

The sober intimacy continues through the intercessory prayer, which is quite extended and prefaced by requests from several in the group. During the closing song, which features God's mighty hand in salvation, an offering receptacle is passed, and people prayerfully offer their gifts. Announcements and benediction in the name of the Holy Spirit complete the service. Quiet chatting occurs at the end, but the mood is not that of hilarity or excitement: both of the young leaders are marked by an earnest but friendly introversion, and the congregation matches this character. The mood may well be subdued because of one of the problems volunteered by a member during the intercessory period. Our Asian visitor goes off with one member, quietly asking questions. Two others of the group continue behind with this young woman, in prayer and support. A few tidy the worship space, and others head to the kitchen to do a final clean-up there. The service was not exciting, but the group has reached out into the community, entered more deeply into friendship with each other, gone quite deeply into meditation on the Word, and joined in worship during the singing and the Eucharist. I sensed that their intimacy would continue over the week through phone calls and coffees.

"The Parallel World" of the Chinese Church

Surprisingly, the earnest character of our final North American group, the emergent congregation, reminded me of the Christians that I met several years ago halfway across the globe in China. My visit to China was in the company of other seminary professors, at the invitation of government officials in the department of religion with whom our seminary had a colloquium the previous year. As a result, we visited only the "registered" (legal) churches there, in a few of the major cities; house churches would provide different insights, of course! One of my first responses to this huge country was to register surprise that all this vitality could have been going on my whole life and I knew virtually nothing about it. The sense of something similar-yet-different made me feel as though I had stepped into a parallel universe. I am a city girl myself, but when one speaks about a "major city" in China, it is an understatement. The metropolis that we first visited was immense, a sprawling urban area full of old buildings mingled with contemporary high-rises. Americans should think of Dallas, but more so. And there are many such cities. In China today, there are only two recognized denominations, Protestant and Catholic (and Catholics are not as much in favor with the government, probably because of the perceived—or real—threat of loyalty to a center outside of China itself).

Early on the Lord's Day

Our first visit was to a Protestant church. It took some time to cross the northeastern city to get to the suburban area where this large Chinese church was located. On the forty-five-minute drive, I counteracted the strangeness I was feeling by practicing how to say "Peace," "Jesus is Lord," "thank you," and "please" in Mandarin. On our arrival, I was struck by the unpretentiousness of the church, which was off the street and surrounded by a little courtyard—how could a congregation of over a thousand meet here? We were ushered into a small room where we met with the pastors of the church (one woman and one man) and with the lay leaders and asked and answered questions with the help of our interpreter. We are told that in addition to the Sunday services, they have a meeting of about five hundred young people, ages eighteen to thirty-five, every Friday night. During the week there is a group of eighty-five women studying the Bible in preparation for lay ministry led by a woman minister.

The hospitality is fabulous—at only 8:00 in the morning, we are treated to lichi fruit, cookies, and tea. Of course, the amenities are another matter, for one of Western sensibilities, but there is at least what passes for a toilet that flushes. One of the lay women introduces me to the Sunday school kids, who are just finishing up in time for the service. When I show the children pictures of my three daughters, they are shocked that I have three, and three girls at that. They keep repeating "Three! Three *girls!*" Evidently, the church has internalized the cultural norms for procreation.[41] Indeed, I will find out in a visit to another church that pastors, as well as anyone else, can be fined and disciplined by sterilization if they have more than the prescribed single child. Though religion has been afforded a newfound (but modified) liberty in China in the past decade, clergy remember the revolution and the suffering of the church in the not-too-distant past. It is therefore quite costly to allow the gospel entirely to inform both the church and the culture. But, given our own North American culture of abortion and selfishness, a malady that has also infected the churches, we should not be self-righteous. Both Chinese and Western Christians who retain a sense of entry into a larger company of worshipers may be corrected and repent of the contemporary drive to drastically limit, even by immoral means, the size of families. We have even more cause to put away the disrespect for life that goes along with such pragmatism—a pragmatism that may be nurtured by Western expectations as well as by Chinese law.

In the service itself, there are about a thousand people present. When I express surprise, our guide informs us that there will be yet another service later in the morning, with many more people in attendance. The building presents difficulties for such a crowd; several rooms make up the church, so that the service is projected on screens in two of the smaller rooms adjacent to the small main sanctuary. The inside is as modest as the outer appearance: a concrete floor, a red rug on the platform, a huge cross with plants alone as adornment at the front, and a bench at the base of the platform, running the whole length of it. (I wonder if there will be an altar call.) The choir is dressed in white and red and is quite large, taking up most of the platform. As the service proceeds, I am reminded of my Salvation Army past in some respects: it has the feel of a Methodist service, and it turns out that this church indeed has a Methodist background, though it is now part of the one Protestant church. The hymnal[42] includes an amalgam of hymns from various quarters, some introduced no doubt by English-speaking missionaries, others of the official patriotic type—"We love our Chinese Christian Church, lamp that guides our human search" (Hymn 127). This morning there is not a whiff of this Chinese politically correct hymnody. Instead, they sing nineteenth- and twentieth-century evangelical lyrics well known from my own childhood—"Precious Name, Oh How Sweet," "Just as I Am," "He Leadeth Me."[43] They sing in Mandarin, we in English: the hymn book presents versions for each language face-to-face, a tribute to the catholicity of the Church and the Caucasian missionaries who brought the gospel to China in the past few centuries. The corporate nature of the Church is also indicated in the prayers of the people, by means of an interesting tradition. Voicing the prayers is the minister, but it is clear that the congregation is entering in: as he prays, the congregation firmly says "Amen" together, punctuating every sentence. The solemnity of the responsive Amen has moved from the eucharistic prayers (found in the ancient and liturgical churches) to the prayers in general!

But the main event is surely the preaching of the Word: the fifty-five-minute sermon is given by an elder who has a job as a salesman during the week. Virtually everyone takes notes, as in a lecture. I cannot, of course, understand the sermon, and the fireworks heard in the distance outside (heralding a wedding ceremony, traditionally held on Sundays in China) remind me forcibly that these Chinese Christians, though tolerated by the government, are engaged in a countercultural activity. No wonder they take what is going on so seriously! The choir sings enthusiastically, accompanied by an extremely out-of-tune piano. Then they close with the *Apostles' Creed, the Lord's Prayer, a long period of personal prayers (conducted in whispers by every member sitting in his or her seat), and an extremely long pastoral prayer or benediction. There is no Eucharist today. The announcements follow, including a welcome of four new people attending the church for the first time; if they are not government employees or teachers, these four may be eventually baptized. There is no altar call, either. Instead, some members of the congregation kneel quietly at the altar to offer special petitions at the conclusion of the service, and these are individual prayers only. I am betting that in the old days the Methodists used the prayer bench for more public purposes.

Sunday Afternoon Mass

Our visit on the following week to a Roman Catholic church was possible, I think, by accident. It was a concession to a mistake made by our hosts, who had omitted making plans for us to go to a service that Sunday morning. Only the Catholics had an afternoon Mass. On the way there in the van, I ask if it is the practice to give blessings to Christians who are not Catholic. Our host is surprised and says that of course we should take Communion. One of the professors traveling with us says that we should follow the custom, or we would offend. I am not convinced and wait to see what will happen. Perhaps the government official thinks that the Catholic Church belongs to all the Chinese (and their guests) and should not follow its own rules, and perhaps a Protestant Westerner thinks that the hedge around the Catholic altar doesn't apply here; but if there is no discipline concerning the Eucharist, then it can hardly be Catholic.

The service is the Vatican II service, very familiar to me from North American experiences. It is Pentecost, and I am delighted to follow parts of the liturgy.

The building is quite old and also beautiful. Inside there are great round arches, painted blue. The front *apse over the chapel is draped with great colored banners coming on four sides to form a huge crown—red, green, yellow. The *Stations of the Cross are spotted along the side of the sanctuary in the alcoves, with banners of holy Mary and other scenes on the intermittent pillars. The pews are wooden, and there is a nicely tiled floor in black and white. The crowd is not huge on this Sunday afternoon, perhaps only about 150, but there are young people and some children; it is hard not to compare the attendance with the thousands in the Protestant church. There are several foreigners besides us—white, black, Indian in appearance—making up about 10 percent of the congregation; in the Protestant church, we had seemed to be the only non-Chinese in attendance. As we wait for the service to start, I see the priest hearing confession off to the side in a slightly enclosed prayer station with the penitent visible to the outside. The priest has a warm face and preaches with passion, though he speaks far more briefly than his Protestant counterpart. The choir is quite excellent and sings throughout—a tenor soloist chants verses of the Psalms and leads the choir. Congregational participation in singing and following the text of the Bible is marked (I have not seen the latter in many Catholic Western churches!), though the note taking is not as assiduous as in the Protestant congregation that I attended the week before.

The music is intriguing—East meets West, with a *Taizé style.[44] Some of the chanting has an Asian flavor, while other parts of the service could have been heard in any Western liturgical setting. The atmosphere is reverent, but not stuffy—in fact, it is a bit brisk and straightforward. The Scripture readings and Psalms are read in English as well as in Mandarin. Everything else is in Mandarin, but some key words (for example, the Scripture references) are projected in English on a screen to the side, which is helpful for the 10 percent or more who need it. The liturgy is quite "high": creed and Lord's Prayer are sung, and the people bow and kneel at key moments. Incense is offered to honor the altar, the priest, the deacon, and the people.

Following our conversation in the van, I wait a little nervously for the Eucharist, in line with others. But several before me only receive a blessing, and so I do not receive the elements but cross my arms like them in the fashion of L'Abri, the signal for a blessing which is evidently known here as well as in Europe and America. As we come to the end of the service, there is another cycle of music, this time with contemporary Hebrew-type Scripture songs. At this point, newcomers are called up front and welcomed with a clapping song—the same routine as in the Protestant church, so it must be cultural. They are invited to a Saturday night inquiry class: I suspect that those who asked for a blessing during Mass were *catechumens or inquirers, and that this church is growing, though not with the same explosiveness as the Protestant church we attended the week before. If it is costly to be a Christian in China, it is even more costly to be a Catholic. I am sorry that our Chinese hosts have no personal connections with this church, for I will not have an opportunity to actually converse with these brothers and sisters. I am left to wonder about the similarities and differences, though I have entered into worship with them. Indeed, "hour by hour fresh lips are making His wondrous doings heard on high."

Gathering the Fragments

Our tour during this chapter began with the liturgical and ended with the liturgical but has included widely divergent expressions of Christian worship. As we gather up the fragments of this very full meal, no doubt we are left with questions, some of which we will broach in our next (and final) chapter. We have seen, however, that even where it is not consciously articulated, there is still today among Christians of various contexts a certain remembrance of worship as entrance. Entrance into a common company is seen especially in the common recital of the Lord's Prayer and the creed, as well as in the songs and hymns that span denominations or generations. The continued practice of the communal assent "Amen!" continues in various forms, as well as a diligent welcoming of newcomers, for whom accommodation is made in very different ways. Many of the hymns and praise songs acknowledge the praise of the angels or of creation, and several of the groups (the American Catholics, the Presbyterian congregation, the Chinese Protestants) state explicitly that to be a disciple is to enter into a studying community.

Not all of the groups conceived of their worship as a gradual entrance going more deeply into the presence of God, but some did, and most (with the exception of the Salvationists) understood this deepening entrance to coincide with the Eucharist itself. Not one of the groups isolated itself completely from the rest of the Church—not even the Chinese church, with its concern for self-sufficiency, nor the emergent group with its new departures. Instead, by song and action, Christians in all these congregations enacted entrance into sacred history and into a larger community than their local one. The use of the trinitarian name was found at the benediction in the services we visited. Continued prayer to the Father, by the Son, through the Holy Spirit may lead, upon reflection, to the sense of entrance into and participation in God's own life.

Though all would not articulate it this clearly, it would seem that every one of the congregations that we have visited would concur with the luminous words of Archbishop of Canterbury William Temple, who describes worship in this way: "Worship is the submission of all of our nature to God. It is the quickening of conscience by His holiness; the nourishment of mind with His truth; the purifying of imagination by His beauty; the opening of the heart to His love; the surrender of will to his purpose."[45] It is less clear, however, that all the Christians who gathered in these places that we have "visited" could then go on to affirm the phrase with which Temple concludes his definition: "—*and all this gathered up in adoration, [which is] the most selfless emotion of which our nature is capable.*"[46] This is because, for some Christian congregations, worship is more often conceived as an aid to something else, not as a "selfless" expression directed toward the Lord alone. Indeed, it is this "something else" that has become for some worshiping bodies the "main show," the greatest of human expressions, the supreme action that surpasses even worship itself—whether this be mission, human community, instruction in the Scriptures, individual experience of God, or evangelism. So we move on to our final chapter, in which we will troubleshoot, trying to determine where Christians have, in their communal worship, unwittingly given up their birthright. That is, where does it appear that today's congregations are failing to grasp the primacy of entrance into worship, the wonder of crying, "Abba! Father!"? In the final chapter, we will look for the distractions and the weaker elements of our worship today, suggesting practical steps that pastors and worship leaders can take to help restore worship to its God-given place as the foundation of the Church's full life.

Questions for Discussion

1. We have seen that the traditional term for Eucharist early came to be the *Mass*, a word related to the Latin verb *missio* ("I send"). In what ways are entrance into worship and mission into the world related? Do the different terms *Divine Liturgy, Mass, meeting,* and *service* imply different understandings of the purpose of worship?
2. How important are physical surroundings and actions to worship? Do you think that architecture affects the kind of praise or the implicit theology of a congregation? How significant is the debate concerning whether the priest should face the congregation or the altar during the eucharistic prayers?
3. What are the potential benefits and drawbacks of maintaining a focus on a theme during a worship service?
4. What different ways do various Christian traditions show honor to the written Word and to the Lord during the Communion service?

7

"That Your Prayers Not Be Hindered"

Avoiding Pitfalls in Corporate Worship

In the last chapter, we visited six congregations in North America and two abroad, discovering very different traditions and noticing that the Christian understanding of entrance into worship still persists, even in contexts where it is not consciously articulated. None of the churches described was particularly eccentric in approach, musical style, or constitution, and all of them were, to some extent, prepared to dig into their tradition (or, beyond that, to the Tradition of the historic Church) while responding to the particular needs of their twenty-first-century context. It is likely, however, that anyone reading this book has participated in services less committed to bringing out "of the storehouse [both] what is new and what is old" (Matt. 13:52 EH). Moreover, even in churches that are intent on balance, as my teenaged daughters used to exclaim, "Weirdness happens!"

Sometimes, of course, the weirdness is a comedy of errors, caused by our common humanity and recognized by all for what it is. I well remember the first charge that my husband and I had as Salvation Army officers, back in our midtwenties, when we were mismatched with a small, working-town congregation of mostly senior citizens. We had only a very few young families, who were mostly Sunday-only attenders and not particularly active in the life of the church. After about a month I managed to convince our treasurer, a well-bred and quite retiring thirty-something, to offer the opening prayer in our Sunday morning meeting. It was a *coup*! "Doug" had never done anything but work behind the scenes, and I was very pleased that he was stepping out to do something beyond his comfort zone. When the opening hymn was over, he approached the central pulpit to offer our petitions and intercessions, with me offering an encouraging smile from the piano at the side of the *sanctuary, just below the platform. He started, "Loving and gracious heavenly Father . . ." There was a clatter of toddler feet that registered a surprisingly loud noise on the wood of the central aisle, and then a shrill baby voice cut through his deeper tentative one, "I hafta go POTTY!" I opened my eyes and took in, all at once, Doug's mortified face, the transfixed stare of everyone present, and blond-headed Emily, panties down around her ankles, beseeching her dad for immediate help. Not bothering to figure out where her mother was, I swooped up the little girl who was standing about five feet from the piano and left Doug to regather the congregational mind toward higher matters. I believe that this début in leading public worship was also his last venture.

So much is "up for grabs" in today's world, and so many church traditions are merging and mutating in this "global village" of today, that sometimes we are not even sure whether an element in the liturgy is "weird" and even comical, or whether we are just not used to it. Forty years ago, the presence of *icons in a Reformed church would have been completely out of court—now, no longer. The question remains, of course, as to whether icons really are compatible with Reformed theology, a classically *iconoclastic tradition that would not even, in a past age, permit a doll for baby Jesus in the Christmas pageant. Or we might consider the strange phenomenon of the Canadian Anglican *Book of Alternative Services*, which offers two (incompatible?) versions of the *Nicene Creed for public use—in the service that is more traditional, the creed reads "I believe in the Holy Spirit . . . who proceeds from the Father *and the Son*." In the contemporary service, the congregation is to drop the final phrase and say instead: "I believe in the Holy Spirit . . . who proceeds from the Father." Of course, the omission of the *filioque* ("and the Son") was prompted by ecumenical dialogue with the Orthodox, who point out that this was a later Roman (originally, Spanish) addition to the creed, and that it is both unbiblical (John 15:26) and theologically suspect.[1] It is very odd, however, that twelve centuries of debate between East and West have been obscured by Canadian generosity, which has seen fit to incorporate both versions, as if it were a matter of chocolate or strawberry ice cream for dessert. The substance of the matter seems unimportant, only the form of accommodation and diversity. Sometimes, then, outside traditions have been adopted without the necessary examination of the implications of the "alien" or new element, and the result is an incoherent theology.

And even while this circulation of ideas and practices among the churches is in high tide, we still remain subject, in our small corners, to a kind of isolation.

Still, our churchly and cultural traditions can act as blinkers, or buffers, so that we do not quite notice the problems that we harbor in our worship times but have grown inured to them. Of course, this is only human and is found in contexts other than church. Our family was quite shocked by the deportment of high school students in the public system when we moved from Canada to the United States—in our new US context, we discovered that high-school students cruise the classroom and talk over the teacher and the announcements in ways that would earn them detention in our Canadian home town. Such unhelpful practices and attitudes creep into the churches, too, whether they are of a traditional or nonconformist character. Our ongoing insularity, which is both a matter of geography and of time, means that we frequently accept things that would be unthinkable in many other Christian contexts. In this case, exposure to the whole Church (including the past) and a careful reflection upon our current practice is in order.

When we measure our practices against a foundational idea, such as that of entrance into worship, some things are indeed revealed as weird, or out of place, in an almost absolute sense—those things that systemically distract or even hamper our worship. In 1 Peter, we find sober instructions to husbands concerning their proper attitude and behavior toward their wives, with whom they are "joint heirs of the grace of life" (1 Pet. 3:7). The Epistle is concerned that wrong attitude and action may actually hinder the prayers of the husband, who must live considerately with his spouse. If this is true on the level of the household, how much more must we be considerate in the "household of faith," especially among those of us who have been given the responsibility of leading in worship, at least on a human level. We want to work together within "the grace of life" so that nothing is an ungodly stumbling block, either to those who lead or to any who worship with us, for it is the desire of the Holy Spirit "that [our] prayers not be hindered" (1 Pet. 3:7). In this chapter, we will cite clear examples of practices that hamper corporate prayer as well as actions that might not seem so outlandish but that threaten the integrity of our worship. As we encounter questionable elements in today's worship scene, they may appear to us to be an irregular assortment of bizarre occurrences. In order to help us to think about these difficulties with a critical eye, and to tame the onslaught into something more manageable, we will group them under these areas: atmospherics, human-centered worship, distorted teaching, misshapen liturgy, and "using" worship. Under each category, we will analyze both the serious as well as the more subtle threats to worship today.

Atmospherics: Linen or Kitchen Table?

Many today approach worship as a kind of spiritual meal. Like all metaphors, this language is both helpful and has its limitations. After all, both the Word

and the Eucharist are associated with "bread" that proceeds from the mouth
of God. The downside to this picture, however, is that we limit our understanding of worship to something that edifies or fills us, rather than an action
into which we are called to enter as participants. This can make for an almost
wholly passive approach—indeed, to a belief that worship is something that
we consume. When the table becomes the dominant metaphor, unchecked
by other biblical and traditional views of what worship is, then it becomes
natural to pose the basic question: "What kind of meal and what kind of food
presentation are to my taste?" Do I have a yen for (or would I *always* prefer)
a formal meal, complete with lowered lights, linen cloths, candles, and a full
complement of dishes; or do I favor more of a kitchen-table, no-frills, hearty
meal? Or how about a whacky yellow deli counter, matching the exotic meal
suited to my particular palatte?

These pictures may seem to trivialize the worship of the Church, but they
are not far from the way that many think about such things. "Atmospherics"
becomes as important as the meal itself and is then the main thing noticed
about a service. When mood dominates in this way, strange things take place.
For example, a commitment to upbeat meetings consonant with the "seeker-
friendly" commitment of Rick Warren's Saddleback Church has all but ban-
ished the use of the minor key for that community:

> Ask: how does this tune make me feel? . . . The wrong kind of music can kill
> the spirit and mood of a service. . . . At Saddleback, we believe worship to be
> a celebration, so we use a style that is upbeat, bright and joyful. We rarely sing
> a song in a minor key.[2]

This may seem merely an offhand remark on the part of Rick Warren, and
it has since been clarified by the church's "Pastor of Magnification," Rick
Muchow. His explanation adds nuance to Warren's comment. Yet he still
retains the priority of mood and the significance of feeling as he explains the
decisions in planning worship that they deem helpful for seekers:

> When pastor Rick Warren talks about songs in a minor key, he is addressing
> the issue of how music makes you feel. One of our principles at Saddleback is
> to keep the music and the message upbeat for the seeker-sensitive audience. . . .
> The key of a song is an expression of tonality. Tonality impacts emotion, but
> so do lyrics and tempo. An example of a song considered a minor key upbeat
> song is "Awesome God." The tonality of the song evokes an emotional response
> of reverence and awe. We use that song at Saddleback. There are also major
> key songs that may not be upbeat. We would not use those songs. It's not so
> much about the key of the song as how the song makes people feel, and many
> minor key songs make people feel sad and hopeless. It's about not using sad
> songs for evangelism . . . in either a major or a minor key. As you know, pastor
> Rick speaks to a wide audience. . . . He aims to make the services a celebration

of the resurrection rather than a memorial service. . . . Everything boils down to how the song makes you feel. If the result is that people are drawn closer to God and ready to hear the message, then pastor Rick loves it![3]

It is clear from this interview that Warren's drive for purpose and upbeat evangelism comes from a reaction to services that are funereal and depressing. However, in both Warren's own words and in the explanation of his worship director, we see an emphasis upon atmospherics that may well lead to manipulation and that deforms reality as well as impoverishing worship. Worship, as we have seen, is not celebration alone, but includes the full spectrum of preparation, sobriety, repentance, confession, and lament, as well as corporate witness, reception, joy, and watchful anticipation. At the least, worship is both penitential and celebratory, in honor of the death and life of Jesus, the Lord of our worship. To reduce awe to "an emotional response," as Rick Muchow does, is problematic. So is Rick Warren's guiding question: "Ask: how does it make me feel?" Note that Warren's question blends emotionalism ("feel") with individualism ("me"). (This combination, I submit, is what actually *can* kill worship.) The eschewal of sad music is only the presenting problem: foundational to this diminution of worship are the assumptions that evangelism should set the parameters for worship and that worship is all about feelings and mood. It is helpful to remember St. Paul's stand on this: worship is for believers, and if nonbelievers come into a God-directed and ordered service, they will have their hearts' secrets laid bare (not very upbeat) and so cry out "God is really among you!" (1 Cor. 14:25).

Recently in a worship conference, I came across another eccentric move based on the assumption that mood is primary. This new trend might not seem so very serious, until we probe its implications. I refer to the decision of some pastors in nonconformist traditions to reverse the natural order of worship, putting the time of Communion before the service of the Word. The rationale for this is that Communion brings the congregation together in intimacy, thus preparing the heart to receive the Lord's Word when it is later read and preached. This strategy of the "ice-breaker" Eucharist may appeal to those who believe that changing things around can keep worship fresh. I have myself been surprised, on mentioning this to others, how many have stopped and wondered if it might be a good idea.

In a church context where the service of the Word, and especially the sermon, are understood to be the main course of the banquet, this reversal may also not seem so far-fetched. Anyone who has prepared a serious message for the people is pleased to prepare them as thoroughly as possible to receive it, as we heard about music choices: "If the result is that people are drawn closer to God and ready to hear the message, then [the] pastor . . . loves it!" The first difficulty with such an approach is that leaders are tempted to manipulate the feelings of the congregation and do not trust the Holy Spirit to bring the message to bear upon God's own people. The second is the assumption that Communion is less important than the reading and exposition of the Word. We cannot, in this study, go into detail regarding a theology of the sacraments and the ongoing debate concerning what the Eucharist is or what happens when it is celebrated. (Is its significance located within the minds and hearts of believers, or is there also something that affects the *elements and/or the entire worship service?) At the very least, however, an awareness of entrance into worship will direct us to think about the Lord's Supper, and indeed any worship service, as something more than a mere exercise in memory or emotion.

Without solving this debate, we can also recall what the Scriptures say about the cleansing role of the Word and the seriousness of receiving the bread and wine without due preparation. Let us remember Jesus' own statement, "You are already made clean by the word which I have spoken to you" (John 15:3); and earlier he had warned them "yet not every one of you [is clean]" (John 13:10), while the story shows that it is on reception of the morsel that Judas actually allowed Satan to enter within (John 13:27). We also noticed in this book's third chapter (on the New Testament) that a similar dynamic is found in St. Paul's warnings to the Corinthians: receiving the Supper in an unworthy condition can cause great harm to the individual and to the community. It is not necessary, then, to come to terms with the historic debates of *"transubstantiation" (Roman Catholic), *"consubstantiation" (some Lutherans), "mysterious change" (Orthodox), "(spiritual) *receptionism" (Reformed), and *"memorialism" (other Christian traditions) in order to acknowledge the healing properties of the Word and the serious nature of the sacrament. (This is not to say that the discussion is unimportant!) To reduce Communion to a preparatory exercise is to get things backward; moreover, it may be inhospitable or dangerous to nonbelievers who will either feel like fish out of water, or participate unwittingly in what is holy, before acquiring any knowledge of the One into whose presence they are entering. He is not a tame lion.

Instead, he is the host at this great table, the One who shows us ultimate love in sacrifice, the One who is the very focus of all adoration. In the end it is not a matter of whether we prefer linen or bare counters, but of whose event this is, and of what God's worship entails. "Stars and angels sing around Him, Center of unbroken praise!"[4] Is this the time to be squeamish at the hors d'oeuvres or to lament that there is a main course before dessert? Is this the time to be enchanted with the sophistication of the choir's chosen *anthem? Is the foot of the cross the place to adopt an air of deliberate informality, assuring people that they should feel at home in their pews, as though it were their living room? No doubt there will be things that distract those who worship, for we are only human, and it is hard to "put aside all earthly care."[5] If we are honest, we will concur with the songwriter, who laments, "Prone to wander, Lord, I feel it."[6] In all this, however, there are some attitudes and some practices that we would do well to reconsider, so that the sources of distraction are not systemic in our gatherings.

To begin with, it seems right, in the presence of the holy Lord and all his angels, that we should eschew two extremes: it is neither helpful to adopt a stuffy and self-advertising formality, nor is it truthful to put on a deliberate informality (we are "just folks" here), as though embarrassed by what we are doing. After all, it's not about us. The use of "holy cocktail music" during times of reverence like the Lord's Supper is not a sure way of directing worship, especially when the lyrics or musical line are sentimental and inward-directing. Silence may sometimes be better, even if it "feels" awkward at first. When music is used, it should be selected carefully so that it does not become a distraction either by its tune or lyrics: is it too imposing, or do the lyrics describe "feelings" that may express some, but not all, of the congregation's response? Better to sing of those things that are always true: the Lord's faithfulness and love. Again, the default expression of constant noise and chatter does not always make for a warm and intimate community but may just be a habit in which our congregations indulge. Those leading worship may find ways of encouraging reverence—a written reminder as people enter the sanctuary that this place is "holy to the Lord," the nonmanipulative use of singing into which everyone can enter, even the refusal of the leaders themselves to be distracted as they adopt a God-directed gaze. At all costs to be avoided are comments upon the congregational lack of fervency or the beauty of the song being sung! (Consider how this immediately redirects the worshiper's attention to himself or herself, or to the music and lyrics rather than the Lord for whom these are given.) The enemy to true worship is self-consciousness. Those who are worship leaders may be "doorkeepers" or "ushers," but the Lord is the host, and it is by God's own invitation that we may enter. Perhaps it is time to put down our napkins and to fall upon our faces.

Human-Centered Worship: It's All about Us, Jesus

Already the question of mood has led us to what may well be the deepest problem in today's worship. Despite numerous songs to the contrary, it is very easy for those who gather today to think that it is indeed "all about us" or even worse, "about me." *How does it make me feel?* At its most egregious, this orientation leads worship leaders to co-opt doctrine and worship in order to glorify or showcase humanity, or to push their pet human theory. One obvious example would be what I call "the Wonder-Bread Eucharist," because of the time that I attended a liturgy in which different loaves were used at the communion table—each representing different cultures, or peoples, with "Wonder Bread" representing African Americans. Though there seems to be a tradition in American sermonizing that uses Wonder Bread, both positively and negatively as an image of spiritual nourishment, I rather wonder what African Americans themselves might think of being represented by this cheap sliced loaf, over against a baguette or a whole-wheat offering! But that is not the point. Consider one instance of this kind of service, which has grown popular in some quarters, especially for the observance of "World Communion Sunday":

> We bring arepas to the table. Arepas come from the native people of Venezuela, and are the staple bread in parts of South America. There and throughout the world people struggle to survive through spiraling inflation, income inequality and high unemployment. We eat arepas today to remember people in poverty.
> —Lord, we pray for opportunity.
> We bring pita bread to the table. Pita bread is a staple throughout the Middle East. There and throughout the world, people struggle to maintain hope through war and ethnic and religious tensions. We eat it today to remember all those living in the midst of war and fear.
> —Lord, we pray for peace.
> We bring rice crackers to the table. Rice is a staple in China and many other Asian countries. There and throughout the world, people struggle against political oppression that stifles their religious practice and freedom of speech. We eat rice cakes today to remember those longing for freedom.
> —Lord, we pray for justice.
> We bring injera to the table. Injera is a staple throughout Ethiopia. There and throughout the world, people struggle to survive through famine brought on by natural disaster and political strife. We eat it today to remember those who are hungry.
> —Lord, we pray for compassion.
> We bring whole grain bread to the table. Whole grains are used in the developed world to combat a variety of illnesses. There and throughout the world, people struggle with health problems brought on by too little or too much food, an unhealthy environment and numerous other causes. We eat this bread today to remember those who are sick.
> —Lord, we pray for healing.
> We bring French bread to the table. Baguettes are common in affluent households in the US and Europe. There and throughout the world, people struggle to maintain balance between their own affluence and comfort and their desire to help people in need. We eat it today to remind ourselves to fight for that balance.
> —Lord, we pray for wisdom.[7]

Of course, concern for poverty, illness, and for the indifference of the affluent healthy is meet and right. But note how heavy-handed didacticism has crept into the moment of acknowledging Jesus' offering, to which we join our gifts to God: the Eucharist becomes yet another sermon, rather than a time of God's gift, Christ's offering (and ours), receiving and resting in the Lord. Secondly, there is no distinction made here between the various peoples of the earth and the new people of God who are in Christ. Thirdly, the bread now has become all about us—our affluence, our acceptance of unhealthy environments where others are concerned, our political strife, our poverty. We forget Jesus' words to Judas: "you will not always have me with you." Even the point of mystery, where angels sing the holy song, is bent to a practical teaching purpose. Though we have seen that *one* intent of the classical liturgy is for the bread to represent God's people, gathered together and offering themselves before the Lord, this is not the whole, *nor even the foundational* meaning of Communion. Where is there room in this Eucharist to hear the solemn and thrilling echo of Jesus' words "this is *my* body; this is *my* blood"? Where is the adoration of the Lamb, who takes away the sins of the world, and who by his body heals us? The remembrance, the thanksgiving is misdirected, and we curve inward, retreating into ourselves rather than entering into worship by the veil that Christ has opened. Communion is supplanted by a lesser agenda.

There are, of course, some churches in which this particular distortion could not take place, either because there is a view of the Supper that would not encourage it, or because the elements of the Eucharist are governed by canon law or by very deep tradition. But the same solipsistic tendency is expressed in places of worship besides Communion. There was, for example, the "re-imagining" of the *Stations of the Cross[8] promoted in 2008 by the Episcopal Relief and Development agency (Episcopal Church, USA). In this publication, the number of stations (normally fourteen) is reduced to eight, matching the United Nations' Millennium Development Goals. Instead of offering scenes for meditation upon the suffering and pilgrimage of Jesus to the cross for the atonement of the world, various ills and suffering around the globe are represented at each station. The stations are equipped with "activities and worship experiences": those who visit may care to draw, color faces, or ring a bell to signify the death of another poverty-stricken child. Even the ancient *Trisagion* ("Holy God, Holy Mighty, Holy Immortal"), said at each station in the more traditional services, is reconfigured. Its familiar closing line no longer pleads "have mercy on us," but rather shifts the focus to human effort: "Transform us / That we might transform the world."

A similar move to introspection reigned in a Roman Catholic baptism that I attended about a decade ago at a rather progressive seminary chapel in Canada. There, instead of the recitation of the Apostles' or Nicene Creed as part of the service, the couple whose baby was being baptized gave a personal word of witness. Sadly, their witness amounted to this: how hard it is to preserve faith in God (any god!) in today's secular world, and how brave one has to be in order to continue to attend church and to have one's baby baptized. The Church's bold declaration of the foundational identity of the Trinity and the work of Father, Son, and Holy Spirit for us—the creed that binds Christians together—was preempted for a pallid but self-congratulatory parental statement about the importance of "faith." And "faith" was there presented as a human emotion and confidence, not as a gift of God or as a corporate response of Christ's body to the One who is the great Initiator. The baptism had become all about the courageous "will to believe" of the parents, not about what God the Holy Spirit is doing for this child, in the context of the Church that he is redeeming.

Then there is also the growing practice of using congregational confession as a teaching moment. Instead of a confessional prayer that will fit like a shoe upon the foot of any member of the congregation ("forgive us for the things that we/I have done, and left undone . . ."), specific social ills are listed, with an emphasis upon corporate sin. It may indeed strike us as ironic that in an age when much of the worship is individualistic, here in the confession of sin (the one place where personal responsibility is appropriate), the corporate is emphasized! And of course, as a society and in the churches, we have much to confess. However, this particular move in contemporary worship may unwittingly alienate some worshipers ("I don't agree with that pastor's political stand on this issue"), or provide a route to opt out of actual confession—if the sins being confessed are the fault of everybody, then they may be thought of to be the fault of nobody in particular. "We" should confess, but *I* need not, because I don't approve of grinding the faces of the poor, of exorbitant interest rates, and so on; nor do I have personal power to change any of this, anyway! James Hitchcock offers a perceptive analysis of this "nonconfession" now becoming popular in some mainline churches:

> Social Sins are Easily and Fashionably Confessed . . . [O]f their very nature, most "social sins" are experienced from a distance. A man whose wealth derives from immoral investments or from injustices perpetrated by his ancestors is implicated in something he can know about only through study. But when a preacher condemns "personal" sins—theft, lying, assault, abortion, unchastity—every hearer knows immediately whether or not he is guilty and whether he is obliged to amend his life. . . . [C]onfessing to social sins can actually be a way of avoiding a real sense of one's own moral failure.[9]

There is something in an authentic moment of repentance that cries out, "against Thee, thee only have I sinned" (though we know that our sin affects others); the true penitent will also cry out, "I have done (or not done) this through my own grievous fault" (even though we know that every human being sins). We are, of course, ingenious at keeping the Holy Spirit at arm's length. And so, through the well-meaning efforts of liturgists who would use the moment of confession to remind us of societal ills that need to be changed, confession morphs to become an extension of the sermon and loses its raison d'être. Or even worse, the social confession may encourage worshipers to lose touch with the reality of their own sinfulness, projecting sin upon those with different social views: "Striking one's breast over social sins can even be a pharisaical gesture by which the individual announces that, morally, he is leagues ahead of his fellow Christians who do not even recognize such sins."[10]

A more subtle example of co-opting elements of the faith is the increasing tendency to adopt the Holy Trinity as a mascot for our view of reality. Consider the theology implicit in a verse by the popular hymnist Brian Wren:

> When leaders meet with angry sound, / yet bridle their hostility,
> And bargain to a common ground, / to end with unanimity,
> Then welcome all the hope that's won / in every kind of unity,
> And join the dance in God begun, / whose nature is community.[11]

It is certainly the case that all love and unity is the gift of God—Father, Son, and Holy Spirit. The human virtue extolled in the hymn is that of finding common ground by compromise, since God's very nature is "community." This is, like all appealing ideas, a half-truth. Certainly we have received teaching about the intercommunion of the Persons of the Holy Trinity. But along with this goes also the great mystery that the Son is eternally begotten of the Father, and the Holy Spirit ever proceeds from this same Father. So then, the unity of the Godhead is personal, in the Father, not in an external principle of democracy or the finding of common ground amidst diversity. (As though the divine Persons could ever be at loggerheads and require compromise!) Latent in the hymn is the assumption that numerous positions are valid and that diversity, including diversity of views, is always a good thing, so long as we can get along.

I agree with Wren's move to teach the church about human reality by looking to the sacred foundation of all—the Triune God. But we have seen already that in our love affair with individualism and egalitarianism, we need the *corrective* implied in the mystery of the Holy Trinity, so far as we can fathom this mystery, from what has been taught to us by the Scriptures and by the ongoing Tradition of the Church. In the Godhead, mutuality is not at war with submission, nor does mutual regard destroy order. The Son obeys the Father even while the Father exalts the Son; the Holy Spirit delights to call attention to the glory of the Son even while the Son speaks of the great things to which the Holy Spirit will lead us. Along with their equality and mutual recognition of divinity, there is a deference of Son to Father and Spirit to Son. The Trinity, then, cannot be made a symbol of democratic ideals, of unity through diversity, or of egalitarian social politics. Instead, we perceive in the mystery of the Holy Trinity a call to obedience alongside mutuality: a great mystery that would help us in our families, in churches, and perhaps even in our nations, during this era when there is a great crisis concerning the nature of authority. God's people, by their hymns, are called to adore the Triune God and allow God to speak into their situation. We are invited to enter into reality, not to reimagine God according to our fond ideas. True entry and worship of the *God who is* is prevented when we seize facilely upon one aspect of the doctrine that pleases us (community) and so tame the holy mystery.

Along with the drive for egalitarianism is also the other twenty-first-century malady with which we began this study—our rank individualism. I suspect that we do not even notice how much of our corporate worship has degenerated into a kind of spiritual "parallel play" such as that which we see among toddlers who are not yet socialized. The most obvious example of this that I have witnessed took place in a Vineyard service, where during "ministry" time, a quick look around made it clear that, for an extended period of time, individuals, at the encouragement of the leader, were seeking isolated heightened spiritual experiences without regard for those around them. We must avoid the tendency to imagine worship in a vertical dimension only, "me and Jesus," with the music promoting the experience, the singing designed to speak about "my" Jesus at the expense of "our Lord," the message judged insofar as it furthers my own spiritual growth, the communion service viewed as a locale where the Lord deals with me alone, and so on.

Encouraging this kind of emphasis upon the individual experience can actually cause isolation for those who are in pain, at a difficult time of life, or simply not "in sync" with the "feelings" around them. I remember well the pull on my arm of a concerned four-year-old during an emotive time in a revival service—"Mommy, I don't know if *I* love Jesus!" Some might have seen this as the opportune time to lead my child to Christ. What I saw in those anxious little eyes, however, was a feeling of being left out of the emotional fervor that was being fueled by the very individualistic songs that we were singing. My response to her was, "Honey, what is more important right now is that Jesus loves you, and all of us!" Adults also may be driven to such unhelpful introspection when they cannot easily enter into expansive lines like: "More than all my lips can utter, more than all I do or sing, is the depth of my devotion to my Saviour, Lord, and King."[12] These have their place. But more songs that extol what is *always* true—the majesty, love, greatness, tenderness of the Lord—will truly unite people, for they point us beyond ourselves to *reality*. While those leading worship should not seek to eradicate the personal impact of worship (and if the Holy Spirit is among us, how would this be possible?), they should be aware that many of us are now "experience junkies" and that their planning for the communal dimension of worship must be deliberate. "I" language must be balanced with "we" language, and even better, with "You" language that addresses and extols our holy God. This is much harder than it seems, as any musical director knows who carefully examines the cache of songs and hymns available for singing, both traditional and contemporary. It's not all about us; and leaders must be countercultural in a day that has forgotten this truth, and in which this amnesia has skewed our hymnody and our liturgical expression.

There is, I believe, one ancient tradition of the Church that has all but been forgotten in many quarters. This is to read the Psalms not as expressive of human experience, but as from the mouth of the Lord, or as pointing to Jesus. Certainly, many of the Psalms are intensely personal, with the "I" voicing many of the experiences common to all of God's people. However, from the very earliest times, Christians read the Psalms christologically, believing that as they were associated with David under the old covenant, for Christians they are now associated with the true Messiah, Jesus. We receive this pattern even from the New Testament, which locates Psalm 22 in the mouth of the crucified Lord, or which reads the Psalms in terms of Jesus: think even of Jesus' argumentative quotation of Psalm 110:1, concerning what "the LORD said to my Lord" (Mark 12:36 KJV). Reading the Psalms in this way prevents us from stumbling over those passages that do not articulate my feelings—for example, I may not be, at any one given moment, weighed down, or lifted up. But our Lord Jesus *was* weighed down and *is* lifted up for our sake! Our loss of this christological dynamic is now so thorough that many did not notice when the NRSV version, and some of the contemporary psalters used in liturgical churches, changed third-person singular language to the plural. Of course, the reason for this change was so that the Psalms could be heard inclusively: we must stipulate in English whether it is "he" or "she" in the singular, but the plural "they" does double duty. But notice what happens when we read the contemporary versions of Psalm 1:1–3 (NRSV):

> Happy are those who do not follow the advice of the wicked, or take the path that sinners tread, or sit in the seat of scoffers; but their delight is in the law of the LORD, and on his law they meditate day and night. They are like trees planted by streams of water, which yield their fruit in its season, and their leaves do not wither. In all that they do, they prosper.

But that is not what the psalm says! Rather, it says "happy is the *man* who . . ." (Here in the original language, the masculine-specific word for man is used, not the inclusive word for humanity or a human being.) There are not *many* who meditate day and night on the Torah, and who prosper in all that they do. But there is One who is always and ever so blessed. Psalm 1 is the picture of *the* Human Being, the true human as God intended us to be—and only One has lived in this way. "One is Holy, One is the Lord Jesus Christ," as the Eastern liturgy puts it. Of course, the psalm lays out a good path for all believers, whether male or female. But it is because it has been fulfilled by the One true Man that we can hope to emulate this pattern.

The first time I came to understand this traditional method of reading the Psalms was in my first vesperal service of the Orthodox. The priest, as Psalm 1 was recited (which is usual on Great *Vespers), stood directly in front of the icon of Christ and meditated upon the One who meditated upon the Law day and night. Like a flash, I understood! The Psalm was fulfilled in the Lord, and this Psalm is the introduction to the whole Psalter, which points to him and is fulfilled in him alone. In Christ, we can sing this psalm. As a reference to godly behavior alone, it is merely didactic and loses its power. I have, since that first revelation, had the joy of reading Fr. Patrick Reardon's *Christ in the Psalms*,[13] which is informed by both the Western and Eastern Christian tradition of reading the Psalms so as to see Christ. The very reading of the Psalms in worship is a corporate entry into Christ, not simply an expressive moment of our feelings—individually or as a group.

We can judge, I think, whether or not we have forgotten about the focus of worship by a simple test. How do we respond to our children at the odd times when their service comes to the fore in our liturgies? When the junior choir sings, do we applaud, rather than entering into worship by means of infant voices? When the children come forward for a blessing or a story, does the animator begin with a comment like, "My, how nice you all look today!" (I've heard this kind of superficial approval in two different denominational contexts.) When the teens take the service, or participate in the liturgy, do we expect a culture shock, or anticipate that the spotlight will be placed upon their talent? Or have we encouraged them to participate all through their lives, so that when they are doing more prominent things, they see what they are doing as a service to the Lord and to the Church? If we put our children on parade, showcasing their gifts or their appearance in the name of encouragement, then we need to consider not only how we want them to understand worship but also what we understand worship to be. It's not about us. In authentic worship, however, we discover not only the "pearl of great price" but also who we really are.

Teaching: Itching Ears and Misguided Tongues

These crucial discoveries concerning the nearness of God and our authentic identity among God's people, however, will be hampered if the element of teaching, an integral part of worship, misfires. I had been tempted to subtitle this section "Itching Ears and Crooked Tongues." However, that would imply rather too much direction and knowledge on the part of the many teachers who shape our worship. Often, for example, the teaching takes place in hymnody and songwriting—in the old Latin adage, *lex orandi, lex credendi* ("what is the rule in praying is—or becomes—the rule in belief"). One Christian poet mischievously laments the trends of today's hymnody:

Is Heresy More Harmful
When Preached or When Sung?

'Tis hard to say if greater harm is done
When heresy is preached or when it's sung,
But I will argue that the latter's worse—

More virulent is heresy in verse.
For heresy may do much greater harm
Once melody and rhythm have disarmed
One's judgment, and one's reason has been charmed
(With ease the foe may take the citadel
That's guarded by a sleeping sentinel);
And songs make us partake in heresy
Which makes us guilty of complicity;
And sermons stay not long between the ears
But song words linger in our heads for years
—The music and the metre make them stick.[14]

Few of our contemporary songwriters are intent to pass on heresy; rather, where the songs are weak or in error, these authors are more usually misguided. So, too, with those who edit the hymns from the past for today. Mostly, they are trying to interpret obscure phrases in hymns that will not be readily understandable. "Here I raise my Ebenezer" (from Robert Robinson's "Come Thou Fount") is deemed too obscure for a generation that doesn't know the details of the Old Testament narratives, so someone changes the line to "Here I find my greatest treasure," ensuring that it still scans, and rhymes with "pleasure." Why not, instead, teach the story of 1 Samuel 7:12–14, so that worshipers learn about the "stone of help" erected as a memorial?

Or, there are the well-meaning changes to Charles Wesley's hymns. His profound "And Can It Be?" for example, has been altered in some hymnals. A line that originally exclaimed, "Amazing Love! How can it be! That Thou my *God* should'st die for me?" now reads "That thou my Lord should'st die for me." With this one change, we may easily miss the paradox of the *God* who died, the very reason for sheer amazement by humans and angels alike! The Lord Jesus died, yes. But that is not all. For the Lord Jesus is *YHWH, the LORD, and so we cry out, with Wesley's subsequent verse: "'Tis mercy all, Th'Immortal dies!" Contemporary alterations like this should cause us to wonder whether there are ethical (rather than simply legal) dimensions to honoring the original author, especially when we recall Charles Wesley's own impassioned plea:

> Many gentlemen have done my brother and me (though without naming us) the honor to reprint many of our hymns. Now they are perfectly welcome to do so, provided they print them just as they are. But I desire they would not mend them—for really they are not able. None of them is able to mend either the sense or the verse. Therefore I must beg of them one of these two favors: either to let them stand just as they are, to take them for better for worse; or to add the true reading in the margin, or at the bottom of the page, that we may no longer be accountable either for nonsense or for the doggerel of other men.[15]

Had Wesley written in the twenty-first rather than the eighteenth century, I believe that he would have added "error" to his lament concerning revisionist "nonsense" and "doggerel."

Of course, there is a fairly long tradition of updating familiar hymns, altering "thee" to "you," for example. Such changes are hardly detrimental to worship, though it is unfortunate that contemporary worship has no way of distinguishing between the personal address to "you" singular and the corporate "you." Yet, the editor's pen is often more ambitious. Numerous alterations now include, of course, the move to inclusive language both for human beings and for God. Even John Milton does not escape the axe! So his magnificent hymn, "Let us with a gladsome mind / Praise the Lord, *for he* is kind" is altered in the newest Canadian hymnal to "Praise the Lord, *forever* kind!" But in one sweep, the *reason* for our praise—God's forbearing nature—is dropped. Thus the song no longer mirrors the Psalter, which often supplies a reason for our praise in a phrase beginning "for . . ." "Oh, give thanks unto the Lord . . . *for* his mercy endures forever, alleluia!" Instead we are left with a kind of platitude that, without intent, has impoverished our worship.

But it is also the case that some of the alterations to older hymns are not cosmetic but substantive and theological in motivation. There has been a concerted effort in several mainline Protestant churches to alter the trinitarian name, for example, along the lines suggested by Brian Wren[16] and others. Accordingly, "Mother" is offered to balance or even to supplant Father, or personal language is dropped for "role" language, and the Trinity is described as, for example, "Creator, Redeemer, and Sustainer." Much could be said about these moves, and there is a great deal of literature available to help Christians through the debate.[17] Perhaps three points will be useful for those who continue to worry about this trend in the churches, and who are responsible for deciding which hymnal should be purchased or which version of the overhead song should be projected.

First, we should remember that the Triune God is a reality not dependent upon how God works for us and in our world; our worship language for the Trinity is inadequate if it simply names God in terms of God's work in the world, without recognizing the inner-relationship between Father, Son, and Holy Spirit, as the Church has done for millennia. We explored some of this mystery earlier in the book, where we considered what it might mean to enter into the life of the Holy Trinity by means of our offering worship. To speak only of the "economic" Trinity (that is, God working among the "household of the Church") is inadequate.

Second, the Holy Trinity is a mystery who has been revealed to us through Jesus, the Son: "no one knows the Father except the Son and any one to whom the Son chooses to reveal him" (Matt. 11:27). Because the truth is something revealed, not gained by human speculation, we must be very careful in assuming that the language is "merely" metaphorical ("window dressing") and therefore we can substitute metaphors more to our taste. We cannot be confident that substituting "Mother" for "Father" does no damage because we cannot get to a vantage point outside of the Holy Trinity so as to compare a human father, a human mother, and the Holy Trinity against them. The use of gendered language to describe God and Israel, Christ and the Church, is so knit into the fabric of the biblical text that we might guess that the masculine language is significant, even while we recognize that the Father does not have a body, and so is not "male." It is, in any case, rather cheeky to think that we have better insight than the Lord Jesus who cried out "Abba! Father!" Was the Jesus who argued theology with the Samaritan woman so blinded to the problem of inclusivity that his language must be corrected?

Third, our ancestors in the faith spent long hours poring over the biblical texts and so responded to the challenges of the Church in working through the trinitarian language. Yet we think nothing of encouraging songwriters with little understanding of this mystery to "bring many names"—and forget that what may be an authentic devotional outpouring of their hearts is now teaching the people, who get precious few sermons on the Holy Trinity today anyway.

This brings us beyond hymnody, indeed, to Christian worship as a whole. I wonder if we have considered the crisis of the "disappearing Trinity" in today's worship. Those who do not have a standard liturgy may not even notice how infrequently Father, Son, and Holy Spirit are invoked—and yet, at one time, this was the deepest characteristic of Christian confession! Even those who continue to offer a closing benediction in the trinitarian name do so sometimes as a mere formality. The people are hardly by this one closing cadence drawn into the wonder that we have been shown, by the Lord Jesus and the Holy Spirit, a little of the inner life of God, expressed in this triune name. Indeed, there are Christian thinkers today who join the skeptics and scoff at the "philosophical" language of the creeds (in the vein of Rudyard Kipling's "tangled Trinities"). When folks in the congregation *do* think about the Trinity, they may do so by means of *The Shack*, rather than through careful preaching, or through the long-term language of the prayers and hymnody of the Church. For such preaching is considered obscure, and such prayers and hymns are being abandoned in favor of more easily accessible fare. Our worship of Father, Son, and Holy Spirit, done deliberately and in awe, is a first step to our coming to understand the Triune God better. Worshipers are not done a service by being given "dumbed-down" language that assumes they do not want to lift their minds to such mysteries. Indeed, they may, by the habits of those around them, be encouraged to drop the matter of the Triune God entirely, worshiping only in the name of Jesus, or thinking of a shape-changing ("modalist") God who is at one time Creator, at another Jesus, at another a life-force. Added to this is the very unfortunate tendency, even among clergy, to refer to the Holy Spirit as a "that" or a "which" rather than a "who"—yet Jesus himself spoke of the Holy Spirit in personal terms and encouraged his disciples to do likewise.[18]

Let's close this section on the hindrances of distorted teaching by thinking a bit about the reading and proclamation of the Word of God. We begin with pragmatics and then will move on to a more urgent concern. Initially, we need to ask *how* should the Word be proclaimed? It is helpful to remember that the proclamation of the Gospel has been associated for long centuries with the incarnation of the Word: congregations stand to hear the Gospel reading not because we give more credence to the Gospels than the Epistles, but because they focus particularly upon Jesus. Honor is due to the reading of the Word, then, because by it and through it we see Jesus. (This is, of course, also true of the Epistles, which explain and apply the Gospels.) In classical liturgies, the priest processes into the midst of the congregation with ceremony, and the reader of the Word is given a blessing, for he or she is doing such an important thing. The proclamation is meant to point to the divine voice, not to call attention to itself. Balance, again, is important: neither a lackluster and hurried reading, with the sense of business-as-usual, nor an overly dramatic, attention-seeking reading, does justice to the Word. The one who reads is handling holy things and must allow the voice of the Holy One to be heard. This is perhaps why the Gospel is, in traditional circles, sung—it is difficult for someone singing to place his or her own eccentric emphasis upon the words, so that people think, "My, what an interesting interpretation." Of course, in some contexts singing is not natural. All the same, the one who reads the Word should pray that he or she becomes transparent, so that God's voice is heard. Treating the reading as a perfunctory duty or a performance is equally distracting. Those who are choosing readers should also ensure that they choose those who are proficient but not self-advertising. Instruction in how to read well, and how to read so as to glorify God, should be a natural thing and not considered heavy-handed or intrusive by those who are asked to read.

We move on to something more substantive. Perhaps the most pressing problem today in full worship is the unfamiliarity of our congregations with the entire Bible—not to mention their understanding of it within the Tradition of the Church. Many congregants will wonder out loud about whether the translations are accurate and worry about whether Dan Brown, author of the bestselling novel *The Da Vinci Code*, has perhaps uncovered a truth hushed up for centuries. Yet they do not know the stories of the Bible, nor have they been well instructed about how the parts of the Bible are mutually interpretative. Especially mysterious is the sweep of the Old Testament, which is not generally known today, though it was the Bible of the Church in the earliest years. In some traditions, there is only one Scripture passage read during a service—that which the pastor will expound upon or use to speak about his chosen topic. In other traditions, such as the Orthodox Church, there are still several readings, but the Old Testament is reserved for services other than the main Sunday one, and these are not attended by as many congregants.

From the very beginning, attention to the "teaching of the apostles" and attendance at the "Liturgy of the Word" (the service for the *catechumens) has been considered essential for the health of the Church. The use of God's written Word in worship is very important, then, and should inform not only the preaching but also the worship in general. The lyrics of our music and prayers should breathe the air of Scripture, and all of our readings should in some way direct us to Christ. (Remember how he himself directed the two on the road to Emmaus to the Old Testament Scriptures, showing how they pointed to himself.) Of course, God cares about the whole of life, and Scriptures speak about the whole of our reality—so the exposition of the Word will also touch on other matters, but should always be centered around our adoration of the Triune God.

Whether the preacher and worship leaders belong to a tradition that follows a *lectionary, or whether sermon series are more common, it is very important that the people get a taste of all of the Scriptures over a period of time, not just the pet topics or passages of those who are leading. If the tradition has some built-in flaws, such as a lectionary that intentionally omits difficult texts (as the Revised Common Lectionary does) or a lectionary that prevents the majority of people from hearing the Old Testament, then the one proclaiming the Word can do something about that. The pastor can direct the reader to reinsert the "difficult text" before reading it; Old Testament texts related to the Gospel or Epistle reading can be supplied in the sermon. May I also plead that the biblical text should never be used as a pretext for something else? God's people are hungry for "every word that proceeds out of the mouth of God"; yet often, they are given far less fare than they can manage, or they are given a stone instead of bread. When the congregation is urged to attend to the reading of the Word, people should not be left puzzled about a real problem in the Bible, a text that is confusing or that requires explanation. It is, for example, a very bad idea to read a text about "the unforgiveable sin" and then to preach about everything in that section without illumining the congregation about this troublesome item. This is a little more difficult for those who are in a tradition that has several Bible readings—even if only one of these is to be focused upon in the sermon, it is not helpful to leave the other readings hanging in the air! These readings have been put together with a purpose, and it is the responsibility of the preacher to show how they relate to each other and to the lives of the people, so that they can enter into a deeper understanding. Again, even if something very significant has happened in the world or the country over the past week, the Bible should itself be taught, not simply used as a diving board for the pastor's ruminations about this urgent matter. The congregation has heard the Bible read—they need to understand it and then perhaps be shown how it relates to that event, not have their focus wholly shifted as though the Bible is less important than the world. It may well be that some ears itch for easier and more common stories:

but a constant and balanced diet of the Word creates a hunger for more, so that God's people, when their appetite is whetted and satisfied, will marvel at the wonders of the Scriptures. St. John Chrysostom, in his third homily on Genesis, put it this way:

> Reading the Holy Scriptures is like a treasure. With a treasure, you see, anyone able to find a tiny nugget gains for himself great wealth; likewise, in the case of Sacred Scripture, you can get from a small phrase a great wealth of thought and immense riches. The Word of God is not only like a treasure, but it is also like a spring gushing with ever-flowing waters in a mighty flood. . . . Great is the yield of this treasure and the flow of this spiritual fountain. Don't be surprised if we have experienced this: our forebears drank from these waters to the limit of their capacity, and those who come after us will try to do likewise, without risk of exhausting them; instead the flood will increase and the streams will be multiplied.[19]

We are called, then, to enter into this flood, not simply to sip at the waters, nor to sprinkle them upon our favorite things or subjects.

Liturgical Shape: Worship à La Carte

Some think, however, that the waters are too shallow! So, alongside or instead of the reading from the Gospels, there are churches that feature readings from Siddhartha or *The Little Prince* or the Qur'an. This leads us to yet another problematic approach in contemporary worship, which might be called "Liturgy à la carte." By this I mean that the various elements of Christian worship are understood as stand-alone items to be positioned at will, and perhaps rearranged, without regard for the inner flow or integrity of a service. Even those who have been immersed in a so-called nonliturgical tradition will concede that there is a usual shape to their own worship gatherings. In revival traditions, the meeting begins with a few songs, then an opening prayer, musical item, Scripture reading, and sermon, followed by an appeal, with soft music building to more stirring and joyful music as the service ends. Extemporaneous prayers, too, take on a shape according to their context, with repeated phrases: "that your kingdom might be extended," "for your glory, Lord," and so on. We have seen already that the two basic units of Christian worship are those of the Word and the Sacrament, and we have queried the helpfulness of reversing the order of these for the sake of novelty or effect. Observation of today's worship will disclose other problems that may occur when we approach congregational worship without a respect for its integrity or structure.

Perhaps the most extreme expression of this today is the experiment attempted in a few emergent congregations—that of putting worship stations in various places around the room, for folks to "taste" and experience at their own will. For example, bread and wine are placed on a table, and people visit this to receive them or not; water is placed on another table, so that someone might come and sprinkle, or dip, remembering their baptism; and so on. This is reminiscent of the alternative classroom of the '70s, with the focus upon individual needs; however, emphasis upon the individual in this case actually suppresses the possibility of corporate worship. At the opposite pole to this cafeteria approach is worship as a concert hall, which is equally damaging to the integrity of worship. In some megachurch contexts, young people gather to hear technically brilliant contemporary Christian music, interspersed with prayer and teaching by the worship leaders. Because of the barrage of new songs, constant movement, and the huge size of the gathering, there is no meaningful entry into the action, except on the part of the performers. Worship for those gathered is reduced to a vicarious emotional experience, rather than being truly "the work of the people."

Then there is the tendency to lift up one element of worship at the expense of others. For example, it is not uncommon for evangelical or charismatic Christians to call the extended period of singing at the beginning or during the service "the worship time," as though the preaching and listening, praying and receiving, were not also worship. Or, in more liturgical churches, sometimes folks come into the service late, in time to receive the Eucharist but without regard for the reception of God's Word; or they leave immediately after receiving, without a care as to the conclusion of the service, the benediction, and the word sending them out. Or perhaps the necessity of being prepared for Communion is not well appreciated, so that confession before Communion is not encouraged (either in personal or corporate form), or the children are hustled into the sanctuary after Sunday school to receive with their parents but without a time of prayer and preparation. This careless approach breeds disregard and creates a culture of indifference that affects not only children but also older members. Conversely, there are some traditions that are so didactic that it is difficult to actually enter into them without reflecting on their meaning. One might think, for example, of the worship leader who exerts a great deal of energy in teaching what the Lord's Supper is *not*—not magic, not a substitute for faith, and so on. But by emphasizing this, he makes the negative instruction a liturgical framework for every Lord's Supper and never allows the people to enter into that which the Lord's Supper *is*. (This is not to say that we should expect worship to be self-interpreting: those coming into the Church, and children, need instruction about the meaning of the parts of the liturgy, but if this is done during every service, it is hard to worship. Separate classes and instruction are a better idea.)

We have seen that some traditions depend a great deal upon a unifying theme in worship. But theme itself might be allowed to dominate so that nothing is allowed into the service that does not further this specific teaching; a rigid or exaggerated concern for consistency in theme may mean that the worship service cannot be balanced or may lend the liturgy an air of entertainment or mere instruction. If the congregational eye is *so* fixed upon the message for the day, it will be difficult for the vision of the people to take in other things that the Lord might have for them. An unrelieved theme of joy, for example, may ring hollow for one who is lamenting and will not leave room for necessary repentance, or awe at the sacrifice of Christ. The liturgy, like the body of Christ, cannot be all ear, or all mouth, or all arm, if it is to invite everyone to enter. Then there is the completely free approach, which simply invites members of the congregation to suggest music on the spot, like a potluck. Such a casual design may be wonderful for a singsong; but if it is the usual approach to liturgy, the congregation may end up with a vitamin deficiency.

Some Christians, especially those who gather for contemporary-style worship, have worried about lack of balance in the wake of the new forms and have fastened particularly on the tendency to repeat choruses or praise songs. Those who are decidedly marked by the Reformed and "Protesting" stance react to this practice, which has become very common in the last thirty years in evangelical and charismatic circles. So they snort that it is the newest version of "vain repetitions" in prayer, against which the Lord himself gave warning. They reason: as Protestants we have spoken against the vain use of repeated prayers when our Catholic friends use the rosary—how is this new practice any different? God hears us the first time—we don't need to say it over and over again. Or, there is an even more cogent objection that has been registered (with some irritation) more than a few times by the evangelical patriarch John Stott, that we sing *"Alleluia! Alleluia!" but "What are we alleluia-ing *about*?" His plea is that we need to retain the purpose clause found in many psalms, that very clause removed by the reviser of Milton's hymn: "Let us with a gladsome mind praise the Lord, *for He is kind*!" Alleluia! Praise the Lord! But *why*? For *what* are we offering our praise? Praises without reason can be mindless, reduced to a mantra, or grist for the mill of ideologues without a sound understanding of the Lord.[20]

Though repetition can be vain, and though repeating, "Praise the Lord" without giving thought to what we know of him can be dangerous, I do not think that this is the major difficulty with most contemporary repetition in songs. Nor is there much danger in the repetition of contemporary songs that they will be treated as magic, giving rise to the vain thinking that by repetition we'll get God's attention. And, of course, repetition is not an evil in itself; after all, the Psalms continuously repeat refrains, and Jesus gave an actual prayer to be repeated, rather than speaking generally, "here are the various subjects that you ought to include in your prayers." Israel repeated the *Shema* daily; Christians throughout the ages have repeated the creeds, the Lord's Prayer, special prayers for help ("Lord have mercy!"), historic prayers like the *Magnificat* of Mary or the *Nunc Dimittis* of Simeon, as well as the beloved sayings of their Lord and the apostles. We have seen that both East and West have been content to repeat prayers in the liturgy, and we notice that even "free" churches settle into a way of speaking, a pattern. Human beings require repetition; indeed, they thrive on it. Consider the four-year-old who must have the same bedtime story night after night—and woe to the mom or dad who drops out one single sentence! No one worries that the rereading of a favorite tale will stifle the child's imagination or create a lifelong phobia that prevents him or her from sleeping if the ritual reading is omitted. We assume that the child's desire matches a need, and we acquiesce despite our own adult boredom. Children of time ourselves, we need repetition for the truth to make its mark upon us as we pass through this life. We need for true words to accompany us as everything else moves on. Nor, surprisingly, are we alone in the appreciation of what is said more than once—the angels sing the thrice-holy hymn, perhaps not merely to honor the Triune God, but because one cry of "Holy!" is just not sufficient for them. Think of Revelation 4:9–10, where it tells us that *whenever* the four living creatures give honor and praise and thanks to the Lamb, the twenty-four elders solemnly cast down their crowns and sing the same song of praise—proclaiming that the Creator is worthy.

So, then, are those who have a visceral reaction, a nervousness concerning repetition in contemporary worship, simply off track? I think not. The important issue seems to be the *use* to which repetition is put, the motivation for it. All too often, it is a matter of exploiting the freedom of liturgy à la carte for the sake of effect (atmospherics), and with the result of intensifying human emotion. By way of response, we should, first, think of the amount of repetition and what is being omitted because of it. How many services are dominated by repeated lyrics, often of mediocre quality, to the exclusion of hymns and prayers that are weighty and that express more perfectly who God is and what God has done? Five contemporary songs sung three or four times may leave no room for "Immortal, Invisible, God Only Wise!"[21] or other weighty hymns that recite salvation history. In classical liturgies of the East and West there is a *balance* of repeated phrases with meaty lyrics in the hymns or the prayers—food for the heart as well as for the mind.

Second, we need to pay heed to *which lyrics* are chosen to be repeated. The lyrical "call-out" is sometimes very disappointing. There are many contemporary songs that have some substance to both the verses and the refrain. But then, the bridge comes, repeated so as to create a moment of emphasis and sometimes to build suspense that is resolved in the final verse or chorus. But what do we repeat? "There is no God like Jehovah!" What need have we to convince ourselves of this? This is not even God's true name (*YHWH, the I Am who I Am), and in the song the refrain grows almost frenetically as though we have to be worked up in a spiritual pep rally in order to truly believe that these are indeed the days when the visions of Elijah, Moses, David, and Ezekiel are fulfilled.[22] But if we are worshiping, then we know that God is acting. And we know that these days are the great fulfillment because they are fulfilled in the Lord Jesus Christ, the One who has shown the nature of the great I AM. So it would be better, I think, to be repeating a refrain about Jesus as the One who has brought in this age.

Or consider the luminous contemporary song that begins, "Light of the World, You stepped down into darkness. . . ."[23] Here are lyrics that train our mind upon the One who is and who loves us. Yet the chosen point of meditation leads us a little *away* from the One whom we are praising, to our own response: "And *I'll* never know how much it cost to see *my sins* upon the cross." This is a sentiment worth expressing, but perhaps there is just too much concentration upon "what I know" and upon "me" at this point: what would happen if another moment were to be chosen to be the transition, the place of stillness upon which the song turns? Concentration upon the One who is the Light, rather than what we know or don't know, would prevent worshipers from sentimentally turning *in* upon their own sense of wonder and move them instead *toward* the Lord.

The fault does not ultimately lie with these talented songwriters but with the "tradition" of many free churches who, in a long-term reaction against formalism in the mainline church, have now formalized the moment of self-reflection. In an environment like this we assume that true worship occurs when I engage in introspection, thinking about *me and Jesus*—or even better is when I have an emotional experience while considering this. It is surprisingly easy for us to actually make such a moment of heightened passion an idol and to think that this is what worship is all about. There will indeed be times when God deals with us personally: but he does this so that we may turn around, so that we may stand outside of ourselves and cry out, as did Magdalene in the garden, "Rabboni!" or as Thomas did in the upper room, "My Lord and my God!" He transforms us that we might become part of the people of God and cry out, "Alleluia" with a countless host of others, unconcerned about our voice, our feelings, our taste!

So, then, songwriters perhaps should consider very carefully which parts of their lyrics merit a moment of pause and meditation—and the psalms and prayers of the Scriptures can be of help here. "Sing praise to him and highly exalt him forever!" (Song of the Three); "Then they cried to the LORD in their trouble, and he delivered them from their distress" (Ps. 107, throughout); "Be exalted, O God, above the heavens! Let thy glory be over all the earth" (Ps. 57:5, 11). Music directors and pastors should also consider with care which songs it might be helpful to repeat and why they want to do this. If it is merely a matter of creating an effect—stirring the emotions, or creating the desire for introspection—then better not to do it. God has his own ways of calling each of our names. But if we need time to pause and think about a certain truth, or to gaze upon the beauty of the LORD, then repetition can be an aid to true entry into the place where we are being called. Repetition, like silence, can sink deep into our minds and hearts. It can also, when misdirected, be a mere distraction or worse, an impediment, turning us in upon ourselves.

Using Worship: Marketing and Magic

A final obstacle to full worship goes beyond being a mere hindrance and becomes an actual stumbling block. I refer to the *use* of worship as a means to something else, rather than acknowledging worship as an action with its own purpose and value. (This is the corporate parallel to that now-familiar phrase "the family that prays together stays together," now rendered something like "the church that worships well grows quickly." Are we to pray *only* to unify our family? Are we to worship together *only* to see "results"?) I suspect that there are more examples of this phenomenon than can be registered in this book, but I will consider three instances—one from a fringe denomination, one from a liturgical denomination, and one found frequently in free-church settings.

The most grotesque example that I have seen is the marketing of the elements of the Eucharist from an e-mail-order site called "Post the *Host."[24] The Web site claims that "God inspired the members of the Open Episcopal Church" to begin this project and gives the following rationale:

> We live in an age when people do not live in the shadow of their priest or the church. They negotiate life and choice according to the information made available to them and they draw down the resources they believe are potent. The Host needs to be readily available for them to be able to make it their primary source of inspiration and direction.

In appealing to readers of the Web site, this enticement is also given:

> We want to encourage people to start the day with Jesus.
> We want people to wake up and smile because Jesus is waiting for them.
> Before they start the day we invite them to receive Jesus in the Host.
> Earth connecting with heaven.
> The visible with the invisible.
> This dimension with another dimension.
> Natural power charged with supernatural power. . . .
> Its power is spiritual.
> It is the plug going in to the socket.
> It is switch on time.

Most Christians reading this advertisement would be appalled and probably not appeased even when they are told that the endeavor is not a profit-making scheme. To divide the elements from the gathered people of God, as though they may stand alone, ready to be used at the will of a single man or woman, is a huge departure from the practice of the Church. This is not the same as bringing the elements to persons confined to their homes by illness or infirmity, who cannot be physically present with the church. It is more reminiscent of some of the extremes of the Middle Ages (e.g., when some spirited away the host to use it as fertilizer in the garden), which ironically this Protestant group seems to have forgotten. But, in fact, this is really only a very radical presentation of the "open table" position that is more commonly commended among Christians today. The members of the Open Church are simply rigorously consistent with their view:

> The central act of "Communion" and the sharing of the Body and Blood of Christ is made available to anyone and everyone without the prerequisite of Baptism and Confirmation. This not only means all Christians, including children and babies, but those of other persuasions. . . . This inclusive principle governs everything.

Asked about whether Communion ought to be practiced in community, they agree heartily, according to their Web site. They insist that the host is consecrated during a service, and that those who partake of it outside that context are "tugged" into the Christian community by the act of reception. The host is therefore the ultimate evangelistic tool, and if it should fall into the wrong hands, "Jesus can take care of himself." We need to ask why they think Communion should serve evangelism, and whether the receiver might not be harmed by their "generosity." (The Web site's facetious response to those who are concerned for the sanctity of the Eucharist—"Jesus can take care of himself"—fails to recognize that Jesus' power or vulnerability is not the point.) Moreover, is it truly inclusive to think that a nonbeliever might become a part of the Church by an action that they do not truly understand, "tugged" against their will, so to speak? The Holy Spirit certainly has ways and means to woo us, but God is personal and does not work in the mode of magic.

Only slightly less alarming than the Post the Host endeavor is the report that I received of a liturgical church that made substitutes for the elements of the Eucharist, not by necessity (as with, for example, the Lord's Supper conducted in a desert or in a prison camp), but in an attempt to enhance the theme or focus of the service. On Pentecost 2009, one Anglican parish served angel-food cake and champagne at the altar—because it was a celebration, the birthday of the Church! So many questions might be asked of this action that it could open up into a book on the significance of the Eucharist and the place of the elements in the Church's action. Surely God can use anything by which to bless us, and we know of incidents in prison camps where water and crackers were used because that was all that was at hand. We know, too, that there is debate between East and West concerning leavened and unleavened bread, that some churches have used grape juice instead of wine, that in some places sensitivities to gluten are honored, and so on. None of these issues are really material to the alteration that was made for this service, however. It was not a matter of conviction, nor of concern for those receiving, in this case. Rather, the focus was upon effect and even upon entertainment in the liturgy. This was something *fun* to do, something celebratory to match the balloons also used for the occasion, and something that fixed the congregational mind upon the enjoyment of "being church."

One wonders what Mary the mother of the Lord, or Mary Magdalene, would have thought had someone offered them champagne at the foot of the cross. Yet again, we see a misfiring of the imagination, a redirection of the congregation toward *themselves*, rather than the adoration of the One who suffered and died for us. The Lord is no angel, to be represented by angel-food. He became one of us and only received sour vinegar when all was accomplished. He is our food and our life-blood, not our dessert.

This disregard for the sacred, for the solemnity of it all, is not so very uncommon in the churches, even where such strange happenings as the angel-food Eucharist would not be tolerated. For example, there is another church where the prayers leading up to the Eucharist were interrupted as the children arrived in the sanctuary; the children were called up to the chancel, and the entire congregation was treated to a dramatized advertisement for Vacation Bible School, complete with clowns and humor. While this was going on, one active little boy ran his tinker toy up and down on the table/altar, and a young lady of three performed pirouettes (not part of the drama) at the front of the church, while the adults dissolved in laughter. After this "word from our sponsor," we proceeded to the "Our Father" and the reception of the elements.

Of course, it is difficult for pastors to always make the right decisions about how to inform congregations about the life of the church (where do we put the announcements?) or about how to encourage families to teach children about reverence. It is clear, however, that in the aforementioned case, the officiating priest had not considered the fallout in interrupting the flow of the service and whether this would hinder his people from preparing for Communion. It was also clear that the "welcome" extended to the children in the service was of the sort that assumed that children cannot truly enter into worship; simply their bodily presence in the sanctuary should be a delight for the congregation. This is actually quite condescending; children often see more in the worship than we do. There are congregations in which children perceive, with the adults, that something big is going on, and they respond—albeit with the level of distraction that we must anticipate in a group of mixed ages and concentration spans!

The difficulty of managing or commending services among the broad family of the church has led some pastors (especially in free churches) to adopt a sequestered approach to worship. In this, they follow the wisdom of the age that like-minded groups do better together. But what does the systematic adoption of "just like us" services say about the nature of the Church? It implies that taste and comfort level should dominate over the body and that Christ cannot bridge generational gaps. So, though we confess that there is in him now "no male and female, slave or free, Jew or Gentile," there apparently remain "twenty-somethings" and grown-up "yuppies." In some churches, then, we often find that the multiple services offered at different hours tend to accommodate to specific age groups (early traditional service for the older group; contemporary service for families at 11:00; evening service for the teens and twenties who don't like to get up on Sunday morning). This is accentuated in other (usually very large) church settings, where the leadership has *deliberately* scheduled parallel services to run simultaneously in different rooms—hymnody and easy-listening contemporary for the adults; straight-edge Christian rock for younger ears; junior church for the school-aged group. Sequestered services may seem practical, responding to the tastes and needs of a diverse church, but we need to think very carefully about the implications, especially if this is the main or the most common way that members engage in worship. It would be very hard for worshipers in a "just like us" service to grasp the enormity of cosmic worship and to see themselves as one among many bringing "peculiar honors to our King."[25] Instead, the actions of the leadership might be thought to suggest that worship happens best with same-group dynamics, rather than in the midst of a host called together from the east, west, north, and south.

This is a matter not of rule, but of wisdom and motivation. As we saw in a previous chapter, there are surely times for special services with special emphases, as for instance when unchurched youth and young adults are introduced to worship. Some may be called to serve and lead worship in a missional situation that requires a particular approach. Those churches that have concern for young parents, and offer a parallel time apart for young children during the service, are called most blessed by young moms with wiggling and vocal two-year-olds. But where these special opportunities are made, they should not be allowed to rule with absolute sway and so rob God's people of the richness of worshiping together, in all the messy complexity and glory of the body of Christ. Children of all ages should participate in worship and in the Eucharist, too, to the degree that they are allowed within the discipline of their church. Teenagers are robbed of their roots when they infer from our church schedules that hymns are not suitable for them. Adults of all ages need the youth, and each other, as they come before the Lord.

In my mind's eye, I see that marvelous scene in *The Lion King* when the whole of the animal kingdom gathers to pay homage to the newly anointed Simba. Whatever one thinks of the animism and ideals of this Disney movie, the weighty effect of its opening scenario is undeniable. The music, with its chant undecipherable except to the few who know Zulu, nevertheless communicates its message of anticipation and welcome:

Nants ingonyama bagithi Baba [Here comes a lion, Father]
Sithi uhm ingonyama [Oh yes, it's a lion]. . . .
Siyo Nqoba [We're going to conquer]

The music swells, coming to a climax as the priestly primate presents the new-born prince to the host of animals far below. "Oh yes, it's a lion; we're going to conquer!" The lion cub looks down, wide-eyed, as animals of every kind stamp for joy. A ray of glory from the unveiling cloud-cover is trained upon the young lion messiah, and the whole assembly bows the knee and closes their eyes in reverence. The first time I saw this, its joyous sobriety brought tears to my eyes, despite the accompanying trite lyrics about the "circle of life." The juxtaposition between old and young, awkward and beautiful, big and small, open and closed eyes, near and far, is evocative of life with all its complexity and simplicity—of each according to their kind, as the Lord made them. And the whole extravaganza, the spectacle of it all, is an apt preparation for the epic leonine drama to follow: even the unwilling are ushered into the story.

We have been wooed by wonder. Worship is interconnected with awe, with being overcome by astonishment. One of the wonders is how the Lord joins together worshipers from many different backgrounds, all one because of their gaze upon him and because of the transformation that he is bringing to us as we become "living stones" in his temple (1 Pet. 2:5). In the best of worship, all those around us become windows or icons, transparent so that we see the glory of Christ through each other, because each of us personally and all of us together are created after the image of the Son. So, for those who for various reasons are involved in smaller situations of worship, I believe that it is important that they enter into the great assembly, from time to time—a grand *synaxis* that will enable them to perceive the great cosmic worship into which we always enter when we kneel before the throne.

Of course, even this worship in the great congregation can become a snare, if we allow it. We can dwell upon the *experience*, or look upon the great assembly itself as the reason for it all, rather than focusing upon the Lord. Those leading the worship might be tempted to lift up God's people, the great mystery of the Church, as the main thing, or speak in hushed tones of the marvelous experience that we are having. If we are tempted to do this, then let us remember that living and praising together requires hard work sometimes! C. S. Lewis displays his usual wisdom when he speaks about the importance of expressing love when there is disagreement among worshipers. Writing in an era before there was a full-blown expression of the "worship wars," he makes invaluable comments "On Church Music":

> There are two musical situations on which I think we can be confident that a blessing rests. One is where a priest or an organist, himself a man of trained . . . taste, humbly and charitably sacrifices his own (aesthetically right) desires

and gives the people humble and coarser fare than he would wish, in a belief (even, as it may be, the erroneous belief) that he can thus bring them to God. The other is where the . . . unmusical layman humbly and patiently . . . listens to music which he cannot . . . appreciate, in the belief that it somehow glorifies God. . . . To both, Church Music will have been a means of grace; not the music they have liked, but the music they have disliked. They have both offered, sacrificed, their taste in the fullest sense.[26]

It is clear from the parenthetical remarks that Lewis himself has opinions about what is truly helpful in worship. But his comments here remind us that motivation is key and that "love covers a multitude" of errors. This is not an excuse for unbalanced worship, confused teaching, ignorance of the Bible, or poor lyrics; it is a reminder that the quality of our life together is seen in how we negotiate the difficult matters that we have spoken of in this section. If we cannot love our brothers and our sisters whom we do see, we cannot love the God who is mysterious and who reveals himself to us as we come together before him.

Here, then, are twelve practical suggestions to remedy the diagnoses that we have attempted above. Some of these are more directed to those in the "free-church" tradition, but some are, I think, applicable to any with the responsibility for worship. I hope that these will be helpful for pastors and those involved in leading worship, as they attempt to treat common maladies due to atmospherics, human-centered worship, distorted teaching, misshapen liturgy, and our penchant for "using" worship.

- Give opportunities for preparation before the service, in the service of the Word, and before the Communion service. Such preparation is the answer to both careless presumption and fearful scruples. Prepare yourself, and those who will serve, prior to serving.
- Read the lyrics of the songs and consider carefully the musical setting, avoiding theological fads or jarring music that does not fit the moment or the liturgy.
- Pastors and worship leaders with some theological training should "vet" their praise songs and hymns for the ubiquitous first person and for an overemphasis upon "feeling." If possible follow an "I" verse with a "we" verse, even adding this spontaneously, if the lyrics permit.
- Choose and encourage songs, hymns, and prayers that are replete with Scripture, so as to direct the mind and heart to the Lord.
- Encourage worshipers by means of example and approach to give praise to God, rather than applauding when there is an anthem or personal offering: avoid the habits of a concert hall.
- Respect the flow of the service and avoid interruptions for commentary, instructions, or announcements. (Instructions in the bulletin can help,

if your people are used to a running commentary, or if various service books are used, e.g., "Please stand, if you are able.")

- If you are a congregation that plans services by means of "theme," pay attention also to the need for balance in every service, so that every part gets its due, whether confession, or praise, or reflection upon the Word.
- Allow for silence, time, and familiarity. Retain long-standing and key practices from your tradition, explaining these to newcomers (but without interrupting worship). Avoid novelty for its own sake and avoid repetition for the sake of stirring emotion. Even if the liturgy is long, do not rush the hymns or prayers, but allow time for them to sink into the heart. Better fewer prayers said with the whole person than many said with wandering minds.
- Scripture readings and sermons should aim to cover much, if not all, of the Scriptures over a period of time (yearly or bi-yearly?); go beyond simply those passages and themes that are well known. Ensure that the congregation is exposed to the whole Word of God.
- Give honor to both the Word and to the table/altar. Pay attention to how the Word may best be read, and give instruction to readers. Consider also, within your own tradition, how to welcome guests without assuming that they are in a place to receive Communion. How to safeguard the holiness of Communion is a matter for the laity (and parents as they instruct their children) as well as clergy.
- Keep the focus on the Triune God in every area of the service—even children's time. In doing this, consider where the physical focal point is: Is worship deflected by the screen or the worship leader? What are people likely to see as they are worshiping?
- Make it possible for the leaders themselves to worship. Do this by becoming familiar with a pattern, so that constant "looking ahead" is unnecessary, and/or by working closely as partners, bearing each other's burden.

Life as Worship

We close our study with a final word about the connection of corporate worship with the rest of our lives. This book has sought to show that worship is best understood in terms of a "grand entrance" into the mysterious presence of the Holy Trinity. Such an entrance means that we recognize the mystery of holiness: we need to "lay aside" earthly care and look to "the one thing that is needful." Yet, human entry into God's presence is only possible because God has fully entered our world in the Son and continues to be intimately present in our midst through the Holy Spirit. Moreover, we are a "royal priesthood," and so, when we pray, we mirror the action of the High Priest Jesus, bearing the world before the throne in our hearts and on our lips. Heaven is not jealous of its peace, but heals and brings wholeness.

In the fullest sense, every Christian is called to worship at all times in his or her life, and the Church is worshiping whenever it serves or tells the gospel or goes out in mission. "To work is to pray" (*laborare est orare*) for those whose life is conducted in the presence of the Lord. There is, then, a seamless robe of worship and life, made actual by God's deep presence with us and among us; yet there is the center, the holy of holies—the Lamb with the Father (and the Holy Spirit) on the throne, before whom we draw nigh, and whom *alone* we worship. All of life is holy; One is Holiness in his very self! We therefore should not separate out our worship from the rest of life, in one respect; yet we must hallow our specific times of worship as all-important. If our congregational worship times are not joined to a weeklong life of service, then there is something wrong: "Seven whole days, not one in seven, I will praise thee!"[27] But if we belittle the times we meet together and reduce these in our imaginations to mere times of restoration, education, a request to "fill 'er up!" then we are not perceiving the grandness of the entrance to which we have been called. So, I plead with those who have a keen sense of mission that they not finish the service with a dismissive "Now go on, get out of here!" (Probably I am not the only one who has heard such a comical "benediction" offered at the end of a retreat!) For, gathering together, we have been in the presence of the Ruler of the Universe, the One who died for us, the One who can be grieved by our indifference to glory and mystery. And this One goes with us into the world, as we remain joined to each other in communion and as we extend our worship into our more "ordinary" moments. We have glimpsed the glory in our worship together! May we see God now in everything and everyone touched by his radiance. May we hear the Word echoing in the voices, sounds, and silences of our daily lives.

Questions for Discussion

1. The scholars of Trent tried to reduce the embellishments of the medieval service in order to allow the people to worship without distraction. What aesthetic, musical, or other embellishments might be distracting in your context for worshipers today?

2. How can your congregation make newcomers welcome without jeopardizing the sanctity of the worship or taking the focus of worship away from God?

3. What practices, songs, hymns, or prayers are there in your church's life that can be enhanced in order to recall worshipers to the mystery of the Trinity?

4. How can children and newcomers both be included in worship and instructed as to how to worship, given the composition and customs of your congregation?

5. Are there musicians or poets in your church who could work on settings to reintroduce the congregation to ancient hymns such as the "Song of the Three," or the songs of Miriam, Simeon, Mary, or the angels (e.g., the *Trisagion*, the *Gloria*, or hymns found in Rev. 4–5)?

6. To what extent and at what points in our worship is it appropriate to sing about ourselves—that is, about our feelings, needs, or actions before God? Is it ever necessary or helpful? Why or why not?

7. What are the dangers of praising God without giving a reason for this praise?

8. In what ways do you tend to "use" worship as a means to an end? Imagine now that worship *is* the "chief end";[28] what difference might this make for how you structure your week, how you prepare for and anticipate worship, and how you then relate this worship to the rest of your life?

Conclusion

"To Sing Is a Lover's Thing"

Can you hear them?

They're singing, singing a song as strong as the sea, as sure as the rock, as heartrending as a glimpse of sapphire sky caught through a tear in an ominous bank of clouds.

Can you hear them?

> Holy, holy, holy,
> Lord God Almighty,
> The One who was, and who is, and who is to come . . .
> Worthy art thou, our Lord and God,
> To receive glory and honor and power:
> For thou didst create all things,
> And by thy will they came to be, and were created. (Rev. 4:8, 11 EH)

The song surrounds John, directed by the cherubim who sing the thrice-holy hymn, and entered with abandon and reverence by the twenty-four elders, representative of God's people. Encircled by the celestial singers, John weeps, lamenting the death, deceit, and evil of this world, crying out because of the impurity of God's people, in extremity because he is afraid there is no one who can open the scroll that explains the meaning and resolution of all this.

This conclusion is an adaptation of an address first given at my installation as the William F. Orr Professor of New Testament at Pittsburgh Theological Seminary, and has also appeared in a modified form as "To Sing Is a Lover's Thing: Toward a Biblical Theology of Worship," *Trinity Journal for Theology and Ministry* 3, no. 1 (Spring 2009): 131–44.

Perhaps like Isaiah of old, he weeps also for himself, frail and sinful, snatched up into a vision that is just too much for human eyes.

Yet he is not left to his own devices. Even amid this scene of sublimity, his sorrow is not ignored. One speaks tenderly to him, words of comfort that indicate the source of his hope. He is directed, for help, to the conquering Lion of Judah—but before his eye appears the Lamb, "standing as if it had been slaughtered." The song surrounds John again, as the elders present before the Almighty all the prayers of the saints. And the song has modulated, for it is new. Can you hear them? "Worthy is the Lamb who was slain," they sing.

> "Worthy art thou . . . for Thou wast slain,
> And by thy blood Thou hast redeemed for God
> People from every tribe and tongue and race and nation.
> And thou hast made them a kingdom and priests to our God:
> And they shall reign upon the earth." (5:9–10 EH)

Can you hear them? The whole creation joins the song now, all the animals and saints and angels together in a great jumble. They're singing our song. They're singing *his* song—the song of the Lion-Lamb, whose proper place is on the throne, but who also remains with us, in our midst.

In tracing the theme of entrance into worship during this study, we may be able to appreciate, with John the seer, how it is that the entrance of God the Son into our world has provided the means by which we may, even now, enter into heavenly worship. Yet we still may harbor the suspicion that complete harmony between disparate peoples could only be engineered by force. How is it possible for twenty-first-century Christians, who cannot even agree with each other, to gather with abandon around the throne? On top of this, we are surely now, in this post-Christian age, singing the Lord's song in a strange land, among a people who have almost forgotten the Lion-Lamb, among a generation to whom lambly sacrifice and lionish monarchy are equally abhorrent, among a society afflicted by an allergy to grand narratives that move to a climax, resolution, and conclusion.

In the Beginning

Sometimes it helps us to envision the end, the fulfillment, by going back to the beginning. So let us move back from the Apocalypse's song of victory to the very beginning. Here, at the utter beginning, in *protological time—the time before the beginning—we learn *why* it is that creation may sing in joy without devolving into sentimentality or unreality. No one could rightly accuse the book of Job of being glib or inculcating mindless high spirits. "Don't worry, be happy!" is the antithesis of this Old Testament book. It is in the very context of this ancient, dark, and probing drama, at the very climax of its laments and disputes, that the Almighty himself gestures to the primordial place of song: "Where were you when I laid the foundation of the earth? . . . When the morning stars sang together, and all the sons of God shouted for joy" (Job 38:4, 7). At the very beginning, God tells Job, the great unseen powers and principalities hymned *in response*, offering angelic appreciation for the handiwork of the Lord, for the dawning of the light. Yet this was not their first song, it would seem, for even before the light of creation was seen, there was the uncreated light to adore. "Meet it is that you should *at all times* be worshiped with voices of praise."[1] Indeed, before the beginning of our world, there was song: remember the eternal "Holy, holy, holy" chanted before the face of God. The archangels sing, and then nature herself sings, clapping her hands, rejoicing at the bounty of the LORD. Their song is joined with our song, and the creation enters into the joy of heaven.

Bittersweet Response

Singing, then, is a *response* of a heightened sort. Because the Lord enters into our midst, we may approach him. Perhaps, because song is by nature responsive, it is an activity proper to us, belonging especially to the created order. God speaks—and the world is created. But the angels sing, we sing, because of the life and love that God has showered upon us. As St. Augustine put it: *Cantare amantis est* (*Sermo* 336,1): "To sing is a lover's thing."[2] St. Augustine spoke about the lover's song as the "new song" that responds especially to the joy of salvation. But love may sing in other modes, in response to the vicissitudes of love and of life. Since, in our great story of salvation, the next major act after the Creation is that of the Fall, God's people have never been strangers to the minor key—though we have seen that there are some contemporary Christian communities who, afflicted by an unreal approach to faith, would like to banish the minor key from the repertoire of their worship! Over against such artificial happiness, Pope Benedict XVI has wisely commented that, this side of the new Jerusalem, our "love is always marked by pain at the hiddenness of God."[3] Indeed, if our response is to be authentic, it must learn also to lower the third of the chord and weep. Consider this lament uttered by an unknown visionary just after the destruction of the *second temple in AD 70:

> For you see that our sanctuary has been laid waste, our altar thrown down, our
> temple destroyed; our harp has been laid low, our song has been silenced, and
> our rejoicing has been ended; the light of our lampstand has been put out, the
> ark of our covenant has been plundered, our holy things have been polluted,
> and the name by which we are called has been profaned; our free men have
> suffered abuse, our priests have been burned to death, our Levites have gone
> into captivity, our virgins have been defiled, and our wives have been ravished;
> our righteous men have been carried off, our little ones have been cast out, our

young men have been enslaved and our strong men made powerless. And, what is more than all, the seal of Zion—for she has now lost the seal of her glory, and has been given over into the hands of those that hate us. (2 Esdras 10:21–23)

Here is a paradox: "our song has been silenced," yet the prophet continues, against his better instincts, to sing. He cannot help himself, for he is in love; like the psalmist he has "set Jerusalem above [his] highest joy" (Ps. 137:6). Indeed, he hopes that, despite all appearances, the Lord of the temple may still act on behalf of his people. Of course, this lament, coming to us from the margins of the Christian canon, from the book of 2 Esdras, does not know that God has already responded to this desolation—for the seal of Zion's glory is now to be found in a Person and not in that great temple made with kingly and human hands. But even in his unenlightened longing, this first-century visionary typifies the poignancy of lament, that dark response born of love and of loss.

Let us turn to Psalms, the book of all singing, of joy and lament. Psalms 42 and 43, though separated into two psalms from our very earliest renditions, seem by literary analysis to form a whole.

To the choirmaster. A Maskil of the Sons of Korah.

As a hart longs for flowing streams, so longs my soul for thee, O God. My soul thirsts for God, for the living God. When shall I come and behold the face of God? My tears have been my food day and night, while men say to me continually, "Where is your God?"

These things I remember, as I pour out my soul: how I went with the throng, and led them in procession to the house of God, with glad shouts and songs of thanksgiving, a multitude keeping festival.

Why are you cast down, O my soul, and why are you disquieted within me? Hope in God; for I shall again praise him, my help and my God.

My soul is cast down within me, therefore I remember thee from the land of Jordan and of Hermon, from Mount Mizar. Deep calls to deep at the thunder of thy cataracts; all thy waves and thy billows have gone over me. By day the LORD commands his steadfast love; and at night his song is with me, a prayer to the God of my life. I say to God, my rock: "Why hast thou forgotten me? Why go I mourning because of the oppression of the enemy?" As with a deadly wound in my body, my adversaries taunt me, while they say to me continually, "Where is your God?"

Why are you cast down, O my soul, and why are you disquieted within me? Hope in God; for I shall again praise him, my help and my God.

Vindicate me, O God, and defend my cause against an ungodly people; from deceitful and unjust men deliver me! For thou art the God in whom I take refuge; why hast thou cast me off? Why go I mourning because of the oppression of the enemy?

Oh send out thy light and thy truth; let them lead me, let them bring me to thy holy hill and to thy dwelling! Then I will go to the altar of God, to God my exceeding joy; and I will praise thee with the lyre, O God, my God.

Why are you cast down, O my soul, and why are you disquieted within me?
Hope in God; for I shall again praise him, my help and my God.

In order to highlight the themes of singing, we must attend to the structure
of the entire poetic diptych, or two-tableau scene. Psalm 42 is written, for the
most part, as a description of the human plight: "As a hart longs for flowing
streams, so longs my soul . . . my soul thirsts for God, for the living God."
Psalm 43, on the other hand, addresses the Lord directly throughout: "Vindicate me, O God . . . deliver me . . . send out thy light." Throughout the ages,
the people of God have, in the psalmist's words, expressed the pilgrimage of
those who long to see the face of God.

The song begins by expressing deep hunger and thirst, flashes back to a time
when God was present in corporate worship, meditates upon the paradox of
separation from the Lord even while God remains steadfast, and mourns over
the mockery that comes from the mouths of those who do not acknowledge
God. Then the psalmist cries out for vindication and deliverance (42:1–4),
reminds God of the desperate situation (42:7–10; 43:1–2), begs for a journey
out of the darkness into the light, from the valley onto the hill (43:3), and
envisages a time of ecstatic abandon before the Lord (43:4). Throughout the
song, we hear the psalmist talking not just about the *situation*, not just ad-
dressing *God*, but also speaking to *himself*. Both the first part, which mourns
the human plight, and the second, which cries out for help, are punctuated
by the psalmist, who addresses his own soul and encourages himself to hope.
Three times we listen in to his internal dialogue (42:5, 11; 43:5): toward the
beginning, the middle, and at the very end. Indeed, though the poem moves
toward a resolution and climax—"I will praise thee with the lyre, O God, my
God" (43:4b)—the psalm ends on this note of reality and introspection. "Why
are you cast down, O my soul, and why are you disquieted within me? Hope
in God; for I shall again praise him, my help and my God" (43:5).

There is something else to notice. Twice the psalmist actually speaks about
hymnody, about song. If we have been well-trained in the liturgical tradition,
we expect that singing will be the result of God's deliverance: so we are not
surprised that after our pilgrimage with the psalmist through the terrains of
longing, separation, remembrance, mockery, crying out for help, and being
led up the mount, that he should finally make music. But this anticipated song
of joy is matched by a darker song that comes earlier in the sequence, in the
midst of pain: "Deep calls to deep at the thunder of thy cataracts. . . . The
Lord commands his steadfast love; and at night his song is with me, a prayer
to the God of my life" (42:7–8). Who, we may wonder, is doing the singing
here? We could assume that since this is "a prayer to the God of my life," the
song is that of the psalmist himself, whistling in the dark. But I am not so sure
that is the whole answer. For the psalmist uses a curious turn of phrase: "The
Lord *commands his steadfast love*; and at night *his* song *is with me*." Is it,

after all, the psalmist's song, or is it a *given* song (*God's* song) that he makes his own? And with whom, after all, was he having his internal conversation throughout the psalm?

All of us, of course, carry on an internal monologue every day. Left to our own devices, it is not always a conversation of hope, of encouragement, and of direction; all too frequently our human prattling and deadening words circle round and round in our heads, cultivating worry, fear, and even hopelessness. How is it that the psalmist has been able, during all these seasons, to continue to ask "why are you cast down?" and to advocate within the heart "Hope in God!"? Surely, as an anointed psalmist, he has invoked the presence of God's very own Spirit. Deep calls to deep, producing the dialogue of the Spirit of God within the spirit of the one who laments, who remembers, who confesses, who mourns, who calls out, and who hopes. Does God himself enter into the minor key? Can it be, after all, that singing is not proper to the creation alone, but that it is, like everything else, the *poiēma* ("poem, handiwork," Eph. 2:10) of God?

Magnifying the Lord

The answer to the question just posed appears to be both yes and yes. Since God is the great Alpha, the great initiator, and the creation is called to answer to God, we must first say that God is such that he will merely *speak*, and it will be done. Response is proper to creation, who sings her song in the music of the spheres. Our God has no *need* of incantation, or response. And so the divine words in the Genesis creation story are solemnly spoken; yet the seven-day sequence reminds us of the liturgical life of the Hebrews, ending on the Sabbath, whose liturgy was always *sung*. More than that, our God is one who visits, who in the fullness of time comes to dwell with those created ones who are made after his image. And so the mother of Jesus rejoices in wonder:

> My soul magnifies the Lord, and my spirit rejoices in God my Savior, for he has regarded the low estate of his handmaiden. For behold, henceforth all generations will call me blessed; for he who is mighty has done great things for me, and holy is his name. And his mercy is on those who fear him from generation to generation. He has shown strength with his arm, he has scattered the proud in the imagination of their hearts, he has put down the mighty from their thrones, and exalted those of low degree; he has filled the hungry with good things, and the rich he has sent empty away. He has helped his servant Israel, in remembrance of his mercy, as he spoke to our fathers, to Abraham and to his posterity for ever. (Luke 1:46–55)

"My soul magnifies the Lord." Many of us enter into worship by repeating holy Mary's words in our evening prayers. But have we ever stopped to think about this? What cheek to speak about "magnifying the Lord." How can it be possible that a human being—even this most-blessed one!—should magnify the Lord of all things, the Lord of all magnifying glasses, the Lord whose delight it is to magnify and whose prerogative it is to cast down? Of course, it is only through the divine humility of one who stoops to enter our world that this is possible, that *we* should bless or magnify the LORD. The soul magnifies the Lord, because he has regarded us, body and soul, and had mercy upon all those who fear him. It is out of his great might that he shares his blessedness and does great things; he is the One who blesses, and so he is, by us, ever blessed. We find ourselves here on holy ground: the greatness of God is such that it cannot ever be diminished by his exaltation of others. The humility of God is such that he comes to dwell with the lowly and meek.

The *Theotokos Mary knows about the character of this God, both by report and by personal revelation. Through the Scriptures, through the worship of God's people, she knows the promises, the actions, the *responsiveness* of her God to "Abraham and our ancestors"—and even overflowing to the "stranger" connected with the people of God. She knows from the ancient stories of Israel that God has mercy "from generation to generation." We hear, in her words of joy, echoes of the great victory hymns, especially the songs of Moses and of Miriam after the crossing of the Red Sea: "The Lord is my strength and my song, and he has become my salvation; this is my God, and I will praise him, my father's God, and I will exalt him. . . . Who is like thee, O LORD. . . . Thou hast led in thy steadfast love the people whom thou hast redeemed, thou hast guided them by thy strength to thy holy abode. . . . Sing to the LORD, for he has triumphed gloriously" (Exod. 15:2–21). Her song echoes their joy in exodus deliverance, and in the character of the living God, who hears the cries of his oppressed people and acts on their behalf. With her imagination, the mother of Jesus has entered into the holy history of her people, of God's people. At the same time that Mary's song has this corporate dimension, it also acknowledges the personal care of the Lord, hearkening back to the plea of another desolate and waiting woman, who in the temple sought a child—her elderly and barren ancestor, Hannah. "My heart exults in the LORD; my strength is exalted in the LORD. . . . There is none holy like the Lord, there is none besides thee; there is no rock like our God. . . . The Lord makes poor and makes rich. . . . He raises up the poor from the dust; he lifts the needy from the ash heap. . . . He will guard the feet of his faithful ones. . . . The Lord will . . . exalt the power of his anointed" (1 Sam. 2:1–10).

Some have thought that Luke, or a scribe, made some mistake in ascribing the song to Mary, rather than to her older cousin, Elizabeth, whose situation more nearly mirrors that of Hannah. I think not, for in this young maiden's song, we hear the response of Israel to that utterly new thing that God is doing. Here is the beginning of the absolutely new song, that song that rejoices in God's full and complete answer to our corporate and personal needs. Mary's song brings together the hopes and fears of Israel's years, while also celebrating God's deep care for all the poor and for each son and daughter. Mary's song, Mary's stance, mirrors for us the way that we may come, personally and corporately, into the presence of the living God: "Here *am I*, the servant of the Lord"; "His mercy is on *those who fear him* from generation to generation." In the particularity of holy Mary's situation we see God's concern for all and God's care for each. With the babe in her womb, she knows that age-old longings for God's action are being fulfilled; yet, a revolution, a subversion, a surprise is also at hand.

And so she sings a song that acknowledges both the mercy of the Lord and the darkness of a human plight to which only God can answer for our good! Those who will not see the situation for what it is (that we are indeed "in darkness and in the shadow of death") are scattered; the construction of imaginary and pretentious worlds cannot stand before the real poetry, before the mighty acts of God. Here is, then, both a song that confirms and that unsettles. We would rather have the former without the latter, but this cannot be, for in a musical piece that has modulated from the major to the minor key, there must be a resolution before the piece can return to its tonic.

Whose Song Is It?

And who, after all, is the singer of this song? If we place the *Magnificat* in its narrative context, we will remember that there has already been a word of prophecy, as Mary's kinswoman Elizabeth, filled with the Holy Spirit, acknowledges the blessedness of the one before her and the unseen anointed babe. Can we doubt that the personal words of the Theotokos are also the words of God, reminding us of his inimitable ways and his heartbreaking mercy? Traditionally, she has been honored in the Church as a picture of the faithful all together; she has presented herself to God, said yes to him, and prepared herself for the holy Presence. It is hardly possible that Luke intends for us to picture Mary as anything other than inspired by the very Spirit of God. And so we learn from holy Mary God's tenderness for the lowly and suffering. St. Paul, considering the whole shape of the salvation story, speaks about how it is that the Holy Spirit is active in God's people, active within us just as the infant Jesus was active within Mary's womb.

In Romans 8, Paul speaks about the Spirit's work within us, leading us together into life, giving voice to our stalled prayers, participating in our pain, and interpreting what is obscure. God acts from the outside, transcendent and sovereign, source of our being, standard of justice and truth, hope of our own glorification, object of our awe and love; God acts from within, so that our capacity for life, light, and love grows. "For all who are led by the Spirit of God are sons of God ["anointed ones," like God's own Son]. . . . Likewise the

Spirit helps us in our weakness. . . . In everything God works for good among those who . . . are called according to his purpose" (Rom. 8:14, 26, 28). The Spirit within us, Christians interceding on behalf of others, humankind giving voice to the inchoate labor of the fallen world—we form a set of concentric circles that will issue in glory (Rom. 8:18–25). It is the prophetic and wooing Spirit who, in Christ, blesses and transforms.

So, then, we return to our question—whose songs are these? They ring out in response to the One who has done all things well. In the end, however, it seems that all songs are inspired by that One, who lamented "where are you?" concerning disobedient humanity, who by the prophets sang sad songs over his desecrated vineyard, who placed hymns of hope in the dark night of the psalmist. Nor are all the songs of God laments: for he promised by the prophet Zephaniah (3:17) to utter his *rinnah*, his ululation or great cry of triumph, when we his people are renewed. As St. Gregory of Nazianzen exalted,

> All things breathe you a prayer,
> A silent hymn of your own composing.
> All that exists you uphold,
> All things in concert move to your orders.
> You are the goal of all that is. . . .[4]

But is this simply a matter of inspiration, of God putting songs on the lips of his prophets, or of *anthropomorphism, of the prophets picturing God as a lamenting lover or exultant warrior? Perhaps. After all, there are precious few places in the Bible where God actually sings himself. I wonder, though, if that is because God's most proper song would be the music made between Father, Son, and Spirit—intimacy known only to them. Yet, at times in the Holy Scriptures we catch a glimpse of a singing God. So we might not think that the inimitable C. S. Lewis has simply imported a foreign element into his Narnian creation story, supposing that the *Word* should *sing*.[5] Why should this not be so?

We hold before us the centerpiece of our great family story, the Incarnation itself. That ancient hymn of the Church found in Philippians 2 (and sung by English-speaking congregations today in F. Bland Tucker's words "All Praise to Thee"), reminds us forcibly of the wonder: God, in his Son, has come nearer to us than our own breath, taking on humanity, dying our death, having the victory, and taking our humanity up with him to the heights. We celebrate that the One,

> Who, though he was in the form of God, did not count equality with God a thing to be grasped, but emptied himself, taking the form of a servant, being born in . . . [human] likeness. . . . And being found in human form he humbled himself and became obedient unto death, even death on a cross. Therefore God has highly exalted him and bestowed on him the name which is above every name, that at the name of Jesus every knee should bow, in heaven and on earth

and under the earth, and every tongue confess that Jesus Christ is Lord, to the glory of God the Father. (Phil. 2:6–11)

In this God, then, who has humbled himself, who was baptized into our corruptible life and our death—in him we anticipate the rescue of all good things and the glorification of all that is truly human, truly made after the image of God. If the song of response is a good thing proper to a creation in love with God, then this, too, is part of what God has taken to himself, and honored, and glorified. Indeed, our Lord Jesus himself practiced the singing of *eucharistia* as well as of lament—worshiping in the synagogue, singing a psalm on the night of his betrayal, taking the psalms to his lips even when on the cross. Singing is characteristic of that dear One who is fully united with the Father.

But there is more. Consider the high points of the Christian liturgy. Even today a solemn service or a contemporary worship time is full of song in response to God's grace. But in the most ancient liturgies, the whole of the prayers are sung. This includes the sung blessings and the giving of peace, where the celebrant sings on behalf of God, "Peace be unto all." And so it is that, in the end, though singing in lament, in joy, in thanksgiving, may be actions that are most fully characteristic of the human family—we are created for thanksgiving!—this, too, comes only through God and has become God's very own. For what we could not do fully, the thanksgiving that we could not offer due to the weakness of our nature, he has himself taught us, by the Advent of his Son, and through the presence of his Spirit among us. When we were too weak to respond, at just the right time, God sent his Son, who offers our response for us and teaches us how to sing.

Entering the Song

Did we think, after all, that response *begins* with the creation? We should know better. This would be true of the general theist but not for those of us who have been let into the mystery of the Holy Trinity. One liturgist puts it this way,

> Music is the language of love. Hence the Church, as the Bride of Christ, has always sung the praises of her Divine Lover, Jesus Christ. Her praises, in turn, are the echo of that ineffable canticle sung in the Godhead from all ages. For the Eternal Word Jesus Christ is a Divine canticle singing the Father's praise. This is the infinite hymn that ever sounds "in the bosom of the Father," the canticle that rises up from the depths of the Divinity, the Living Canticle wherein God eternally delights, because it is the infinite expression of His perfection.[6]

Response itself begins with the One who is Alpha and Omega, as Son and Spirit respond to the Father, and as the Father responds to Son and Spirit.

Some of late have waxed eloquent about the "perichoretic dance" that goes on between the Persons of the Father, Son, and Holy Spirit. This notion may be picturesque, but it is actually based, as we have seen, on a misunderstanding of the word *perichōresis*. There has even been talk of our entry into "the great *perichoresis* that flows between" Father, Son, and Spirit. Such discussion is, I believe, too glib. It is perhaps even a category error. For the relationship of the Persons of the Trinity—Father, Son, and Holy Spirit—is a far deeper spiritual communion than anything that we know. We are here at the Holy of Holies, attempting to understand something that is proper to the Godhead and not known (perhaps, not *ever* fully known) to humanity. *Perichōresis* implies an *indescribable* ecstasy and intimacy, a "song" that is, in its fullness, known only in that holy place, among that holy Three-in-One.

Yet, if we are not to enter into the very inner relations of the Godhead, still there is such a divine hospitality toward us, so that we may be taught by them how we might reflect, in our lives together, their mysterious and abundant life. Indeed, music provides the perfect analogy by which we can understand how God can remain God and yet bring humanity into the fullness of life. There is the tonic note, the center of all things, that One who remains always the foundation of all that is good and lively and illumined. In relation to this, we who are in Christ find ourselves in relation to that tonic, and in harmony with each other—notes sounded together, heard together, yet distinguishable and particular in that very moment of harmony. In the end, it seems that the imaginary creation of Lewis in the *Magician's Nephew* is consonant with the Christian view, and not simply nostalgia imported from Scandinavian ancient stories. For, after all, the creation is the word of Father, Son, and Spirit, who by the Christian reckoning of Genesis deliberate together, "let us make *Adam*." And so, through Lewis's artistry, we think in a different way about the primordial time when the first created light emerged, as the Logos responded to this divine deliberation. In Lewis's depiction of the creating Lion who is also the re-creating Lamb, we encounter him first as a Voice sounding after a long time of darkness—the Voice comes from the distance, and it is difficult to determine from where it is coming. Perhaps it is coming from all directions at once! The sound even seems to be more fundamental than the ground beneath the listeners' feet. The Singer is unique in beauty and mystery, and yet does not remain alone:

> The Voice was suddenly joined by . . . more voices than you could possibly count
> . . . singing in harmony with it. . . . [N]ew stars and the new voices began at
> exactly the same time. If you had seen and heard it, you would have felt quite
> certain that it was the stars themselves who were singing, and that it was the first
> Voice, the deep one singing, which had made them appear and made them sing.[7]

The light of the stars and their singing begin at the same moment: to become is to respond! Seeing this, a humble character in Lewis's story declares, "Glory be!" and then remarks that he would have been a better man throughout his life if he had known there were "things like this." He hears the song and enters into the wonder of it all, adding his own cockney cry of "Glory!"

Can you hear them? Can you hear *Him*? Through Christ Jesus, we *do* know that there are things like this, so let us be better men and women—no, let us allow the Spirit to make of us better sons and daughters—so that we enter into that grand action, company, and place, singing with the Spirit and the whole Church: "Even so, Come, Lord Jesus!"

Notes

Preface

1. C. S. Lewis, *Letters to Malcolm: Chiefly on Prayer* (New York: Harcourt, 1964), 5.

Introduction

1. Leontius of Byzantium, *Against Nestorius and Eutychius* 3.19 (J.-P. Migne, ed., *Patrologia graeca* [=*Patrologiae cursus completus: Series graeca*], 162 vols. [Paris, 1857–86], 86:1368C).
2. See Darrell L. Guder, ed., *Missional Church: A Vision for the Sending of the Church in North America* (Grand Rapids: Eerdmans, 1998); and Christopher J. H. Wright, *The Mission of God: Unlocking the Bible's Grand Narrative* (Downers Grove, IL: IVP Academic, 2006).
3. St. Irenaeus, *Against Heresies* 4, preface.
4. C. S. Lewis, *An Experiment in Criticism* (Cambridge: Cambridge University Press, 1961), 141.
5. In 1 Cor. 1:10, Paul appeals to the Corinthians that they might all say "the same thing" (Gk., *to auto*), but this is translated as "that . . . you agree" in the RSV and even more innocuously as "be in agreement" in the NRSV. See also 2 Cor. 13:11.
6. I follow the NRSV translation, using its alternate reading for verse 3, but have supplied the more exuberant RSV punctuation.

Chapter 1   "Teach Us to Pray"

1. This song was retrieved in the international archives of the Salvation Army. It is entitled, "Thy Kingdom Here," words by Brigadier Mrs. Ivy Mawby and music by Lt. Commissioner E. Grinsted. Published in *Favourite Songs for Young People*, No. 4 (London: Salvationist Publishing and Supplies, 1957).
2. This idea of each human heart as a microcosm, or kingdom, is perhaps seen best in the poignant words of the fourth century St. Macarius, who said, "Within the heart are unfathomable depths. . . . Dragons and lions are there. . . . There likewise is God . . . and the Kingdom" (*Homilies* 15.32; 43.7). For a more recent example, see the helpful exposition of the Eastern Church's teaching on the internal Christian life, as represented by (*Metropolitan) Kallistos Ware, *The Inner Kingdom* (Crestwood, NY: St. Vladimir's Seminary Press, 2000).
3. Robert F. Taft, *Beyond East and West: Problems in Liturgical Understanding*, 2nd ed. (Rome: Pontifical Oriental Institute, 1997), 246.

4. "Forms of Prayer to Be Used in Families," in *The Book of Common Prayer According to the Use of the Anglican Church of Canada* (Toronto: Anglican Book Centre, 1962), 729. Available online at http://www.prayerbook.ca/the-prayer-book-online.

5. This is the final stanza of "Praise, My Soul, the King of Heaven," by Henry Francis Lyte (1834).

6. This is the translation from J. B. Phillips's 1958 translation of the New Testament, published by MacMillan.

7. C. S. Lewis, *Till We Have Faces: A Myth Retold* (1956; Grand Rapids: Eerdmans, 1996).

Chapter 2   "Praise God in His Sanctuary"

1. Many commentators consider chapter 6 as representing the initial call of Isaiah, while others disagree—see, for example, John D. W. Watts, *Isaiah 1–33*, Word Biblical Commentary 24 (Waco, TX: Word Books, 1985), 70—and argue that this was a striking vision that shaped Isaiah's ministry but not his first calling as a prophet.

2. Christopher R. Seitz, *Isaiah 1–39* (Louisville: Westminster John Knox, 1993), 54.

3. Some readers may be startled that I am interested not only in reading the Hebrew (*Masoretic) text but also in the wording of the old Greek or *Septuagint (LXX) version. This version cannot be ignored, especially when the worship tradition of the Church is in view, for it was the earliest Bible of the ancient Church, rather than the Hebrew text. Moreover, it is being considered more seriously for its readings by scholars, since we have discovered some very ancient Hebrew readings of passages that are closer to the LXX than to the Hebrew medieval (Masoretic) version, which previously was used almost exclusively in academic circles. The LXX of Isaiah 6 has been extremely important, since it is in the Greek that the text came over into the New Testament writings.

4. (*Protopresbyter) Alexander Schmemann, *The Eucharist* (Crestwood, NY: St. Vladimir's Seminary Press, 1987), 45.

5. Scholars continue to discuss the exact meaning of covered feet, here and elsewhere in the Old Testament, and whether the heavenly beings here are conceived as possessing the equivalent of genitalia.

6. The Hebrew is strange, vacillating between the "dual" and the plural. Matters are further complicated by the singular "the voice of the one calling" in the subsequent verse.

7. St. John Chrysostom, *Against the Anamoeans* 3.24; 1.35, in Steven A. McKinion, ed., *Ancient Christian Commentary on Scripture, Isaiah 1–39*, Old Testament, vol. 10 (Downers Grove, IL: InterVarsity, 2004), 49–50.

8. St. John Chrysostom, *Concerning the Statues*, in McKinion, ed., *Ancient Christian Commentary*, 50.

9. Brevard S. Childs, *Isaiah* (Louisville: Westminster John Knox, 2001), 56.

10. Visionary imagery of this sort goes far in declaring mysteries. Here, we see how it is that God's presence can be both immediate to us and mediated, how God the Word is ultimately our only help and yet God uses his servants to bless us. The Eastern Orthodox celebrate this mediate immediacy in an ancient hymn that remembers the meeting of St. Simeon with the infant Jesus: "Christ the coal of fire, whom holy Isaiah foresaw, now rests in the arms of the Theotokos ["God-bearer" Mary] *as in a pair of tongs*, and He is given to the elder."

11. This is actually a respectable scholarly position, made famous by F. C. Baur, who engaged in a quest for the earliest church, prior to its complex stages. He traced a trajectory from St. Paul's liberty, through the rigid reaction of the Jewish Jerusalem apostles, to an "early Catholic" compromise.

12. For a description of these three modes of operating, common among Protestant (especially Evangelical) scholars, see Michael A. Farley, "What Is 'Biblical' Worship? Biblical Hermeneutics and Evangelical Theologies of Worship," *Journal of the Evangelical Theological Society* 51, no. 3 (2008): 591–613.

13. Ibid., 610.

14. The phrase is that of C. S. Lewis, made memorable in the title of the autobiography of Sheldon Vanauken, *A Severe Mercy* (New York: Harper Collins, 1980).

15. (*Metropolitan) Anthony Bloom, *Beginning to Pray* (Mahwah, NJ: Paulist Press, 1970), 26–27.

16. C. S. Lewis, *The Lion, the Witch and the Wardrobe* (Middlesex, England: Penguin, 1950). Mr. Beaver so describes Aslan on pages 75 and 166.

17. Exodus 24 is stressed by Hughes O. Old, *Themes and Variations for a Christian Doxology* (Grand Rapids: Eerdmans, 1992); John Witvliet, "The Former Prophets and the Practice of Christian Worship," *Calvin Theological Journal* 37 (2002): 82–94; Michael Horton, *A Better Way: Rediscovering the Drama of God-Centered Worship* (Grand Rapids: Baker, 2002). It is even more explicitly used as a patter, and amplified by texts such as Leviticus 19, by Jeffrey J. Meyers, *The Lord's Service: The Grace of Covenant Renewal Worship* (Moscow, ID: Canon, 2003).

18. C. S. Lewis, *The Weight of Glory* (New York: Harper Collins, 2001), 42–43.

19. From *The Book of Common Prayer According to the Use of the Anglican Church of Canada* (Toronto: Anglican Book Centre, 1962), 453–54.

20. For a study of the theme of ecstasy in the Christian tradition, see Edith M. Humphrey, *Ecstasy and Intimacy: When the Holy Spirit Meets the Human Spirit* (Grand Rapids: Eerdmans, 2005).

21. C. S. Lewis, "The Weight of Glory," was first preached as a sermon in Oxford in 1942 and is available online at http://www.doxaweb.com/assets/doxa.pdf. As the first of a collection of essays by Lewis, it also is the title of this collection, *The Weight of Glory* (New York: HarperCollins, 2001).

Chapter 3   "In Spirit and in Truth"

1. Paul F. Bradshaw (*The Search for the Origins of Christian Worship: Sources and Methods for the Study of Early Liturgy* [New York: Oxford University Press, 1992], 44–55) points out that both *berakah/eulogia* (blessing) and *hodayah/eucharistia* (thanksgiving) forms of prayer were used in the early Christian worship and have parallels in the *Second Temple Jewish period. The two actions of blessing and giving thanks are not "simply synonymous" and seem to point to a "different liturgical construction" (44). In time, Christian worship seemed to give precedence to the thanksgiving motif. However, to trace this development or to speak confidently about the relationship between Jewish and early Christian formulae of worship is no easy task. It is difficult to know whether the breaking of the bread described here was accompanied by a blessing or a thanksgiving or both, and Luke does not give us specifics. Luke's description of the Lord's actions in the Last Supper (Luke 22:17) does not clear up this matter. It is difficult to know whether Jesus' initial action of breaking was accompanied by a blessing (as is detailed in Mark 14:22) so that Luke's account has been colored by the later (but still early) Christian action of "giving thanks," and then read back into the first supper. Or perhaps both actions were in fact common in the Second Temple Jewish and early Christian period, and so Jesus both blessed and gave thanks: in Mark's Gospel, the bread is blessed, while thanksgiving is given for the cup (Mark 14:23).

2. See Jeremias's discussion in *The Eucharistic Words of Jesus*, trans. Norman Perrin (London: SCM, 1966), 118–22.

3. See especially chapter 2 of Paul F. Bradshaw, *The Search for the Origins of Christian Worship: Sources and Methods for the Study of Early Liturgy* (New York: Oxford University Press, 1992), 30–55.

4. Fr. Patrick Reardon, "Saint Mary of Egypt," *Father Pat's Pastoral Ponderings*, All Saints Antiochian Orthodox Church, April 5, 2009, http://www.allsaintsorthodox.org/pastor/pastoral_ponderings.php.

5. Ibid.

6. For those who doubt that Paul was as aware of the divine status of Christ as we are in our post-Trinitarian context, consider his restatement of the Jewish *Shema* in 1 Cor. 8:6. For the Christian, Paul has argued in 1 Corinthians 8 that to worship the one God includes acknowledging Jesus as the bearer of the divine name (LORD, *Kyrios*, here translates Deut. 6:4's *YHWH*). This Kyrios Jesus is, indeed, the agent of creation! Paul does not use our creedal language ("consubstantial, co-eternal") but certainly gives Jesus "the name above every name" (Phil. 2:11) to which worship is due, and yet remains a monotheist. The Father and the Lord Jesus are not two gods, but One.

7. Paul has, however, been misread by many on this score, including the great English poet John Milton, who in *Paradise Lost* restates this passage so as to establish a graded scale of being. Indeed, Milton also distinguished between God and Jesus in terms of their essence—Jesus was not quite God, he believed—and so he made the same mistake in talking about the Godhead as he did about humanity.

8. Several good exegetes have argued that verses 33b–36 are not original to Paul. They have influenced, for example, the editors of the NRSV, who placed this section in parentheses as though it were an aside and not part of Paul's flow of argument. However, the verses are found in every ancient manuscript and have been read as authentic throughout the centuries. It would seem that the judgment to excise them only provides a "solution" in the case of readers who attribute authority only to original manuscripts as reproduced by scholars and as though God does not continue to lead the Church. I myself do not think that we can find an easy solution by removing the offending verses (and, indeed, what will we do with 1 Tim. 2:11 and 1 Pet. 3:1, which also associate women with silence?). Rather, we must read this difficult section in such a way that it does not neutralize what Paul says elsewhere—that women do pray and prophecy in the assembly and that they should comport themselves in a particular way when they do so. In the same letter, in an early chapter, Paul has assumed, without critique, that women will speak. It therefore seems reasonable to assume that Paul is not enjoining absolute silence here in chapter 14—or else he would have done so also in 1 Cor. 11, rather than fastening upon the matter of the woman's head. Instead, a particular type of silence must be in view—refraining from debate or from chattering in a disruptive way.

9. The phrase comes from Reepicheep, but it is also the title of chapter 15 of *The Last Battle* (England: Bodley Head, 1956).

10. William T. Cavanagh, *Torture and Eucharist: Theology, Politics, and the Body of Christ* (Oxford: Blackwell, 1998), 224.

11. St. Gregory of Nazianzen, Epistle 101, "To Cledonius the Priest Against Apollinarius," in Philip Schaff and Henry Wace, *Nicene and Post-Nicene Fathers of the Christian Church*, vol. 7, *Cyril of Jerusalem, Gregory Nazianzen* (Grand Rapids: Eerdmans, 1955), 439–42. The famous declaration is found on p. 440. Available online at http://www.ccel.org/ccel/schaff/npnf207 .iv.iii.iii.html.

12. Graham Kendrick, "Jesus Let Me Meet You in Your Word," © 1991, 1993 Make Way Music (Administered by Music Services in the Western Hemisphere). Used by permission. All rights reserved.

13. Standard translations render this as "has made him known." In fact, the Greek verb is associated with our word *exegesis*, that is, the art of "drawing out" the meaning of something.

14. William P. Young, *The Shack* (Los Angeles: Windblown Media, 2007), 145.

15. This prayer is based upon an Anglican *collect for the second Sunday after Epiphany, Proper 2. It may be found in the *Canadian Book of Alternate Services*, online at http: d1.dropbox .com/u/4905842/Liturgy/BAS.pdf.

Chapter 4   "From You Comes . . . Praise"

1. W. O. E. Oesterley, *The Jewish Background of the Liturgy* (Oxford: Clarendon, 1925); *Dom. Gregory Dix, *The Shape of the Liturgy* (London: Dacre, 1945); Louis Bouyer, *La vie de la*

liturgie: Une critique constructive du mouvement liturgique (Paris: Cerf, 1956); idem. *Liturgical Piety* (Notre Dame, IN: University of Notre Dame Press, 1955); Aidan Kavanagh, *On Liturgical Theology* (New York: Pueblo, 1984); Frank C. Senn, *Christian Liturgy: Catholic and Evangelical* (Minneapolis: Fortress, 1997); Paul F. Bradshaw, *The Search for the Origins of Christian Worship: Sources and Methods for the Study of Early Liturgy* (New York: Oxford University Press, 1992).

2. This procedure has its flaws, as there was considerable cross-fertilization between the East and the West, not only in the early years but up until Nicaea and beyond, and even (strangely!) after the Great Schism. However, since the mature liturgies are quite different in shape and ethos, this seems the best way to go forward.

3. The translation used is that of the *New Advent Church Fathers*, found at http://www .newadvent.org/fathers/0714.htm. The emphasis is mine, here and throughout this discussion.

4. "Apostolic Constitutions: Didascalia Apostolorum Book I–VI," available online at http:// www.piney-2.com/DocAposConstitu.html. See the references to God's "inheritance" in the pre-sider's prayer and the description of approach to the altar in the east, as if it were a return to Eden.

5. For the text see Philip Schaff, *Ante-Nicene Fathers*, vol. 7, *Fathers of the Third and Fourth Centuries*, ed. Alexander Roberts and James Donaldson (1888; Grand Rapids: Eerdmans, 1970), 380. Available online at http://www.ccel.org/ccel/schaff/anf07.viii.iii.ix.html. Thanks is given for "the holy Vine of thy servant David," a prayer is made that the scattered church be "gathered into one," and access to the holy Eucharist is hedged.

6. A. S. Wood, "Creeds and Confessions," in *International Standard Bible Encyclopedia*, vol. 1, ed. Geoffrey W. Bromiley (Grand Rapids: Eerdmans, 1995), 808.

7. Careful observations concerning the continuity of themes and elements from the *Didache* through to Serapian are made by Senn, *Christian Liturgy*, 63.

8. *The Anaphora of the Holy Apostles Addai and Mari* may be found online at http://www .oxuscom.com/liturgy.htm#Anaphora. This version is reproduced from the text provided by William Macomber, "The Ancient Form of the *Anaphora of the Apostles*," in *East of Byzantium: Syria and Armenia in the Formative Period*, ed. Nina Gargoian, Thomas Mathews, and Robert Thomson (Washington, DC: Centre for Byzantine Studies, 1982), 73–88. One of the difficulties of working with such texts is to determine how much is of ancient origin and which portions have been added by connection with other liturgical traditions. Senn believes that some of these parts of the Anaphora actually come from a later time, such as the addition of the Sanctus after the Trisagion. However, it is clear that even the earliest version was influenced by Isaiah 6 and sounds forth the theme of entrance into mystery. See Senn, *Christian Liturgy*, 80–81.

9. Gerald Moultrie, "Let All Mortal Flesh Keep Silence," 1864.

10. This beginning to the Great Entrance of the *Liturgy of St. James* may be found in the version at http://web.ukonline.co.uk/ephrem/lit-james.htm.

11. Senn, *Christian Liturgy*, 120.

12. This distortion of the meaning of the entrances has been made not only by visitors to Eastern churches but by members too, and the Church is indebted to Father Alexander Schmemann for fighting a battle to restore the original meaning in the imaginations of Orthodox.

13. My emphasis. These phrases are taken from two versions of the liturgy, the first academic and the second popular: http://web.ukonline.co.uk/ephrem/lit-james.htm and http://elibron .com/cgi-bin/pview_pdf.php?fpt=L3UwOC91c3IvdXBsb2FkL3B2aWV3X3R4dDAwMy8xMDAy MzI5Ny82MzMwMwNA==.

14. There are many translations of this ancient, but consistently and currently used, liturgy. The most popular English version is available online at http://www.ocf.org/OrthodoxPage/ liturgy/liturgy.html. For a more complete compilation of Orthodox worship, consult (Archbishop) Lazar Puhalo, trans., *A Clergy Service Book: For Service with Priest and Deacon*, 4th ed. (Duvall, WA: Theophany, 2007). Those interested in seeing the Greek online may find it, along with the English translation, a commentary, and a musical setting, at http://www.newbyz .org/complete_liturgy_book.pdf.

15. Schmemann, *The Eucharist*, 63.

16. The origin of Great Vespers is difficult to ascertain, but many scholars would date a service of this sort as having a place in Christian worship before the sixth century. Its best-known hymn, *Phos Hilaron* (Hail, Gladsome Light!) is most likely the oldest Christian hymn not of biblical derivation.

17. St. John Chrysostom's explanation is quoted by (*Metropolitan) Kallistos Ware, "Approaching Christ the Physician: The True Meaning of Confession and Anointing," October 18, 2004, on Communion: Web site of the Orthodox Peace Fellowship, http://incommunion .org/?p=100.

18. All of the quotations from *Kairon* are taken from Puhalo, *A Clergy Service Book*.

19. This version of the prayer is taken from the *Service Book of the Holy Eastern Catholic and Apostolic Church According to the Use of the Antiochian Orthodox Church Archdiocese of North America* (Englewood Hills, NJ: Antiochian Orthodox Christian Diocese of North America, 1971), 91.

20. This phrase comes from stanza 8 of Isaac Watts's 1719 hymn "Jesus Shall Reign."

21. Dix, *Shape of the Liturgy*, 118. Dom. Dix is speaking specifically of Roman rite which, after the end of the fourth century, added a priestly prayer that commended the people's own offering, not his own actions. In the East, too, the entire congregation is understood as making the offering, with God himself being the main actor, though the priest "lends his hand and provides his tongue" (so says St. John Chrysostom, quoted in Kallistos Ware, "Approaching Christ the Physician").

22. Schmemann, *The Eucharist*, especially chapter 3, 49–64.

23. Ibid., 61.

24. In both Orthodox and Roman Catholic tradition, these were the parents of Mary, the mother of Jesus. That they can be called the "ancestors of God" may be shocking to Protestant ears, just as Theotokos ("bearer of God") is too bold a title in some minds for Mary herself. If Jesus is truly one, however (the God-Man) and not divided or fragmented in nature, these titles are both appropriate.

25. The use of dramatic metaphors to describe worship is helpful, though it has its limitations. Of late, biblical scholars such as N. T. Wright, throughout *The New Testament and the People of God* (Minneapolis: Fortress Press, 1992), have referred to the entire story of salvation history in terms of an ongoing drama, in which we participate: worship is, if anything, an intensification of our human experience and in traditional liturgies actually re-presents the salvation story. Some might complain that the idea of drama gives a sense of removal, or distance, from reality, as when we speak of "play-acting." We may think, however, of the play of children, which is generally quite serious, and which, in some ways, forms children into the adults that they are becoming. Especially in the Orthodox Divine Liturgy, we see a complex interplay between acting and becoming. At the beginning of the Eucharist proper, the congregation understands itself in these words, "We who mystically represent the cherubim, and who sing the Thrice-Holy Hymn." The worshipers are, it seems, "putting on" angelic garb—and so, in worship, they become like the angels. Surprisingly, it seems that the cherubim themselves "put on" human dress while they adore God, for they are described as four "living creatures" in Rev. 4:6–7, one with the face of a human being, and all of them together presenting the needs of creation before God. When creatures worship, it seems, there is a mutual sharing of identities, a bringing together of the whole created order. We enact this communion in the liturgy, beginning as "actors" who re-present each other, and thus becoming the healed creation that God has in mind for us to be.

26. Again, it is a complex matter to determine how much of the liturgy now said has been developed since the time of St. Basil. The liturgy as it is now said in parishes that use English may be found in various translations, but one such version is available at http://www.goarch .org/chapel/liturgical_texts/basil#divine.

27. For a discussion of the relationship between the liturgies, and an analysis of their roots, see especially pp. 196–97 in Robert F. Taft, SJ, "St. John Chrysostom and the Byzantine Anaphora

That Bears His Name," in Paul F. Bradshaw, ed., *Essays on Early Eastern Eucharistic Prayers* (Collegeville, MN: Liturgical, 1997), 195–226; and Robert F. Taft, SJ, "The Authenticity of the Chrysostom Anaphora Revisited: Determining the Authorship of Liturgical Texts by Computer," *Orientalia Christiana Periodica* 56 (1990): 5–51.

28. This praise to Mary, which begins *Axios estin*, "It is meet and right" is not of St. John's own composing but was added under the influence of the monks of Mt. Athos, perhaps by means of the eighth-century St. Cosmas the Hymnographer. Here is an example of a living liturgy that takes on new life throughout the centuries.

29. Schmemann, *The Eucharist*, 88.

30. Fr. Patrick Reardon, "Fourth Sunday after Pentecost," *Father Pat's Pastoral Ponderings*, All Saints Antiochian Orthodox Church, July 5, 2009, available online at http://www.allsaints orthodox.org/pastor/pastoral_ponderings.php.

31. St. John Damascus, in the midst of the *iconoclastic controversy, was worried that some might read St. Basil as suggesting that the mysteries were only images or symbols, and so says that the term is used of the *elements before they are consecrated. They are not simply types (he exclaims, "God forbid!") and as "antitypes" they both participate in and point forward to the intimacy with God that is to come. (*An Exact Exposition of the Orthodox Faith*, 4.13). St. Cyril of Alexandria uses both type and antitype to refer to the outer and inner nature of the mysteries in his Catechetical Orations. (See the notes found in Edwin Hamilton Gifford, DD, *Writings of Cyril. The Catechetical Lecture: The Catechetical Lectures of St. Cyril, Archbishop of Jerusalem*, ed. Philip Schaff (New York: Christian Literature, 1893). Available online at http://mb-soft.com/believe/txuc/cyril34.htm.

32. In this suggested translation, I read the genitives in the phrase "antitypes *of* thy holy Body and Blood" (*ta antitypa tou hagou sōmatou kai haimatos tou Christou sou*) as *defining* the word "antitypes"—for grammar buffs, as "epexegetical genitives." My suggestion is similar to that of sixteenth-century Bishop of the Catholic Reformation Robert Bellarmine, who had qualms over the use of *type* for the elements but was less concerned with *antitype*, since "not all figures are called antitypes, but only those who differ scarcely at all from the truth" (*De Sacr. Euch.*, cited in Scudamore, *England and Rome; A Discussion* [London: Rivington's, 1855], 364). For the Greek language of St. Basil's Liturgy, see http://analogion.net/glt/texts/Oro/Basil_Liturgy.uni.htm.

33. St. Gregory of Nanzianzen is cited in Geoffrey Wainwright, *Doxology: The Praise of God in Worship, Doctrine, and Life: A Systematic Theology* (New York: Oxford University Press, 1980), 466, concerning the Alexandrine Anaphora.

34. The ambon is the area directly in front of the Royal Doors, that is, on the congregational side, in the center of the iconostasis. This is also where Communion is regularly administered, at the place of entrance.

Chapter 5 "In the Great Congregation"

1. Dix, *Shape of the Liturgy*, 116.

2. Again, see ibid., 114–15.

3. 1 Clement in Philip Schaff, *Ante-Nicene Fathers*, vol. 1, *The Apostolic Fathers with Justin Martyr and Irenaeus*, ed. Alexander Roberts and James Donaldson (1885; Grand Rapids: Eerdmans, 1973). Available online at http://www.ccel.org/ccel/schaff/anf01.ii.ii.xxix.html. All subsequent references to Clement come from this edition.

4. Some of the arguments mounted by Clement, for example, his restriction of worship times and places, may appear to us as very rigorous and as imposing a "legal" dimension upon the Church. Others have seen in this letter an implicit suggestion that Clement saw himself, the Bishop of Rome, as having jurisdiction over Corinth. That he is assuming universal jurisdiction is not wholly clear, though certainly Clement expected that his authority as a bishop would be recognized in Corinth among the dissidents there. Clement's appeal to *taxis* (order), in the assembly and in the life of the Church, stands alongside organic metaphors of the body and of a

vital, growing community, which he yearns to see at Corinth. His perspective is not, therefore, simply that of the Church as an institution to rule, but as something interdependent and living.

5. See his *First Apology* 26:7.

6. Justin Martyr, *First Apology* 1:67, in Schaff, *Ante-Nicene Fathers*, vol. 1, *Apostolic Fathers*, 186, my emphasis. Available online at http://www.ccel.org/ccel/schaff/anf01.viii.ii.lxvii.html.

7. Ambrose, *Epistles*, 70.4–5 (Epistle to Marcellina his sister) in Fathers of the Church Series, vol. 26, *Saint Ambrose Letters*, trans. Sister Mary Melchior Beyenka, OP (New York: Fathers of the Church, 1954), 366; Egeria, *Pilgrimmage of Egeria* 24.11 and elsewhere; H. A. Wilson, *The Gelasian Sacramentary* (Oxford: Clarendon, 1894). We will look at the possible meanings for the term *Mass* later in this chapter.

8. Justin Martyr, *Dialogue* 117, in Schaff, *Ante-Nicene Fathers*, vol. 1, *Apostolic Fathers*, available online at http://www.ccel.org/ccel/schaff/anf01.viii.iv.cxvii.html.

9. For a thorough but readable discussion of how the work has been accepted by many scholars as that of Hippolytus, on literary and archaeological grounds, see the helpful Grove booklet by Geoffrey J. Cuming, *Hippolytus: A Text for Students: With Introduction, Translation, Commentary and Notes*, Grove Liturgical Study 8 (Bramcote, Nottingham, UK: Grove Books, 1976), 3–4.

10. Marcel Metzger ("Nouvelles perspectives pour le prétendue Tradition apostolique," *Ecclesia Orans* 5 [1988]: 241–59) first argued this case, which has been taken up in the new Hermeneia commentary by Paul F. Bradshaw, Maxwell E. Johnson, and L. Edward Phillips, *The Apostolic Tradition: A Commentary* (Minneapolis: Fortress, 2002), 13–15. See also the edition produced by Alistair Stewart-Sykes, *Hippolytus: On the Apostolic Tradition* (Crestwood, NY: St. Vladimir's Seminary Press, 2001), who sees Hippolytus as the last of several compilers and editors who integrated traditions and prescriptions for worship and church order during a time of conflict concerning whether the Roman Church was to be led by a single bishop.

11. Some believe that this passage is of very early origin, possibly early second century, since it uses ancient terms such as "Child" (also used in the *Didache*) for Jesus. Others believe it to be based on early material but edited by a later author, since the Eucharist is folded into the description of the episcopal consecration. One influential author, Bradshaw, believes that some of the service has been added as late as the fourth century.

12. Of special note is Dom. Gregory Dix, who has produced a thorough annotated edition and translation of the work, reconstructed from the various languages: Dom. Gregory Dix, *The Treatise on the Apostolic Tradition of St. Hippolytus of Rome*, reissued with corrections by Henry Chadwick (London: Alban, 1937; Ridgefield, CT: Morehouse, 1992). Also helpful is the synoptic version offered in the Hermeneia series: see Bradshaw, Johnson, and Phillips, *The Apostolic Tradition*.

13. This translation of *Apostolic Tradition* 4 is that of Kevin P. Edgecomb, available online at http://www.bombaxo.com/hippolytus.html. It corresponds mostly to the Latin version of what was originally a Greek text, though the latter has been lost. To this helpful work, I have added a few paragraph markers; I have also put his footnoted alternate translations in square brackets and given one other important alternate translation in doubled square brackets. The emphasis also is mine.

14. It is important to note, however, that the "in the Church" wording is not found in the Latin text, where we might have expected it, given Cyprian's arguments about there being "no salvation outside the Church."

15. The kiss of peace is described just prior to the rite that we have quoted and is found also in the *synaxis*, or meeting for liturgy described elsewhere in *Apostolic Tradition* 18. That it was a well-known feature of Western worship, both in Rome and in Carthage, is seen in the comments of both Justin (*First Apology* 65) and Tertullian (*De Oratione*, 18).

16. Joseph Metzinger comments: "Even as late as 426 the Roman liturgy began abruptly with the Scripture readings; St. Augustine describes an Easter Sunday Mass where the first scripture reading is preceded only by a simple greeting." See "Western Catholic Liturgies: Gregorian

Reforms," Liturgica.com, http://www.liturgica.com/html/litWLReform.jsp?hostname=null. In case we think, however, that this indicates a lack of interest in preparation, it is important to remember that in the early days of the Church, the catechumens, along with their sympathetic sponsors, underwent a rigorous training prior to Easter baptisms.

17 *On the Mysteries*, in Philip Schaff, *Nicene and Post-Nicene Fathers*, vol. 10, trans. H. de Romesin (Grand Rapids: Eerdmans, 1955), 323. Online at http://www.ccel.org/ccel/schaff/npnf210.iv.v.html. This translation, though not contemporary, is helpful because it views the congregation as a whole, as one.

18. *The Sacraments*, 4.6.27 in *The Fathers of the Church: A New Translation,* Vol. 44, *Saint Ambrose Theological and Dogmatic Works* (Washington, DC: Catholic University of America Press, 1963). The authorship of *The Sacraments* continues to be disputed but is defended as Ambrose by translator Roy J. Deferrari on pp. 265–67 of this volume. There is an online version of the Fathers of the Church series, including many of the ancient texts studied in this book, at http://www.orthodox.cn/patristics/frchurchnewtrans_en.htm.

19. Augustine, *Sermons on the Liturgical Seasons*, trans. Mary Sarah Muldowney, Fathers of the Church: A New Translation, vol. 38 (New York: Fathers of the Church, 1959).

20. Helpful information on the missal, plus spirited commentary and discussion, are found in the essays collected by Yitzhak Hen and Rob Meens, eds., *The Bobbio Missal: Liturgy and Religious Culture in Merovingian Gaul* (Cambridge: Cambridge University Press, 2004).

21. In the thematic collects, as with the hymns, we see the particular genius of the West. We will consider the structure of collects in a later chapter when we look at contemporary Anglican worship that has preserved this element of the ancient West.

22. Louise P. M. Batstone, "Doctrinal and Theological Themes," in Hen and Meens, *Bobbio Missal*, 173.

23. Sermon 69 in *St. Caesarius of Arles, Sermons 1–80*, trans. Mary Magdeleine Mueller, Fathers of the Church Series, vol. 31 (New York: Fathers of the Church, 1956), 325.

24. The Old Testament Apocrypha is the term used to describe those books and passages that were considered noncanonical by Protestant Reformers, who followed the decision of the Jewish community in this regard: the books in the collection are a mixture of genres, and there are also passages that amplify, in particular, the book of Daniel, such as the Song of the Three. The Roman Catholic and Orthodox communities accept these books with some variations, calling them "Deuterocanonical" or "Readable Books." Even the Reformers thought that the apocryphal books had value for fostering piety and prayer; they simply should not be used for doctrine. However, they are much neglected today. A helpful resource for Protestants interested in an introduction to the Apocrypha has been written by David deSilva: *Introducing the Apocrypha* (Grand Rapids: Baker, 2002).

25. The Latin text may be seen in Hen and Meens, *Bobbio Missal*, 148, where it is compared with a less verbose liturgy.

26. Those who would like to have a taste in English of the liturgical prayers in the Bobbio missal may read pp. 201–3 (Appendix 1) of Hen and Meens, *Bobbio Missal*, where there is reproduced the "Mass for the Ruler" (*Princeps*). Here, the thematic element is very strong, referring to the King of kings, to Abraham as the head of his servants, to Melchizedek, to the arms of Moses held by Hur, to the hosts of heaven, to Joshua's victory, and to Goliath.

27. Online versions of this rite, in both Latin and English, are available at http://justus .anglican.org/resources/bcp/Sarum.

28. A helpful study of the manuscripts that set forward the tradition of Sarum processionals has been written by Terence Bailey, *The Processions of Sarum and the Western Church* (Toronto: Pontifical Institute of Mediaeval Studies, 1971).

29. We might suspect that the English translator has provided the addition "and sisters" for the sake of today's reader. In fact, the rites of Sarum, Bangor, and York make explicit mention of women who are worshiping as well as of women saints. See John Theodore Dodd, *The*

Ordinary and Canon of the Roman Mass According to the Use of Sarum (London: Joseph Masters, 1872), 25.

30. We should note, however, that the invocation of the Holy Spirit occurs in this older Western rite as a general *offertory invitation, without the request that the elements be changed: "Come, O Almighty and Eternal God, the Sanctifier, bless this sacrifice."

31. Dix, *Shape of the Liturgy*, 15.

32. For a trenchant Eastern critique and admission of Eastern fault in this matter, see Schmemann, *The Eucharist*, 195–227. Though Communion is received far more regularly among Orthodox laity today, there are still some Eastern traditions where children are brought forward for Communion while their parents and other lay adults tend to refrain, apparently out of scrupulous attention to their state of preparation.

33. Anne Roche, *The Gates of Hell: The Struggle for the Catholic Church* (Toronto: McClelland and Stewart, 1975).

34. This document, which gives the Tridentine teaching on Communion, is found online at http://www.catholicapologetics.info/thechurch/catechism/Holy7Sacraments-Eucharist.shtml.

35. After the reforms of Trent, the bishop's mass retained this custom of processing out while reading from the prologue of John's Gospel.

36. Theodor Klauser, *A Short History of the Western Liturgy: An Account and Some Reflections*, trans. John Halliburton (New York: Oxford University Press, 1979), 37 (originally published in German in 1965). Some of Klauser's reflections on Roman practice and liturgy are less complimentary than this statement about entry into corporate worship!

37. An e-version of both the Latin and English translation of the Tridentine Mass is available at http://www.ewtn.com/library/LITURGY/TRIDMASS.TXT.

38. For more information on these developments, see http://www.katapi.org.uk/Singing Church/Ch5.htm.

39. Pope St. Pius V, "Apostolic Constitution: Quo Primum," July 14, 1570, http://www.papalencyclicals.net/Pius05/p5quopri.htm.

40. The quotation is from Henry Francis Lyte's *Praise My Soul, the King of Heaven*, but this stanza is frequently omitted when the hymn is sung today.

41. Though *theosis is more associated with the East than the West, we see in this prayer the association of the Eucharist (sharing in Christ) with 2 Pet. 1:3–11, the biblical foundation of the doctrine. More about theosis can be learned in the glossary.

42. The scholarly literature on this debate is staggering. A helpful article that sets out the tradition and the debate concerning the meaning of *missa est* is available online: Adrian Fortescue, "Liturgy of the Mass," *The Catholic Encyclopedia*, vol. 9 (New York: Robert Appleton, 1910), http://www.newadvent.org/cathen/09790b.htm>.http://www.newadvent.org/cathen/09790b.htm.

Chapter 6   "Your Church Unsleeping"

1. There are several publications now that have "corrected" the lyrics by pluralizing them ("And I will raise *them* up"), in order to avoid the masculine pronoun "him." The revisers have not noticed that they have also stripped the song of its particularity (the story of raised Lazarus) and of its personal impact for the sake of political correctness. We might also note that the female lyricist was not worried by the pronoun, and that the revision is tantamount to correcting the Lord—or the fourth evangelist—from whom the words are derived.

2. The third scenario (the Anglican parish) is a composite, derived from my memory of a past visit there and from observations of several who attended that service, including the memory of the music leader/pastor. The final two scenarios from China (based on a trip in 2006) are specifically obscured in order to guarantee the security of the church leadership. All the other scenarios are more recent, drawn from my visits, specifically with an eye to this project. In the case of the fourth scenario (the Presbyterian congregation), my visit was a virtual one (tapes and photos) though I have experienced worship under the direction of their pastor/music director in the context of a conference.

3. This hymn is by Michael Perry, 1988.

4. For an explanation of these ministers and guidelines for their service in the North American Catholic Church, see http://www.usccb.org/liturgy/girm/lit4.shtml.

5. *Vatican II was a solemn general council of the Roman Catholic Church that opened under Pope John XXIII on October 11, 1962, and closed under Pope Paul VI on December 8, 1965. Responding to various critical issues of the twentieth century, the bishops deliberated especially on the doctrine of the Church, the liturgy, and the nature of revelation. One of its legacies was a revised Eucharist of which the Latin and English versions are to be found at http://www .preces-latinae.org/Libelli/Missa.pdf.

6. Ted Rosean, "Two Rites Make a Wrong," *USCatholic*, July 14, 2009, http://www.uscatholic .org/church/2009/07/two-rites-make-wrong?page=0%2C0.

7. Perhaps my visceral reaction to the song is borne out by Carter's own admission: "By Christ, I mean not only Jesus; in other times and places, other planets, there may be other lords of the dance. But Jesus is the one I know of first and best. I sing of the dancing pattern in the life and words of Jesus." This statement is quoted in his obituary, demonstrating that the songwriter did not have a secure grasp of the uniqueness of Jesus the Messiah and the God-Man. If he can honor him in song, he cannot worship him as the One who is alone to be worshiped, with the Father and the Holy Spirit. The creaturely and folk quality of his minstral Jesus cannot command such adoration. The popularity of the lyrics, put to a Quaker tune, among Anglican and Protestant circles perhaps made it inevitable that it should have been discovered by Catholic musicians. For Carter's obituary see http://www.guardian.co.uk/news/2004/mar/17/guardianobituaries.religion.

8. As this book goes to press, I have been notified of the forthcoming work by Benedictine Anscar Chupungko, *What, Then, Is Liturgy? Musings and Memoir* (Collegeville, MN: Liturgical, 2010). Father Chupungko's contribution to the discussion in Catholic circles is positive with regards to the "gift" of Vatican II—namely, "active participation in the liturgy" (24), even while he ruefully recognizes that in some places since the council there have been eucharistic celebrations that have "the features and qualities of showbiz" (30). In speaking of the very study of liturgy, he traces our theme of entrance: "Studying the theology of liturgy is like entering a forest of doctrines, symbols, metaphors, and poetry. We may take delight in the loftiness of a doctrine, or in the beauty of a symbol, but we should not lose sight of their deeper spiritual meaning … to discover the face of God in …worship" (lxi). Others echo the fundamental question that underlies his helpful discussion of the Vatican II *aggiornamento* ("updating"): "Is there a need to reform the reform?" (xv).

9. "The median church in the U.S. has 75 regular participants in worship on Sunday mornings," finds a recent study done by the Hartford Institute for Religion Research, http://hirr .hartsem.edu/research/fastfacts/fast_facts.html.

10. A "troparion" is a short thematic hymn, intended to be repeated throughout a particular feast. Sometimes these are printed in the church bulletin for the week, but more often, they are simply known by the worshipers as they go through the church year. Any visitor who doesn't know the troparion for a specific feast is sure to know it by the end of the feast, if they attend all the services!

11. Orthodox worship typically is more embodied than many Western expressions. On the importance of the body in Christian worship, see Steven R. Guthrie, "Temples of the Spirit: Worship as Embodied Performance," in *Faithful Performances: Enacting Christian Tradition*, ed. Trevor A. Hart and Steven R. Guthrie (Aldershot, UK: Ashgate, 2007), 91–107.

12. I quote here from the NKJV, that version used for the New Testament in the Orthodox Study Bible, in order to retain the flavor of the service.

13. When I was regularly preaching as a Salvation Army officer, I was tempted several years running to adopt this second text for Mother's Day, as a warning against the sentimentalization that can occur in thematic worship. It is interesting that even among the Orthodox, who honor the Theotokos, there is no shrinking away from Jesus' seemingly harsh statements about what brings blessing.

14. John Chryssavgis, *Light through Darkness: The Orthodox Tradition* (Maryknoll, NY: Orbis, 2004), 20.

15. Ibid., 39.

16. Ibid., 20.

17. Steve James's music is known mostly in Britain, where he now serves as priest to a congregation and musician in various conferences. He is also chair of *Jubilate Hymns*. His music and life story may be seen at http://www.stevejamesmusic.com/sjmusic.html.

18. An opening excerpt of this song is available as selection number 10 of the album "All My Ways" and also number 10 of "Voices in the Desert," at http://www.stevejamesmusic.com/sjdownloads.html. The full song is available for order on this site and also on iTunes.

19. This parish prefers to follow the classical *Book of Common Prayer*, in its revised (Canadian) 1963 format, for its services, unlike many Canadian parishes that reserve the older form for the early morning service and use the *Book of Alternative Services* for their major service(s). The choice of the BCP over the BAS is made here not because of a predilection for archaic language but because the BAS has altered the tone and structure of the original Anglican service, which has an impact upon the theology as well; the newer forms are far less penitential, for example. American readers should know that the liturgies given in their 1979 (American) *Book of Common Prayer*, commonly used in Episcopal churches in the United States, are more akin to those found in the Canadian BAS. Even "Rite I" in the American book, which retains some of the archaic language, does not preserve the same structure as the classical Anglican eucharistic liturgy. American parishes, therefore, do not have easy access to the earlier liturgy, whereas in Canada, parishes may have both the BAS and the BCP in the pews. For a helpful set of resources on the common prayer tradition in Anglicanism including American and Canadian Books of Common Prayer and the BAS, see http://justus.anglican.org/resources/bcp/.

20. George E. Mims, DM, Organist and Director of Music Interim, St. Paul's Episcopal Church, Mobile, Alabama; Organist and Director of Music Emeritus, St. Martin's Episcopal Church, Houston. This statement was made in a discussion group, and I have asked Dr. Mims for his permission to quote it.

21. For these prayers and others, see the version of the 1963 Canadian Book of Common Prayer at http://justus.anglican.org/resources/bcp/. In this evening service, the antiquated language (thee, thou) was modified by the one praying.

22. S. Trevor Francis's traditional words (1875) usually are set to the tune "Ebenezer," composed by Thomas J. Williams (1880).

23. This hymn is by James Montgomery, 1820.

24. Hymn by Casey Corum, 2003.

25. Patterns for the free-style prayers of the presider are given at W-3.3613 of the *Book of Order*, which is Part II of *The Constitution of the Presbyterian Church (U.S.A.)* (Louisville: Office of the General Assembly 2007), and also on p. 156 of *Book of Common Worship* (Louisville: Westminster John Knox, 1993).

26. "Go to Dark Gethsemane" is by James Montgomery, 1820; "Draw Me Nearer, Precious Lord" is by Frances J. Crosby, 1975.

27. The words of this hymn are by Jackson W. Van De Ventor, 1886; music by W. S. Weeden, 1896.

28. For more information on these songs and other contemporary settings for ancient hymns such as the *Phos Hilaron* and the *Agnus Dei*, contact Robert Austell at http://robertaustell .blogspot.com. Of real interest is also Robert Austell's *Biblical Worship through Music* (n.p.: Robert Austell Publishing, 2009), available at lulu.com. His book tackles the worship wars from a Presbyterian but small "c" catholic perspective, providing helpful insights, statistics, and planning strategies for those whose role is to supervise or lead worship.

29. This statement, and all those that follow, are taken from the pastor's answers to a questionnaire sent to him (and others) as part of my research.

30. This song is by Rufus McDonald, 1914.

31. This carol is by John W. Work Jr., 1907.

32. From the praise song by Bob Fitts, "Blessed Be the Lord God Almighty," 1985.

33. Words for this hymn are by Charles Wesley, 1739; music by Mendelssohn, 1840.

34. The benediction, "O Father, Let Thy Love Remain," is the English translation by Salvation Army officer William F. Palstra (1904–73), who also put to music this Dutch benediction of Henrik Ghysen (1660–93). It first appeared in the *Musical Salvationist* (London: Salvationist Publishing and Supplies, 1949) and started to appear in North American Salvation Army songbooks in the mid-1950s.

35. This is the opening stanza to a beloved Army hymn, "My Life Must Be Christ's Broken Bread," by General Albert Orsborn, a Salvationist poet laureate.

36. This praise song is by David Moody, 1974.

37. C. S. Lewis, *Reflections on the Psalms* (Glasgow: Collins, 1961), 48.

38. The best known writer of the *emergent movement would be Brian McLaren, whose writings speak both of the importance of novel approaches in a changing culture and of a recovery of the ancient traditions of the Church. See his first and last books, for example: *The Church on the Other Side* (Grand Rapids: Zondervan, 2006); *Finding Our Way Again: The Return of the Ancient Practices* (Nashville: Thomas Nelson, 2008). For a recent description of the movement see Eddie Gibbs and Ryan Bolger, *Emerging Churches: Creating Christian Community in Postmodern Cultures* (Grand Rapids: Baker Academic, 2005). For a critique, see D. A. Carson, *Becoming Conversant with the Emerging Church* (Grand Rapids: Zondervan, 2005). It is important to remember that we are speaking of a movement and that not all emerging or emergent communities would agree, for example, with all the philosophical and theological declarations of its most prominent members.

39. From the song "Forever," by Chris Tomlin, 2001.

40. These words are from the song "Let My Words Be Few," 2000.

41. Since 1979, the one-child policy has been rather strictly enforced in China, leading to an unbalanced population of young men or boys to young women or girls. (Families allowed only one child have aborted more female children than male, leaving room for the desired sex.) This is of great concern at this point: how ironic that a policy meant to bring social aid is now causing sociological trouble. Here would seem to be a strong indication that a society that routinely flouts moral law will reap the difficulties inherent in its choices. The church's role in systemic societal sin is complex, but indicated, as we are called to be both "salt and light." It is, of course, far easier to see societal sin from a distance than to recognize that in which we are immersed.

42. The hymnal used by the Protestant *"Three-Self Patriotic Movement" or Church was presented to me by one of the university professors of religion in Nanjing. In China there are only two state-sanctioned Christian denominations—the Roman Catholic and the Protestant (an amalgamation of the various mission churches that once existed)—and these are subject to government intervention. The hymnbook contains many hymns known in the West, but also some more recently written hymns that express the three-self philosophy of self-governance, self-support, and self-propagation, as well as themes arising from Chinese culture. In *The New Hymnal* (The Chinese Christian Hymnal Committee, 1983) one finds several hymns, for example, on respecting the elderly and filial piety (e.g., numbers 188 and 189) but also hymns glorifying the new Chinese church in its "self-reliance" (hymns 127 and 128): "Guide Thou Our Church, 'Three-self' Goals to Sustain."

43. "Precious Name, Oh How Sweet," is by Lydia O. Baxter, 1870; "Just as I Am," is by Charlotte Elliott, 1835; "He Leadeth Me," is by Joseph H. Gilmore, 1862.

44. Taizé was a religious community composed of about a hundred monks from Roman Catholic, Orthodox, and Protestant traditions who gathered in Taizé, Saône-et-Loire in Burgundy, France. Many young people make pilgrimages to the community to share in their prayer, study, and communal work. Its music, made up of simple yet profound repetitive refrains, has

been of help in bringing quiet reverence and a focus upon Christ into various denominations. The movement's Web site is found at http://www.taize.fr/en.

45. William Temple, *Readings in the Fourth Gospel* (London: MacMillan, 1955), 68.

46. Ibid., my emphasis.

Chapter 7   "That Your Prayers Not Be Hindered"

1. This is not the place to engage fully in this debate. For those who are interested, here is a sketch. Both the Eastern and Western Church are concerned about authority (does Rome have authority to establish a change in the creed, without the consent of the rest of the Church?) and about trinitarian doctrine (what *is* the mysterious inter-relationship between Father, Son, and Holy Spirit?). Some have also argued that what we believe about the Trinity affects our understanding of the structure of the Church: the structural differences between West and East (e.g., papal infallibility over against the authority of bishops in a council) are then seen as directly related to this debate. Others have said that the matter of the procession of the Spirit is not so serious a division, and that East and West need to understand what the other means by their different phrase. Some have looked for a new formulation from the ancient past, agreeable to both sides: "The Holy Spirit . . . proceeds from the Father *through* the Son." But such a change would require a worldwide ecumenical council! Many Protestants remain unaware or detached from the debate, though some are wholly committed to the Western formula that they have received (found also in the *Athanasian "creed")* while others insist that, out of fairness alone, we should revert to the original wording.

2. Rick Warren, *The Purpose-Driven Church: Growth without Compromising Your Message and Mission* (Grand Rapids: Zondervan, 1995), 286–87.

3. See "Ask Rick Muchow: Burnout and Songs in Minor Key," Rick Warren's Ministry ToolBox, April 1, 2004, http://www.pastors.com/blogs/ministrytoolbox/archive/2004/04/01/Ask-Rick-Muchow_3A00_-Burnout-and-songs-in-minor-key.aspx.

4. This poignant line is from Harry Van Dyke, "Joyful, Joyful, We Adore Thee," 1908.

5. This injunction is made in the Orthodox Divine Liturgy.

6. This sentiment is found in Robert Robertson's "Come, Thou Fount of Every Blessing," 1757.

7. This service is found at http://www.indymenno.org/bulletins/bulletin2008_10_05.doc. For other examples of these "out of the box" services, see also http://www.liturgyoutside.net/Breads.pdf.

8. Meditating upon the passion, suffering, and death of Jesus in stages is a very ancient practice in the Western Church and is called "the Stations of the Cross," the Way of Sorrows, the *Via Crucis*, or the *Via Dolorosa*. It may be done in personal devotion or as a congregation, with clergy leading the responses as the congregation visits each station (usually fourteen): many Catholic churches, and some Anglican, too, actually have representations of the various stages on the walls around the sanctuary, beginning with Jesus' condemnation to death and ending in his burial. The most famous of these would be, of course, the large scale representation of the *Via Dolorosa* in the Old City of Jerusalem, beginning with the Monastery of the Flagellation. For an article on the Millennium stations, see the March 2008 article by Susan Wunderink, http://www.christianitytoday.com/ct/2008/marchweb-only/110–42.0.html.

9. James Hitchcock, "Citizen, Heal Thyself: Social Sins Are Easily and Fashionably Confessed," *Touchstone: A Journal of Mere Christianity* (November/December 2009): 3.

10. Ibid.

11. Brian Wren, "When Minds and Bodies Meet as One," *The New Century Hymnal* (Cleveland, OH: Pilgrim, 1996), 399. I do not intend to disparage the manifest talent of this poet-musician, and I have myself used some of his songs. Rather, because Wren's offerings are so popular in the mainstream today, and because his artistry is impressive, when the Christian message is altered, the effect can be serious. In an interview, Wren outlines his perceived vocation to "speak truth by stepping beyond the church's limits of comfort and convention" (Ruth Vander

Hart, "Poet of Faith: An Interview with Brian Wren," *Reformed Worship* 17 [September 1990], http://www.reformedworship.org/magazine/article.cfm?article_id=305). See also his program to alter "KINGFP [King-God-Almighty-Father-Protector]" language for God so that it fits more easily in our inclusivist culture, as outlined in his book *What Language Shall I Borrow?* (New York: Crossroad, 1989). Those who share the theological views implicit in his lyrics may use them without reserve; those who do not should be aware of the implications, so that they do not simply use an artistically pleasing song without a view to the contents.

12. The lyrics are those of General Albert Orsborn, "In the Secret of Thy Presence," Song 531 of *The Song Book of the Salvation Army* (London: Salvationist Publishing and Supplies, 1955). Though this verse is not known outside of Army circles, there are numerous contemporary Christian songs with the same effusive language that may focus our minds upon the depth of our devotion, rather than upon the One being worshiped. This is not a critique of Orsborn's offerings but meant to register a potential danger.

13. Patrick Henry Reardon, *Christ in the Psalms* (Ben Lomond, CA: Conciliar, 2000).

14. Braddon Upex, "Essay on Hymnody," *Hippocampus Extensions* 8, January 2004, http://hippocampusextensions.com/issues/08/an_essay_on_hymnody. Used by permission.

15. "Preface and Selection of Hymns from the 1780 Handbook," in Frank Whaling, ed., *John and Charles Wesley: Selected Prayers, Hymns, Journal Notes, Sermons, Letters and Treatises* (New York: Paulist Press, 1981), 176–77.

16. See note 11 for this chapter.

17. For searching critique of inclusive language for God, see Alvin F. Kimel Jr., ed., *Speaking the Christian God: The Holy Trinity and the Challenge of Feminism* (Grand Rapids: Eerdmans, 1992); Elizabeth Achtemeier, "Female Language for God: Should the Church Adopt It?" in *The Hermeneutical Quest: Essays in Honor of James Luther Mays on His Sixty-fifth Birthday*, ed. Donald G. Miller (Allison Park, PA: Pickwick, 1986), 97–114; Susanne Heine, *Matriarchs, Goddesses and Images of God: A Critique of Feminist Theology*, trans. John Bowden (Minneapolis: Augsburg, 1989). Most lately see Andrew Purves and Charles Partee, *Encountering God: Christian Faith in the Turbulent Times* (Louisville: Westminster John Knox, 2000), esp. 23–32; and Andrew Purves and Charles Partee, "A Name Is Not a Metaphor: A Response to 'The Trinity: God's Love Overflowing,'" *Theology Matters* 12, no. 2 (March/April 2006): 1–4. Available online at http://www.theologymatters.com/MarApr06.pdf.

18. This is even more striking when we consider that the Greek noun for the Spirit is neuter in gender. Yet throughout John 14–17, Jesus uses the pronoun *ekeinos*, which is personal, rather than neuter, to refer to the Comforter who is to come.

19. John Chrysostom, "Homily 3" on Genesis, in *Homilies on Genesis 1–17*, trans. Robert C. Hill, Fathers of the Church Series, vol. 74 (Washington, DC: Catholic University of America Press, 1999), 39.

20. Walter Brueggemann addresses the problem in "Doxology without Reason," chapter 5 of *Israel's Praise: Doxology against Idolatry and Ideology* (Philadelphia: Fortress, 1988), 89–122. Brueggemann argues that praises offered without a foundation of reason can fall prey to ideology and give no reason for hope.

21. This hymn is by Walter C. Smith, 1876.

22. "These are the Days of Elijah," by Robin Mark is the song in question. There are some excellent lyrics here, when they are understood as Jesus fulfilling the promises of the Old Testament so as to give a field of harvest for the Church. I have attended services where the bridge was altered to "Who was, and is and is to come," but I wonder if such alterations are not an infringement of copyright.

23. Tim Hughes, "Here I Am to Worship." Here is a devout and talented author whom I do not intend to criticize. I only offer this as an example of how easily we have become accustomed to pausing at the point of introspection, rather than at the point where we see the Lord.

24. The site, run by a group called "The Open Episcopal Church," which boasts itself to be a member of the World Council of Churches, is found at http://www.postthehost.net/701.html.

25. This phrase comes from stanza 8 of Isaac Watts's 1719 hymn "Jesus Shall Reign."

26. C. S. Lewis, "On Church Music," in *Christian Reflections*, ed. Walter Hooper (Grand Rapids: Eerdmans, 1967), 94–99, quote at 96–97.

27. The declaration is that of the seventeenth-century Anglican priest George Herbert, from his poem "King of Glory, King of Peace," a work put to music and sung in some places even today.

28. This phrase comes from the first question of the Westminster Shorter Catechism, "What is the chief end of man?... Man's chief end is to glorify God and to enjoy him forever."

Conclusion

1. The phrase is from the vesperal hymn of the Church, East and West, *Phos Hilaron* ("O Joyous Light").

2. I offer thanks to Pope Benedict XVI, whose happy English translation of Augustine's phrase, "Singing is a lover's thing" has evidently influenced my own translation. For a taste of his 2000 book (translated from the German) *The Spirit of the Liturgy*, see http://www.ignatiusinsight .com/features2006/ratzinger_sotlmusic_jun06.asp.

3. Cardinal Joseph Ratzinger, "Music and Liturgy. How Does Music Express the Word of God, the Vision of God?" *Adoremus Bulletin* 7, no. 8 (November 2001). Available online at http://www.adoremus.org/1101musicliturgy.html.

4. A. Hamman, ed., *Early Christian Prayers*, trans. W. Mitchell (London: Longmans Green, 1961), 162.

5. C. S. Lewis's creation story is told in *The Magician's Nephew* (Glasgow: Collins, 1986).

6. Stephen Thuis, OSB, *Gregorian Chant: A Barometer of Religious Fervor* (private publication). Excerpts available online through *Una Voca America*, http://unavoce.org/uva-ar chive/gregorian-chant-a-barometer-of-religious-fervor/. This particular passage is also cited in Scott A. Haynes, SJC, "The Spirituality of Sacred Music: What Does It Mean When the Church Sings?" *Adoremus* 14, no. 7 (October 2008). Available online at http://www.adoremus .org/1008SacredMusic.html.

7. Lewis, *The Magician's Nephew*, 93–94.

Glossary of Foreign and Key Terms

a cappella—Singing in the "style of the chapel," that is, without instrumental accompaniment.

Adonai—Hebrew for "Lord." See YHWH.

Agnus Dei—"Lamb of God, who takes away the sin of the world, have mercy on us." A prayer said or sung in the Western rite of the Eucharist, introduced in the seventh century by Pope Sergius I.

alleluia—Latinized Hebrew for "Praise the LORD" (*Hallelu-jah!*). In liturgy, the repeated singing of Alleluia, usually three times, occurs at key points, such as the reading of the Gospel.

Anaphora—The "lifting up" prayer that begins the solemn part of the Eucharist: "Lift up your hearts!"

anthem—A special musical piece sung by the choir alone.

anthropomorphism—In theological discussion, this means to picture God as a human person, for example, to speak of God's hands or mouth.

antidoron—(literally, "The gift *instead of . . .*") The remaining blessed bread from the loaf after that which is to be used for the Eucharist has been removed. It is given in Eastern churches to guests who are not communicants and is also given and taken by communicant members after they have received the Eucharist, as an expression of love one for the other.

antitype—(Gk., *antitypos, typos*) A way of seeing relations between persons, things, and events in the history of salvation, most often between the Old and New Testaments. "Type" means quite literally a "stamp" or "mold" and refers to the person, thing, or event that points toward the real thing (usually something to come in the future). For example, the "burning bush" of Exodus is understood in Orthodox thought as the "type" of the Theotokos, who is the "antitype," or reality to which the bush corresponds. The bush bore the majestic presence of God, manifesting the I AM to Moses; Mary bore the God-Man, Jesus.

Typology is seen in the New Testament itself, as when St. Paul speaks about Adam as the type of the true man, Jesus, who was to come.

Apocrypha, Old Testament (Deuterocanonical Writings, Readable Books)— Books and passages considered noncanonical by Protestant Reformers. They are called "Deuterocanonical" in the Catholic tradition, and "Readable" in the Orthodox Church.

apology—(Gk., *apologia*) A written work or speech intended as a careful defense of a position or person.

apophatic—A theology that considers God without the use of terminology or words, or by saying what God is *not* like.

Apostles' Creed—An ancient statement of faith, less complex than the Nicene-Constantinopolitan Creed, that goes back at least to the fourth century. It is used in Roman Catholic and Anglican churches for baptism and recited at other times both in those Communions and in other Protestant churches. It is not said in the East but is used in Western rite Orthodox churches.

Apostolic Tradition—A work associated with Hippolytus (second to third century AD) that was discovered in the nineteenth century and has been influential in the twentieth-century "liturgical renewal."

apse—The semicircular vault at the front inside wall of an Eastern church, visible rising above the iconostasis, on which an icon of the Theotokos (with Christ-child) is painted.

Asperges—The "sprinkling" with water and the prayers that accompany this, at the beginning of the (Western) liturgy.

Athanasian Creed—Also known by its Latin beginning, *Quicumque vult*. This is not by Athanasius, since there is no evidence that it circulated in anything but Latin (Athanasius wrote in Greek). Nor does it appear to actually be a creed in the same sense as the Apostles' and Nicene, since it has a rhythmic and lyrical structure, much more like a poem. Unlike the other creeds, it also has anathemas attached to it, that is, statements of excommunication of those who do not accept it. It gained acceptance in Western Christianity at about the sixth century, is one of the three creeds recited in traditional Anglican and Lutheran circles, and is formally accepted by Rome, though has not been recited frequently since Vatican II.

Benedicte es—(literally, "blessed art thou") The Prayer of Azariah and the Three, found in the LXX (ancient Greek) text of Daniel and in the Apocrypha of Protestant Bibles in the book entitled, *The Prayer of Azariah*. The song is sometimes known as "The Song of the Three" (also "The Song of the Three Children" or "The Song of the Three Young Men").

Benedictus—(literally, "blessed") The Song of Zacharias, father of John the Baptist, found in Luke 1:68–79 and sung in the liturgy, probably from apostolic times.

Bobbio missal—A seventh- or eighth-century book, helpful in demonstrating a Western rite used probably in southeastern Gaul.

Book of Common Prayer—The title of various prayer books of the Anglican tradition, beginning with Cranmer's work in 1549 and reformulated in various editions, from 1552, 1559, 1662, 1962 (Canada), 1892, 1928, and finally 1979 (last three, USA). The 1979 USA prayer book is a very substantial revision of the former liturgies, changing the structure of the main service. In the Book of Common Prayer are found not only the Communion service, but also the Morning and Evening Prayer, the service of Baptism, prayers for other various occasions, a lectionary, family prayers, and the historic "Thirty-Nine Articles of Religion."

Canon of the Mass—The Roman Catholic name for the Eucharist itself, that is, the Service of the Sacrament, Communion, or Lord's Supper.

catechumen—Someone who has expressed a formal desire to become a member of the Church, whose intent has been recognized by the Church, and who is learning church doctrine with a view to baptism. The "catecumenate" is a formal "order" or class in the Roman Catholic and Orthodox Churches.

catholic, catholicity—(from the Greek, *kat'holon*, "according to the whole") A practice, thought, church order, or approach that is consonant with the whole Church, across space and time.

chrismation—An anointing with oil that follows immediately after water baptism and is connected with the gift of the Holy Spirit. Baptized converts to the Orthodox Church from trinitarian traditions outside of the Orthodox Church are usually received through chrismation alone, rather than by means of baptism.

Christophany—Just as a "theophany" is a special manifestation or revelation of God, a Christophany is a revelation of Christ.

Chronicles of Narnia—A series of seven children's novels by C. S. Lewis. The most well known is *The Lion, the Witch and the Wardrobe.*

collect—A prayer with a threefold format: address, petition, and ascription of power to God. It is an ancient form of prayer adopted by Cranmer for use in the Anglican Church. The collects are often specific to church seasons and feasts.

Communion—(Gk., *koinōnia*) This term refers (1) to fellowship among Christians and between the Church and God, (2) to the Holy Eucharist, (3) and to a body of Christians that identifies itself in terms of those who share the sacraments—for example, "the Anglican Communion."

communion of saints—The belief that all members of the body of Christ, whether living or "asleep in the Lord" remain in fellowship with each other and can pray for each other.

Confiteor—(literally, "I confess") A confession made by priest and deacon at the beginning of the Mass.

consubstantiation—A view proposed by the scholar Duns Scotus, in which the body and blood of Christ are said to be mysteriously present alongside the bread and the wine. This view of the Eucharist is held by many Lutherans, though there is debate concerning whether it faithfully represents Luther's own teaching of "sacramental union" of the elements with the body and blood of Christ.

Contestatio—Part of the eucharistic prayers in the Western tradition that vary with the feast.

corps—A local congregation in the Salvation Army. The building in which the corps meets might be called a citadel, or a temple.

Council of Trent—The famous sixteenth-century Roman Catholic council of reform. Decisions made at this council are referred to as "Tridentine."

didachē—(literally, "teaching") It is also the name of an ancient book, the *Didache*, written in the late first century or early second century.

Didascalia Apostolorum—(literally, "teachings of the apostles") A third- or fourth-century church order of Syrian provenance.

Divine Liturgy—The Eastern term for Mass, Communion, or Lord's Supper. It refers also to the whole service of Word and Sacrament, joined together.

divinization—See theosis.

Dom.—An abbreviation of Dominican.

Dormition—The belief that shortly after her death Mary was assumed, body and soul, to paradise, without her body being corrupted. In Roman Catholicism, the parallel teaching is called the "Assumption of Mary." Some Catholics do not believe, however, that Mary died before this event.

doxa, doxology—*Doxa* is the Greek word for "glory" (and also for "opinion," or "teaching"). A doxology is a prayer that gives glory to God, typically offered at the end of a service. *Orthodox* can mean, variously, "right teaching" or "right glory/praise/worship."

elements—The bread and wine of the Eucharist, or Lord's Supper.

emergent—A contemporary movement of nontraditional worshiping communities.

epiclesis—(literally, "calling to/upon") The prayer that asks the Holy Spirit to come upon the elements of the Eucharist and the people gathered.

Gallican rites—A group of Western rites, more ornate than that found in ancient Rome.

Gloria, Gloria in Excelsis—The traditional prayer, sung in East and West, that begins with the Song of the Angels from Luke 2:14:

> Glory to God in the highest, and peace to his people on earth.
> Lord God, heavenly King, Almighty God and Father,
> We worship you, we give you thanks,
> We praise you for your glory.
> Lord God, Lamb of God, you take away the sin of the world,
> Have mercy on us.

You are seated at the right hand of the Father—receive our prayer!
For you alone are the holy One, you alone are the LORD,
You alone are the most high, Jesus Christ, with the Holy Spirit,
In the Glory of God the Father, Amen.

Gregorian rite—The Roman rite established by Pope Gregory I. Sometimes the Tridentine rite is also called Gregorian, since scholars of Trent aimed to restore Gregory's liturgy.

Hosanna!—A Hebrew cry found in the Psalms and uttered as Jesus entered Jerusalem on Palm Sunday. It is a cry of acclamation, but means, literally, "Lord, save!"

host—The word used in the Catholic tradition for holy bread which "hosts" Christ.

icon—A representation of Christ, angels, or members of the household of faith, either from Old or New Testament, that is "written" according to specific rules (canons) and is intended to draw the worshiper to God.

iconoclastic—Literally, the tendency to "smash icons," because they are considered to be idolatrous. Iconoclasts faced off with "iconodules" (those who reverenced icons) in the tenth century. The Church, East and West, ratified the use of images on the theological basis of the incarnation of Christ. Iconoclasm reappeared in the Reformation.

iconostasis—The screen that marks the sanctuary of an Eastern Church from the congregational area and holds icons of the faithful. Typically as one faces the iconostasis, the Royal Doors in the center have Mary the Theotokos directly to their left and Christ directly to their right. Over the top is usually a representation of the Lord's Supper.

immanence—From the Latin *in manō*, "to remain in," this word refers to God's presence with us and with creation and is applied most usually to the Holy Spirit. It is contrasted with transcendence.

Jacobite—An adjective meaning "of James." Used in many contexts, both in the ancient world (e.g., the followers of sixth century Jacob Bar'adai, a bishop who formalized the separation from the Church of "non-Chalcedonians") and more recently (e.g., the English "Jacobites" who championed the claim of James II and VII to the throne). It is also the adjective used to refer to an ancient Eastern rite (the Liturgy of St. James/Jacobite liturgy), especially associated today with the Indian Church.

kairos, Kairon—(literally, "time, moment") *Kairos* is distinguished from *chronos* in that it refers to a specific time (cf. Rom. 5:6) whereas *chronos* refers to the flow of time ("chronology"). *Kairon* (also known as "Entrance prayers") is the Eastern preparatory service for the Eucharist and is linked to the Divine Liturgy with the deacon's words, "It is time for the Lord to act!"

kataphatic—Theology that uses words (distinguished from "apophatic" theology).

koinōnia—See Communion.

Kyrie eleison—(short form, *Kyrie*) The cry for help used throughout the service, "Lord, have mercy!"

lectionary, Revised Common Lectionary—A lectionary sets out the scriptural readings to be used throughout the church year or over a cycle of several years. The Revised Common Lectionary is the 1983 publication used by the North American and British Roman Catholic Church and a number of mainline denominations and has a three-year cycle.

Lent, Great Lent—The period of preparation (usually forty days) before Easter. In the Eastern Tradition, this period is called "Great Lent," because the period preceding Christmas is also a fast time, called sometimes "Little Lent."

Magnificat—(literally, "it [my soul] magnifies") The song of Mary, found in Luke 1:46–55, sung or prayed especially in Morning Prayer.

Masoretic—The Masoretic text of the Hebrew Old Testament refers to the version copied, edited, and passed on by Jewish scholars known as "Masoretes" (literally, "Traditioners") from the seventh through tenth centuries AD.

Mass *(missa est)*—The term used for the Eucharist, or for the entire Service of Word and Communion, in the Roman Catholic and Anglo-Catholic contexts. It derives from final dismissal given in the service, the Latin phrase, "Missa est. . . ."

memorialism—A view of the Lord's Supper associated with the Reformer Zwingli and commonly held among Protestant churches. The sacrament is a means of remembering the death of Christ and his power to conquer over sin and death.

Metropolitan—In Greek usage, the bishop of a large city ("metropolis"). Elsewhere, the archbishop who is responsible for an entire jurisdiction in Orthodoxy.

mystery—The Orthodox term for "sacrament."

narthex—The lobby of the church.

Nicene Creed—Properly known as the Nicene-Constantinopolitan Creed, it is the ecumenical creed recited and believed by most Christians, formed in the councils of 325 and 381, and was ratified by the Church subsequent to that time.

Nunc Dimittis—(literally, "Now you are dismissing/Now dismiss . . .") Simeon the elder's prayer, from Luke 2:29, used traditionally in evening prayer or Vespers.

offertory—At the offertory, the bread and wine are presented for use in the Eucharist, collection may be taken from the people, and often special music (an anthem or hymn) is sung.

Orthros—The first service on Sunday morning in Eastern Tradition.

PCUSA—The Presbyterian Church USA, a mainline Reformed domination in the United States.

perichōresis—The word used by ancient theologians to refer to the intimate interrelationship between Father, Son, and Holy Spirit. Wrongly translated as "dance."

Phōs Hilaron—The ancient vesperal hymn of the Church, "O Joyous (gladsome) Light."

Prothesis—(also known as *Proskomedia*) The service when the elements are prepared by the priest for the Divine Liturgy. This often takes place simultaneously with *Orthros*.

protological—The opposite of "eschatological." Literally, teaching about the very beginning, concerning matters at the Creation and prior to the Creation.

Protopresbyter—A priest who has earned deep respect in the Orthodox Church and who is a leader among priests.

psychopomp—One who directs, or leads the soul to the afterlife, or in the Christian tradition, to heavenly places.

receptionism—A view of Communion associated with Reformed churches. The reception of the elements in faith means that the believer also spiritually receives the body and blood of Christ by means of the Holy Spirit working in the Sacrament. Calvin said that the physical elements were a seal that the Lord truly gave himself to believers in the Eucharist.

reserved sacrament—Elements of bread and wine, consecrated in the congregational Eucharist, that are taken to the ill who cannot be present, or left in the sanctuary for those who will meditate and worship.

Royal Doors, Royal Gates—The double doors in the middle of the iconostasis, which, when opened, allow a view of the altar.

Saint John Chrysostom—A renowned Orthodox theologian, priest, and teacher from Antioch (c. AD 347–407) who earned the nickname "Golden-Mouthed" ("Chrysostom") and became the archbishop of Constantinople. His name is associated with the most common Eastern liturgy.

sanctuary—In Protestant churches, the entire place where worship takes place, including where the congregation sits. In Orthodox contexts, the holy place behind the iconostasis.

Sarum rite—An English version of the ancient Roman rite, dominant in Britain during the eleventh century.

second temple—The Jerusalem temple built and enlarged in the time after the Jewish people were allowed to return from Babylonian exile, until it was destroyed in AD 70. The phrase "Second Temple Period" refers to the period between this return until the final destruction (536 BC to AD 70).

Septuagint (LXX)—The term used for ancient Greek text of the Old Testament, translated from the Hebrew between the third and first centuries BC. Its name comes from the story that seventy (Gk., *Septuagint*) or seventy-two independent translators miraculously rendered the Hebrew text into the same Greek version.

Shema—The declaration of faith in the LORD God, beginning with the word "Hear!" (*Shema*), found in Deuteronomy 6:4 and recited at least twice daily by observant Jews.

soteriology—A subdivision of Christian theology that deals with the doctrine of salvation.

Stations of the Cross—Portrayals of Jesus' suffering and death, at which personal and congregational prayers are made, especially during the season of Lent.

Sticheron, stichera—This is a hymn in the Eastern tradition, sung in alternation with verses from the Psalms or other parts of Scripture.

synaxis—(literally, "gathering together") The technical word for a gathering for worship.

Taizé—A movement that began in a monastic community in France in the twentieth century and that has bequeathed a contemplative form of worship and style of music that is simple and suited to ecumenical gatherings.

telos—The Greek word for "end," "fulfillment," and "goal." It is also used in philosophical English in the word "teleology."

theōsis—A foundational teaching in Eastern Christianity, the seeds of which may be found in 2 Peter 1:3–11. God assumes humanity (in the Incarnation), so that humanity may be made "divine." St. Basil says that "man is the only creature who has been given the command to become god." Strictly speaking, this is not simply an Eastern doctrine, since it is found also in St. Augustine and implied in the Tridentine Mass. In the East, however, it is more fully explored by theologians such as St. Maximos Confessor and St. Symeon the New Theologian, who distinguish between God who is by nature divine and human beings who receive divine glory by grace. The distinction between God's energies and essence is also made: human beings who are deified only participate in the energies, but never the essence of God. This teaching was partially recaptured in the West by John and Charles Wesley, who read the Eastern fathers and were influenced by them in their hope for complete sanctification.

Theotokos—(literally, "God-bearer") The term used for Mary in Orthodox Tradition. Its equivalent in the Western Church is "Mother of God."

Three-Self Patriotic Movement/Church—The Protestant Church of China, whose philosophy is based on the three principles of self-governance, self-support, and self-propagation.

Tone—The set musical formula in Orthodox Tradition, to which various prayers or acclamations are put, rendering them hymns. There are eight tones, found differently in the two traditions, Slavonic and Byzantine.

transubstantiation—An explanation of the mystery of the Eucharist ratified by the Council of Trent, in which the elements are said to be changed in substance (trans-substantiated), while remaining the same in their outward appearance ("accidents"). The explanation uses the Aristotelian categories of "substance" and "accident," an approach that was naturalized in Roman Catholic theology through the strong influence of Thomas Aquinas. The Eastern Church also believes in a mysterious change, but it is not explained in philosophical terms, nor is it marked temporally in the Divine Liturgy (for example, by the ringing of a bell).

Tridentine Mass—The Mass established by the sixteenth-century Council of Trent, which removed many accretions and looked back to the Gregorian Mass.

Trisagion (*Ajus, Agios*)—The "thrice-holy" song of the angels in Isaiah 6, amplified in the liturgy as: "Holy God, Holy Mighty, Holy Immortal, have mercy on us." It is sung in every Eastern service and is especially sung during Lent in the Western tradition.

troparion, troparia—A short thematic hymn sung throughout a particular feast in the Eastern tradition.

type—(Gk., *typos*, plural *typoi*) See antitype.

Vatican II—This was a solemn general council of the Roman Catholic Church that opened under Pope John XXIII on October 11, 1962, and closed under Pope Paul VI on December 8, 1965.

Vespers, Great Vespers—Vespers is a service said in the evening. In the Eastern tradition, Great Vespers occurs on Saturday evening.

Watchers—A group of angels, associated with Genesis 6, about which much lore was written in ancient times, some of it preserved in books that are noncanonical and collected in the Old Testament Pseudepigrapha. These angels also make an appearance in the recent fiction by Madeleine L'Engle entitled *Many Waters*. The Watchers are generally not considered to be good angels and are said to have married human women and wreaked havoc on earth. In the hymn, "Ye Watchers and Ye Holy Ones," it is clear that only *some* of the Watchers were considered to have fallen. The name is probably derived from their office: to guard the throne of God in its holiness.

Western Rite Vicariate—A special group of parishes under the direction of an appointed "Vicar," who is answerable to the Metropolitan, who have permission to worship according to the Western rite though part of the Eastern Church.

Westminster Catechism—A body of teaching, in long and short forms, produced by British Calvinist theologians in order to aid in the teaching of doctrine. It was adopted by the General Assembly of the Church of Scotland and other Presbyterian bodies.

YHWH, LORD—These four Hebrew letters (the "Tetragrammaton") are used to refer to the true God and can be translated as "I am," "I will be," or "I cause to be." In the tradition of the Hebrew Bible, these consonants were printed with the vowels associated with the title *Adonai* (Lord) as a reminder to the one reading aloud in the service that the holy name (YHWH) should never be uttered. Instead, the reader was to say, "Adonai." This custom is indicated in the King James version by the capitals LORD. When *Adonai* is translated into English, the word "Lord" (without capitals) is written. "Jehovah" is a mistaken English verbalization of YHWH (the four consonants) combined with the vowels of the word *Adonai* and has no legitimate meaning in English or Hebrew.

Bibliography

Achtemeier, Elizabeth. "Female Language for God: Should the Church Adopt It?" In *The Hermeneuetical Quest: Essays in Honor of James Luther Mays on His Sixty-fifth Birthday*, edited by Donald G. Miller, 97–114. Allison Park, PA: Pickwick, 1986.

Aikman, David. *Jesus in Beijing: How Christianity Is Transforming China and Changing the Global Balance of Power*. Washington, DC: Regnery, 2003.

Austell, Robert M., Jr. *Biblical Worship through Music*. N.p.: Robert Austell Publishing, 2008. Available at Lulu.com.

Bailey, Terrence. *The Processions of Sarum and the Western Church*. The Pontifical Institute of Mediaeval Studies: Studies and Texts, No. 21. Netherlands: Royal Van Gorcum, 1971.

Batstone, Louise P. M. "Doctrinal and Theological Themes." In *The Bobbio Missal: Liturgy and Religious Culture in Merovingian Gaul*, edited by Yitzhak Hen and Rob Meens, 168–86. Cambridge: Cambridge University Press, 2004.

Beale, G. K. *We Become What We Worship: A Biblical Theology of Idolatry*. Downers Grove, IL: InterVarsity, 2008.

Bechtel, Carol M., ed. *Touching the Altar: The Old Testament for Christian Worship*. The Calvin Institute of Christian Worship Liturgical Studies Series. Grand Rapids: Eerdmans, 2008.

Bloom, Anthony. *Beginning to Pray*. Mahwah, NJ: Paulist Press, 1970.

Bouyer, Louis. *La vie de la liturgie: Une critique constructive du mouvement liturgique*. Paris: Cerf, 1956. English translation: *Liturgical Piety*. Notre Dame, IN: University of Notre Dame Press, 1955.

Bradshaw, Paul F. *The Search for the Origins of Christian Worship: Sources and Methods for the Study of Early Liturgy.* New York: Oxford University Press, 1992.

Bradshaw, Paul F., Maxwell E. Johnson, and L. Edward Phillips. *The Apostolic Tradition: A Commentary.* Minneapolis: Fortress, 2002.

Brock, S. P. *Holy Spirit in the Syrian Baptismal Tradition.* Syrian Churches Series, vol. 9. Pune, India: Anita, 1998.

Brueggemann, Walter. *Israel's Praise: Doxology against Idolatry and Ideology.* Philadelphia: Fortress, 1988.

Cabié, Robert. *History of the Mass.* Translated by Lawrence J. Johnson. Portland, OR: Pastoral, 1992.

Carson, D. A. *Becoming Conversant with the Emerging Church.* Grand Rapids: Zondervan, 2005.

Cavanagh, William T. *Torture and Eucharist: Theology, Politics, and the Body of Christ.* Oxford: Blackwell, 1998.

Chadwick, Henry. *The Treatise on the Apostolic Tradition of St. Hippolytus of Rome.* London: Alban, 1937. Reprint, Ridgefield, CT: Moorehouse, 1992.

Chan, Simon. *Liturgical Theology: The Church as Worshiping Community.* Downers Grove, IL: IVP Academic, 2006.

Chryssavgis, John. *Light through Darkness: The Orthodox Tradition.* Traditions of Christian Spirituality Series. Maryknoll, NY: Orbis, 2004.

Chupungko, Anscar. *What, Then, Is Liturgy? Musings and Memoir.* Collegeville, MN: Liturgical Press, 2010.

Coventry, John. *The Breaking of Bread: A Short History of the Mass.* London: Sheed & Ward, 1950.

Cuming, Geoffrey J. *Hippolytus: A Text for Students: With Introduction, Translation, Commentary and Notes.* Grove Liturgical Study 8. Bramcote, Nottingham, UK: Grove Books, 1976.

deSilva, David A. *Introducing the Apocrypha.* Grand Rapids: Baker, 2002.

———. *Sacramental Life: Spiritual Formation through the Book of Common Prayer.* Downers Grove, IL: InterVarsity, 2008.

Dix, Gregory. *The Shape of the Liturgy.* London: Dacre, 1945.

Dodd, John Theodore. *The Ordinary and Canon of the Roman Mass according to the Use of Sarum.* London: Joseph Masters, 1872.

Eisenhofer, Ludwig, and Joseph Lechner. *The Liturgy of the Roman Rite.* Translated by A. J. Peeler and E..F. Peeler. Edited by H. E. Winstone. New York: Herder & Herder, 1961.

Farley, Michael A. "What Is 'Biblical' Worship? Biblical Hermeneutics and Evangelical Theologies of Worship." *Journal of the Evangelical Theological Society* 51, no. 3 (2008): 591–613.

Fortescue, Adrian. *The Mass: A Study of the Roman Liturgy.* 2nd ed. London: Longmans, Green, 1913.

Gargoian, Nina, Thomas Mathews, and Robert Thomson, eds. *East of Byzantium: Syria and Armenia in the Formative Period.* Washington, DC: Centre for Byzantine Studies, 1982.

Gibbs, Eddie, and Ryan Bolger. *Emerging Churches: Creating Christian Community in Postmodern Cultures.* Grand Rapids: Baker Academic, 2005.

Gifford, Edwin Hamilton. *Writings of Cyril: The Catechetical Lectures. The Catechetical Lectures of St. Cyril, Archbishop of Jerusalem.* Edited by Philip Schaff. New York: Christian Literature, 1893. Available online at http://mb-soft.com/believe/txuc/cyril34.htm.

Guthrie, Steven R. "Temples of the Spirit: Worship as Embodied Performances." In *Faithful Performances and Enacting Christian Tradition,* edited by Trevor A. Hart and Steven R. Guthrie, 91–107. Aldershot, UK: Ashgate, 2007.

Hamman, A., ed. *Early Christian Prayers.* Translated by W. Mitchell. London: Longmans, Green, 1961.

Harper, John. *The Forms and Orders of Western Liturgy from the Tenth to the Eighteenth Century: A Historical Introduction and Guide for Students and Musicians.* Oxford, UK: Clarendon, 1991.

Haynes, Scott A. "The Spirituality of Sacred Music: What Does It Mean When the Church Sings?" *Adoremus* 14, no. 7 (October 2008). Available online at http://www.adoremus.org/1008SacredMusic.html.

Heine, Susanne. *Matriarchs, Goddesses and Images of God: A Critique of Feminist Theology.* Translated by John Bowden. Minneapolis: Augsburg, 1989.

Hen, Yitzhak, and Rob Meens. *The Bobbio Missal: Liturgy and Religious Culture in Merovingian Gaul.* Cambridge Studies in Palaeography and Codicology. Cambridge: Cambridge University Press, 2004.

Hitchcock, James. "Citizen, Heal Thyself: Social Sins Are Easily and Fashionably Confessed." *Touchstone: A Journal of Mere Christianity* (November/December 2009): 3–4.

Horton, Michael S. *A Better Way: Rediscovering the Drama of God-Centered Worship.* Grand Rapids: Baker, 2002.

———. *People and Place: A Covenant Ecclesiology.* Louisville: Westminster John Knox, 2008.

Humphrey, Edith M. *Ecstasy and Intimacy: When the Holy Spirit Meets the Human Spirit.* Grand Rapids: Eerdmans, 2005.

———. "Grand Entrance: Entrance into Worship as Rhetorical Invitation and Liturgical Precedent in the Older Testament." In *The Old Testament as Authoritative Scripture in the Early Churches of the East,* edited by Vahan

S. Hovhanessian, 79–89. Bible in the Christian Orthodox Tradition Series, vol. 1. New York: Peter Lang, 2010.

———. "To Sing Is a Lover's Thing." Lecture presented December 13, 2005, at the installation of Edith M. Humphrey as the William F. Orr Professor of New Testament. Pittsburgh Theological Seminary. Reprinted in modified form as "To Sing Is a Lover's Thing: Toward a Biblical Theology of Worship." *Trinity Journal for Theology and Ministry* 3, no. 1 (Spring 2009): 131–44.

Jeremias, Joachim. *The Eucharistic Words of Jesus.* Translated by Norman Perrin. London: SCM, 1966.

Jungmann, Josef A. *The Early Liturgy: To the Time of Gregory the Great.* Translated by Francis A. Brunner. University of Notre Dame Liturgical Studies, vol. 6. Notre Dame, IN: University of Notre Dame Press, 1959.

Kauflin, Bob. *Worship Matters: Leading Others to Encounter the Greatness of God.* Wheaton: Crossway, 2008.

Kavanagh, Aidan. *On Liturgical Theology.* New York: Pueblo, 1984.

Kimel, Alvin F., Jr., ed. *Speaking the Christian God: The Holy Trinity and the Challenge of Feminism.* Grand Rapids: Eerdmans, 1992.

Klauser, Theodor. *A Short History of the Western Liturgy: An Account and Some Reflections.* Translated by John Halliburton. 2nd ed. New York: Oxford University Press, 1979.

Lewis, C. S. *Christian Reflections.* Edited by Walter Hooper. Grand Rapids: Eerdmans, 1967.

———. *An Experiment in Criticism.* Cambridge: Cambridge University Press, 1961.

———. *The Last Battle.* England: Bodley Head, 1956.

———. *The Lion, the Witch and the Wardrobe.* Middlesex, England: Puffin Books, 1959.

———. *The Magician's Nephew.* Glasgow: Collins, 1986.

———. *Reflections on the Psalms.* Glasgow: Collins, 1961.

———. *Till We Have Faces: A Myth Retold.* Grand Rapids: Eerdmans, 1996. Originally published 1956.

———. *The Weight of Glory.* New York: Harper Collins, 2001.

Ludlow, Morewenna. *The Early Church.* The I. B. Tauris History of the Christian Church. New York: I. B. Tauris, 2009.

Macomber, William. "The Ancient Form of the *Anaphora of the Apostles.*" In *East of Byzantium: Syria and Armenia in the Formative Period,* edited by Nina Gargoian, Thomas Mathews, and Robert Thomson, 73–88. Washington, DC: Centre for Byzantine Studies, 1982.

Man, Rob. *Proclamation and Praise: Hebrews 2:12 and the Christology of Worship*. Eugene, OR: Wipf & Stock, 2007.

Mazza, Enrico. *Celebration of the Eucharist: The Origin of the Rite and the Development of Its Interpretation*. Translated by Matthew J. O'Connell. Collegeville, MN: Liturgical, 1999.

McLaren, Bruce. *The Church on the Other Side*. Grand Rapids: Zondervan, 2006.

———. *Finding Our Way Again: The Return of the Ancient Practices*. Nashville: Thomas Nelson, 2008.

McPartlan, Paul. *The Eucharist Makes the Church: Henri de Lubac and John Zizioulas in Dialogue*. 2nd ed. Fairfax, VA: Eastern Christian Publications, 2006.

Metzger, Marcel. "Nouvelles perspectives pour le prétendue Tradition apostolique." *Ecclesia Orans* 5 (1988): 241–59.

Meyers, Jeffrey J. *The Lord's Service: The Grace of Covenant Renewal Worship*. Moscow, ID: Canon, 2003.

Miller, Donald G., ed. *The Hermeneutical Quest: Essays in Honor of James Luther Mays on His Sixty-fifth Birthday*. Allison Park, PA: Pickwick, 1986.

Moreton, Bernard. *The Eighth-Century Gelasian Sacramentary: A Study in Tradition*. Oxford Theological Monographs. London: Oxford University Press, 1976.

Moule, C. F. D. *Worship in the New Testament*. Ecumenical Studies in Worship 9. Richmond: John Knox, 1961.

Oesterley, W. O. E. *The Jewish Background of the Christian Liturgy*. Oxford: Clarendon, 1925.

Old, Hughes O. *Themes and Variations for a Christian Doxology*. Grand Rapids: Eerdmans, 1992.

Plantinga, Cornelius, Jr., and Sue A. Rozeboom. *Discerning the Spirits: A Guide to Thinking about Christian Worship Today*. The Calvin Institute of Christian Worship Liturgical Studies Series. Grand Rapids: Eerdmans, 2003.

Puhalo, Lazar, trans. *A Clergy Service Book: For Service with Priest and Deacon*. 4th ed. Duvall, WA: Theophany, 2007.

Purves, Andrew, and Charles Partee. *Encountering God: Christian Faith in the Turbulent Times*. Louisville: Westminster John Knox, 2000.

———. "A Name Is Not a Metaphor: A Response to 'The Trinity: God's Love Overflowing,'" *Theology Matters* 12, no. 2 (March/April 2006): 1–4. Available online at http://www.theologymatters.com/MarApr06.pdf.

Ratzinger, Joseph. "Music and Liturgy: How Does Music Express the Word of God, the Vision of God?" *Adoremus Bulletin* 7, no. 8 (November 2001). Available online at http://www.adoremus.org/1101musicliturgy.html.

————. *The Spirit of the Liturgy*. Translated by John Saward. San Francisco: Ignatius, 2004.

Reardon, Patrick Henry. *Christ in the Psalms*. Ben Lomond, CA: Conciliar, 2000.

Rienstra, Debra, and Ron Rienstra. *Worship Words: Discipling Language for Faithful Ministry*. Engaging Worship Series. Grand Rapids: Baker Academic, 2009.

Roche, Anne. *The Gates of Hell: The Struggle for the Catholic Church*. Toronto: McClelland and Stewart, 1975.

Rognlien, Bob. *Experiential Worship: Encountering God with Heart, Soul, Mind and Strength*. Colorado Springs: NavPress, 2005.

Rosean, Ted. "Two Rites Make a Wrong." *US Catholic*, July 14, 2009, http://www.uscatholic.org/church/2009/07/two-rites-make-wrong?page=0%2C0.

Ross, Allen P. *Recalling the Hope of Glory: Biblical Worship from the Garden to the New Creation*. Grand Rapids: Kregel, 2006.

Schaff, Philip. *Ante-Nicene Fathers*. Vol. 1, *The Apostolic Fathers with Justin Martyr and Irenaeus*, edited by Alexander Roberts and James Donaldson. Grand Rapids: Eerdmans, 1973.

Schaff, Philip, and Henry Wace. *Nicene and Post-Nicene Fathers of the Christian Church*. Vol. 7, *Cyril of Jerusalem, Gregory Nazianzen*. Grand Rapids: Eerdmans, 1955.

Schmemann, Alexander. *The Eucharist*. Crestwood, NY: St. Vladimir's Seminary Press, 1987.

————. *For the Life of the World*. Crestwood, NY: St. Vladimir's Seminary Press, 2000.

————. *Introduction to Liturgical Theology*. Translated by Ashleigh E. Moorhouse. Portland: American Orthodox Press, 1966.

Seitz, Christopher R. *Isaiah 1–39*. Louisville: Westminster John Knox, 1993.

Senn, Frank C. *Christian Liturgy: Catholic and Evangelical*. Minneapolis: Fortress, 1997.

Service Book of the Holy Eastern Catholic and Apostolic Church According to the Use of the Antiochian Orthodox Christian Archdiocese of North America. Englewood Hills, NJ: Antiochian Christian Diocese of North America, 1971.

Stewart-Sykes, Alistair. *Hippolytus: On the Apostolic Tradition*. Crestwood, NY: St. Vladimir's Seminary Press, 2001.

Taft, Robert F. "The Authenticity of the Chrysostom Anaphora Revisited: Determining the Authorship of Liturgical Texts by Computer." *Orientalia Christiana Periodica* 56, no. 1 (1990): 5–51.

————. *Beyond East and West: Problems in Liturgical Understanding*. 2nd ed. Rome: Pontifical Oriental Institute, 1997.

———. "St. John Chrysostom and the Byzantine Anaphora that Bears His Name." In *Essays on Early Eastern Eucharistic Prayers*, edited by Paul F. Bradshaw, 195–226. Collegeville, MN: Liturgical, 1997.

Temple, William. *Readings in the Fourth Gospel*. First and Second Series. London: MacMillan, 1955.

The Book of Common Prayer According to the Use of the Anglican Church of Canada. Toronto: Anglican Book Centre, 1962.

The New Hymnal: English-Chinese Bilingual Edition. Three-Self Patriotic Movement and Chinese Christian Council: Shanghai, China: Nanjing Amity, 1999.

The Song Book of the Salvation Army. London: Salvationist Publishing and Supplies, 1955.

Thompson, Bard, ed. *Liturgies of the Western Church*. Cleveland: World, 1961.

Thuis, Scott. O.S.B. *Gregorian Chant: A Barometer of Religious Fervor*. Published privately. Excerpts available online at http://unavoce.org/uva-archive/gregorian-chant-a-barometer-of-religious-fervor/.

Upex, Braddon. "Essay on Hymnody." *Hippocampus Extensions* 8 (January 2004). http://hippocampusextensions.com/issues/08/an_essay_on_hymnody.

Van Dyk, Leanne, ed. *A More Profound Alleluia: Theology and Worship in Harmony*. The Calvin Institute of Christian Worship Liturgical Studies Series. Grand Rapids: Eerdmans, 2005.

Wainwright, Geoffrey. *Doxology: The Praise of God in Worship, Doctrine and Life: A Systematic Theology*. New York: Oxford University Press, 1980.

———. *Eucharist and Eschatology*. New York: Oxford University Press, 1981.

Ware, Kallistos. "Approaching Christ the Physician: The True Meaning of Confession and Anointing." October 18, 2004. On Communion: Web site of the Orthodox Peace Fellowship. http://incommunion.org/?p=100.

———. *The Inner Kingdom*. Crestwood, NY: St. Vladimir's Seminary Press, 2000.

Warren, Rick. *The Purpose-Driven Church: Growth without Compromising Your Message and Mission*. Grand Rapids: Zondervan, 1995.

Watts, John D. W. *Isaiah 1–33*. Word Biblical Commentary 24. Waco, TX: Word Books, 1985.

Whaling, Frank, ed. *John and Charles Wesley: Selected Prayers, Hymns, Journal Notes, Sermons, Letters and Treatises*. New York: Paulist Press, 1981.

Williams, D. H. *Evangelicals and Tradition: The Formative Influence of the Early Church*. Evangelical Ressourcement: Ancient Sources for the Church's Future. Grand Rapids: Baker Academic, 2005.

Wilson, H. A., ed. *The Gelasian Sacramentary: Liber Sacramentorum Romanae Ecclesiae*. London: Oxford University Press, 1894.

Witvliet, John D. *The Biblical Psalms in Christian Worship: A Brief Introduction and Guide to Resources*. The Calvin Institute of Christian Worship Liturgical Studies Series. Grand Rapids: Eerdmans, 2007.

————. "The Former Prophets and the Practice of Christian Worship." *Calvin Theological Journal* 37 (2002): 82–94.

————. *Worship Seeking Understanding: Windows into Christian Practice.* Grand Rapids: Baker Academic, 2003.

Wren, Brian. *What Language Shall I Borrow?* New York: Crossroad, 1989.

Wright, N. T. *The New Testament and the People of God*. Grand Rapids: Eerdmans, 1992.

Wunderlink, Susan. "Stations of the Cross—Without the Cross." *Christianity Today* (March 2008). Web only. Available online at http://www.christianity today.com/ct/2008/marchweb-only/110–42.0.html?start=2.

Young, William P. *The Shack*. Los Angeles: Windblown Media, 2007.

Scripture Index

Subject Index

Printed in Great Britain
by Amazon

56377820R00154